Empowering Your Life
with
KABBALAH

Jonathan Sharp

ALPHA

A member of Penguin Group (USA) Inc.

To Victoria, Joanne, Sr. C.D., and Fr. A.G.

Publisher: Marie Butler-Knight

Product Manager: Phil Kitchel

Senior Managing Editor: Jennifer Chisholm

Senior Acquisitions Editor: Randy Ladenheim-Gil

Development Editor: Lynn Northrup

Production Editor: Janette Lynn

Copy Editor: Keith Cline

Cover Designer: Bill Thomas

Book Designer: Trina Wurst

Creative Director: Robin Lasek

Indexer: Brad Herriman

Layout: Becky Harmon

Proofreading: Donna Martin

Contents

Introduction

Congratulations, you have taken the first step toward changing your life in a dramatic and all-encompassing way! If you follow the steps in this book, you will find that almost every aspect of your life improves.

We all want to be empowered in our lives, and *Empowering Your Life with Kabbalah* offers every reader the opportunity to not only discover life goals, but also to set about achieving them. As the world in which we live becomes increasingly complex and our personal time squeezed, it is inevitable that many of us feel rather lost and uncertain of our real direction in life. The system of Hermetic Kabbalah provides an easy-to-follow, step-by-step guide to regaining a sense of direction, clarity, and peace of mind in your life.

Although many books on the market promise to improve your life in one specific area, *Empowering Your Life with Kabbalah* can help you to improve your quality of life in a whole range of areas, from your relationships to your spirituality to your work life. What's more, this wide-ranging improvement can be achieved by using a single system: the ancient wisdom of Kabbalah. Packed with practical exercises, meditations, and rituals, what you hold in your hands is a hugely effective combination of authentic esoteric insight and the practicality of a Ten-Step Program.

In recent years there has been an explosion of self-help books. This could be the result of a growing level of independence that comes with the new Age of Aquarius, representing the growing desire within people to find their own solutions to their problems. However, the fact that these books are referred to as "self-help" tells us that the aim of such books is to help, but not necessarily to free, ourselves. The *Empowering Your Life* series moves beyond the notion of self-help, which seems to promise only to make you, the reader, well again. With self-empowerment you are aiming to achieve not only an adequate life or health or relationship, but also to achieve results that go beyond the merely satisfactory, and in a way that increases your own sense of personal power and control.

How to Use This Book

It would be possible to treat this book as a handy source of useful tips for improving different areas of your life as and when you feel they could do with a little nudge in the right direction. However, *Empowering Your Life with Kabbalah* is designed as a step-by-step program, and your success with it will be greatly enhanced by working through each stage fully and in the recommended order.

Many people buy self-development books with the intention of carefully working through all the recommended exercises, but never seem to get started. We have all tried fooling ourselves that we can somehow absorb the information from books without actually reading them—and just as it never worked at college, it's not going to start working now! As with all the best things in life, you will change your life only if you make the commitment to yourself to work through the exercises in the book.

Before you panic, though, let me say that in developing the activities in this book I have tried to recognize the busy lives people lead. This is why you will be able to work through this book with as little as 30 minutes to an hour a day set aside to reinvigorate your world with Kabbalah. Of course, some of you will be able to work with the book only once or twice a week. This is not a problem because there is no required time limit in which you need to complete any section of the program. Self-empowerment should always be seen as a journey and never as a race. The important point here is that none of the practical exercises themselves require more than an hour or so to complete.

You will use a number of powerful empowerment tools to bring about changes in your physical, mental, and emotional worlds. A number of these tools can be used in different settings, especially after you are competent in their use. You may find it useful to keep a journal of your progress. This will help you to keep track of whether you feel you have fully activated the empowerment tools within each chapter. In addition, when you have successfully worked through the whole book, you will be able to look back and see which of the techniques you felt most comfortable with and would like to continue with to maintain your new and much improved life.

Acknowledgments

I would like to thank my daughter, Vicky, for nagging me to finish; Anna Ridley for providing the symbols, the drawing of the Tree of Life, and much appreciated moral support; Barbara and Michael for giving me a space in which I could write; and to everyone I've known within the Western Mystery Tradition for their advice and enthusiasm.

Trademarks

All terms mentioned in this book that are known to be or are suspected of being trademarks or service marks have been appropriately capitalized. Alpha Books and Penguin Group (USA) Inc. cannot attest to the accuracy of this information. Use of a term in this book should not be regarded as affecting the validity of any trademark or service mark.

Chapter 1

What Is Kabbalah?

During the past several years, you've probably heard the term *New Age* used on television, in magazines and books, on the radio, and in general conversation to describe a variety of things. Many different interests and activities have been, or are, described as New Age, from aromatherapy to feng shui, from crystal healing to meditation. So what does New Age actually mean? The best way to describe the concept of New Age is as a way of thinking about ourselves and our environment that recognizes the links among the physical, the mental, and the spiritual.

Those with an interest in New Age philosophies may have heard of Kabbalah as being an ancient source of secret wisdom. If you follow the Jewish faith, you may be aware of Kabbalah as its mystical aspect. Even if you are new to the whole notion of all things New Age, chances are you will have heard about Kabbalah, thanks to its growing popularity among many celebrities. (You may have seen pictures of pop star Madonna, for instance, wearing a symbolic red thread, representing the spirit or ruach, around her wrist. This thread is not worn by all Kabbalists and is an innovation used by one particular Kabbalah group. Many Kabbalists would say that Kabbalah lives within us and so we don't need to wear it on the outside.)

In recent years, Kabbalah has become increasingly popular with all sorts of people. In many ways, this is not surprising. There seems to have been recently an awakened quest for spiritual wisdom, and for a practicable spirituality rather than a spirituality that just requires adherence to beliefs or faith. Although it's hard to narrow down Kabbalah to a simple set of beliefs, one distinct feature it has is that the spiritual and the practical, as well as the human and the Divine, are seen as inextricably linked. Based on the definition of the New Age I've just offered, you can understand why Kabbalah is so popular. Although it is an ancient system of mysticism, it ties together the worlds of the physical, the mental, and the spiritual—and thus provides an ideal example of a New Age approach to self-development.

Although this book is intended to provide you with a number of powerful tools to profoundly change your life, Kabbalah is a system of such complexity and mystery that it can sustain even the most curious with a lifetime of study and practice. Enjoy the journey!

What Kabbalah Can Do for You

No single book details all the secrets of Kabbalah. It's not just a set of particular beliefs to buy into, nor is it a clearly defined set of practices (activities required on a regular basis). Instead, Kabbalah combines *all* of these aspects.

Kabbalah relates to our lives on every level. It's a mystical system, but it speaks to us and assists us in every aspect of our life. One aspect of Kabbalah is the belief that our physical life is as much a part of the Divine as our spiritual life, and so the wisdom that we find within Kabbalistic teachings can help empower our lives as much as it can help bring us closer to the Divine.

A useful way to think about the potential for life improvement Kabbalah offers is to compare it to yoga. When yoga was first developed, it had only one purpose: to bring the yogi closer to an understanding of the Divine. Over the centuries, however, more and more people have been exposed to the benefits of yoga. It's still possible to use yoga as a purely spiritual practice, but for many people it's also a way to be healthier, fitter, less stressed, and more at ease with themselves. Similarly, we can use Kabbalah as a wholly mystical system, but it can also influence major changes in the way we live our daily lives—the way we think, how we express ourselves, and how we relate to those around us.

Kabbalah and the Body/Mind/Spirit Connection

Let's consider the yoga analogy again. If I exercise at the gym three times a week, I will become physically fit. That's undoubtedly a good thing. If I practice yoga three times a week, I will not only become physically fit but also mentally calmer. This is the crux of the New Age approach— that we can do a purely physical activity, or a purely mental activity, that will affect the whole of our life. Kabbalah works in a New Age way because it recognizes the connection among the body, mind, and spirit. If I want to improve my promotion prospects at work, I might stay late, network with the right people, and so on. If I want to use Kabbalah to improve my promotion prospects, I will take a very different approach. Instead of just focusing on the physical or material issue—I want a promotion—I recognize that my mental and spiritual attitude are just as important to getting that promotion as any direct action I might take. Therefore, in addition to doing the obvious things, I also perform certain meditations, burn particular incense, and use special Divine names in my prayers. By doing these things, I bring my mind and spirit into alignment with my physical desire and increase the chances of success.

As you work through this book, you'll find that each chapter addresses specific areas of your life, from your relationships to your career to your own sense of self. The New Age approach to life can seem confusing at first, because there is often no obvious connection between what you are actually doing and the area of your life you are trying to improve. When using this book to work on your emotions, for instance, you will spend a lot of time around and in water. Although you may not immediately recognize a direct link between water and improving your relationships, you will find the link as you explore the New Age approach. As you investigate the nature of water, you are unconsciously exploring your own emotional makeup because the element Water is an ancient symbol of our emotions.

Your activities will stimulate largely unconscious-level responses. Although you may not see the connection as you are performing the activity, you will certainly feel its effects in your life. Remember that Kabbalah is highly spiritual, and throughout this book you will use the names of Divine and angelic beings to give power and certainty to your self-development. Hermetic Kabbalah, discussed later in this chapter, holds that we all have a Divine spark within us and that we can awaken this spark by calling upon the ancient names of spiritual beings.

If this sounds difficult to accept, consider a simple example of how seemingly unconnected activities can impact our lives. A female friend of mine was hugely insecure and shy, which stopped her from advancing in her career, made dating next to impossible, and stifled her social life. I suggested that she try the Self-Massage exercise in Chapter 3. After a couple of weeks, I tried to call her, but couldn't reach her for a number of days. She had started to go out in the evening. She was still nervous, but she had gained that essential boost that allowed her to restart her life. She was at a loss to understand how it had worked; after all, all she had been doing was giving herself a massage every evening and repeating certain simple prayers. I explained that the physical act of giving herself a massage also operated on a mental and spiritual level because it was symbolizing to herself that she was a person of value who deserved to be pampered and appreciated.

Many books form the basis of Kabbalah, and they can provide many thought-provoking hours of reading. However, to really benefit from this treasure trove of mystic wisdom we need to do more than just read. Kabbalah is as much about *doing* as it is about thinking. You can learn a lot about cars by reading a driving manual, but only when you drive do you really begin to understand what driving is all about. You don't need to have any particular religious belief to benefit from the exercises and empowerment tools presented in the following chapters. I believe the great spiritual truths will always transcend the human boundaries of culture and religion. Additionally, as a practitioner myself I can say from experience that when we take steps to empower our physical life in a way that is in tune with Kabbalistic teachings, we inevitably see changes in our spiritual life, too.

Let's return for a moment to our comparison with yoga. A person might sit in the lotus position as a way of increasing physical flexibility; after a while, however, he will find that he also feels much more serene in his daily life. In the same way, you may take up the activities in this book because you want to enhance your career or become more creative, but an inevitable result will be that you also begin to get in touch with your inner spirituality.

> Before enlightenment—chop wood, carry water.
> After enlightenment—chop wood, carry water.
> —Attributed to Siddhartha Gautama, the Buddha (approximately 500 B.C.E.)

The Ancient Roots of Kabbalah

Kabbalah is unique in that it is both ancient and has also continually developed through the centuries. The fact that Kabbalah has continued to be actively practiced as a form of mysticism for centuries sets it apart from almost all other systems of practical mysticism.

As Kabbalah has developed and changed, inevitably different sorts of Kabbalistic practices and beliefs have emerged. In the same way that there are many different interpretations of Buddhism and Christianity, there are a number of ways of practicing Kabbalah. Each is valid in its own way and will suit a particular mindset. As one Great Master said, "My Father's house has many mansions"; in other words, there is no single "true" way to the Divine. You may be surprised to learn that the Great Master in question was none other than Jesus, a member of a group known as the Nasorean Essenes; it is likely that he was involved in Kabbalistic forms of mysticism.

Hands-On Kabbalah

This book focuses on the general mystical power and message of Kabbalah. In addition, we will be engaging in the secrets and mysteries of Kabbalah in a very "hands-on" way. This sort of approach is the way I was introduced to Kabbalah, and it is the best way to work with it if we want to make empowering changes in all aspects of our lives.

Think of Kabbalah as being a tree with many branches. Even though some of those branches look quite different from each other, they are all attached to a single, central trunk. Think of this trunk as the heart of

Kabbalistic thought. The roots of this tree reach deep into the past, possibly back to the very first civilizations.

Just like any mystical system, whether it is the Tarot, crystal healing, or alchemy, Kabbalah has been the subject of much debate and discussion. At a basic level, there are debates about how its name should be spelled. Over the centuries, it has been spelled Cabbala, Qabala, Kabala, and even QBLH. The wide range of ways of even spelling the name Kabbalah is perhaps to be expected given how long this system has existed. (I use the spelling *Kabbalah* throughout this book.)

There is also debate about the very origins of Kabbalah as a system of spiritual insight. Many believe that Kabbalah is entirely Jewish in origin. However, the history of our mystical inheritance is never quite that simple. The true origins of Kabbalah will always be shrouded by the mists of antiquity.

What we do know suggests that Kabbalah draws on a whole range of ancient mystery religions and magical insight. It seems likely, for example, that the early development of Kabbalah would have drawn on the priest craft of the ancient Egyptians. Although a number of different systems of mysticism were woven together in Kabbalah, until the Renaissance period the actual practice of Kabbalah was almost exclusively Jewish.

A Secret Tradition

During the Renaissance period in Europe, a number of Christian thinkers became interested in Kabbalah and found that they could relate its esoteric secrets to their own mystical versions of Christianity. In the centuries that followed, Kabbalah in various forms has been adopted by many different groups and this process continues today. By the same token, each tradition that has absorbed Kabbalah has also given something to Kabbalah. In this way, much like our image of a tree with many branches, the system of Kabbalah has developed in the same way that a person grows and develops organically over a period of time.

The word *Kabbalah* means "tradition." This points to its ancient status, but also reminds us that Kabbalah is a growing and expanding group of beliefs and practices. All traditions change little by little as they are handed down, and this is certainly true of Kabbalah. What is also true is that while certain things may change, the core of the tradition remains unchanged.

The word from which Kabbalah is derived is the Hebrew word *Qibel*, which means "to receive." This connection reminds us of the secret oral tradition that kept Kabbalah alive for hundreds of years. It also tells us that the mysteries of Kabbalah are a gift from the Divine to the people of the world that can only be fully "received" when we engage with this gift.

Secrecy has played a part in many mystical traditions and societies for a number of reasons. In Europe it was very important that those interested in mysticism kept their interests and activities a closely guarded secret; otherwise they faced imprisonment or even death. But even if Kabbalists hadn't been in danger of persecution, the idea of secrecy would still have been important. One of the easiest traps to fall into when working in the realm of the magical and spiritual is that people start to feel that little bit more special and important. By keeping Kabbalah secret, the danger of using this new knowledge in the interests of personal vanity was greatly reduced. Although Kabbalah today is not secret, you can maintain your own personal level of secrecy to prevent yourself from falling into the same trap. It can be helpful to work on the Kabbalah as a group or with a partner, but ask yourself whether you are sharing ideas or just trying to impress others.

Kabbalah Through the Ages

The first Kabbalists were the so-called Merkabah mystics. Through a strict regime of fasting and secret breathing techniques, the Merkabah mystics hoped to attain a vision of God. One of the reasons why these breathing techniques were kept secret was because it was thought that they were so powerful that that they could be dangerous in inexperienced hands. The main period of activity for the Merkabah mystics was from about 100 B.C.E. to 800 C.E. The Merkabah mystics tried to re-create the experience of the vision of the Divine described by the prophet Ezekiel. They were a loose association of Jewish mystics based in Palestine. We know very little about them as individuals, but one of the most important Kabbalistic documents, the *Sefer Yetzirah*, is said to have been revealed during this period of Kabbalistic exploration.

The focus on intense meditation was continued and greatly developed by Abraham Abulafia in the twelfth century. Abulafia was something of a character who had a reputation for intense mystical activity and insight. Abraham Abulafia came from a wealthy and scholarly family in Spain.

One of his most important contributions to the development of Kabbalah was in the area of trancelike meditation. He popularized, among Kabbalists, the practice of meditating on combinations of Hebrew letters in order to achieve a trancelike state.

It was the publication of the *Zohar* by Moses de Leon in the thirteenth century that made the spread of Kabbalistic wisdom possible. Like Abulafia, Moses de Leon was a Spanish Jew, and this area of Europe was a hotbed of Kabbalistic activity during this period. The *Zohar* was not written by Moses de Leon, but as a scholarly individual he was responsible for piecing together and committing to paper a huge array of Kabbalistic wisdom that had previously been passed down only by word of mouth. Some Kabbalists claim that Moses de Leon found the entire text of the *Zohar* in a cave in Israel.

Popular Kabbalistic practice today is intended to bring about changes in the way we live our day-to-day lives as well as in our spiritual development. This practical approach was first advocated by the Safed school of Kabbalists, who were led by the hugely influential Isaac Luria. Luria is one of the most famous pre-Renaissance Kabbalists. He was born in Jerusalem in 1534, and spent most of his life at Safed in Palestine. He was the head of a school of Kabbalah, which in a sense we could see as the equivalent of an ashram or modern New Age spiritual community. His followers saw him as a saintly character in spite of his very rigid rules. Although Luria himself was a mystic with no real interest in publishing his ideas, much of his philosophy of Kabbalah has been preserved through the records of his followers.

Around the time of the Renaissance, however, a number of Christian philosophers became interested in this powerful mystical system, and the Western Mystery Tradition as it exists today began to form. The Western Mystery Tradition combines Kabbalah with a range of other mystical and magical practices, including alchemy, astrology, and talismanic magic, along with traditions of mysticism from the ancient Greek and ancient Egyptian cultures.

No fixed beliefs make up the Western Mystery Tradition; it is a broad term used to cover a range of often-secret mystical and magical societies that developed in Europe from the Renaissance onward. The Western Mystery Tradition has continued to expand right up to the present day. Just think about groups such as the Golden Dawn, the Aurum Solis, and even esoteric Freemasonry and Wicca—all of these owe their existence to some degree or other to the Western Mystery Tradition.

Although the Western Mystery Tradition draws on a number of mystical systems, it is generally true that the most important influence has been Kabbalah. Although in today's culture science tends to poke fun at the claims of the New Age, for many centuries science and the Western Mystery Tradition went hand in hand. For instance, it is a little-known fact that Sir Isaac Newton was an expert alchemist. In fact Newton himself saw his mystical work as far more important than his scientific discoveries.

When I meditate in my astral temples, it feels as though I really am touching the feet of the angels.

—From a modern-day member of a Western Mystery Tradition group based in England

Orthodox and Hermetic Kabbalah

From the Renaissance onward, the number of Kabbalistic schools continued to multiply in the form of two broad traditions. The first tradition is what might be termed Orthodox Kabbalah. This is the tradition that has remained strictly within the Jewish faith. It is extremely rare for a Gentile to be inducted into the secrets of an Orthodox school of Kabbalah, and its practices tend to be directly linked to the main Kabbalistic documents such as the *Zohar* and the *Sepher Yetzirah*.

Whereas Orthodox Kabbalah has remained largely unchanged and hidden from the uninitiated, the second tradition that we might call Hermetic Kabbalah has become increasingly public and is now one of the most popular forms of alternative spiritual practice. It is Hermetic Kabbalah that this book focuses on, particularly because Hermetic Kabbalah is open to everyone regardless of religious beliefs. Hermetic Kabbalah retains the historical Kabbalistic documents and practices, but tries to understand and use them in a way that is not tied to one particular religion.

One consequence of this is that Hermetic Kabbalah has always looked to many other mystical traditions as a means to widening and deepening the level of spiritual understanding. The term *hermetic* refers this form of Kabbalah to the Western Mystery Tradition. There are two relevant meanings of the word *hermetic*. On the one hand, it means something that is completely sealed, and this relates to the often secret nature of Kabbalah. The other meaning of hermetic relates to the mythical Hermes Trismegistus (Hermes the Thrice Great), who is supposed to have first revealed the great secrets of existence to mankind.

The Four Aspects of Kabbalah

In every school of Kabbalah and within both the Hermetic and the Orthodox traditions, Kabbalistic wisdom is divided into four broad areas:

1. Literal Kabbalah
2. Practical Kabbalah
3. Dogmatic Kabbalah
4. Unwritten Kabbalah

The focus of this book is on Unwritten Kabbalah. As you journey from chapter to chapter, however, you will develop personal-empowerment tools that originate from each of the four broad strands of Kabbalistic wisdom.

Literal Kabbalah is concerned with an ancient practice known as gematria. This practice uses the fact that all Hebrew letters also have a value to explore the mystical relationships between words that have the same numerical value. For instance, the Hebrew word meaning "Adam" has the same value as the Hebrew word meaning "Earth," which draws attention to a number of insights about the nature of mankind, including the fact that ultimately we all return to the earth.

Practical Kabbalah deals with ways in which Kabbalah can be applied to the physical as well as the spiritual world. It deals with the ancient secrets of talismanic magic and other magical processes that are available to the experienced Kabbalist. Kabbalistic magic is properly referred to as theurgy because all Kabbalistic ceremonial magic is performed under the authority of the Divine.

Dogmatic Kabbalah is perhaps the most important aspect of Kabbalah to the Orthodox Kabbalist. Dogmatic Kabbalah refers to the key texts that underpin the Kabbalistic tradition. These texts include the *Zohar*, *Sepher Yetzirah*, and the *Bahir*. The *Pentateuch* from the Jewish Bible is also included in Dogmatic Kabbalah partly because of the number of secret meanings that can be found within the books of the *Torah*.

Finally, we have *Unwritten Kabbalah*. This title refers to the fact that until the insights that make up Unwritten Kabbalah were committed to paper, they were passed down from mouth to ear, from teacher to student. The material that makes up Unwritten Kabbalah was considered for a long time to be too powerful to be written down, for fear that it might fall into the wrong hands. Unwritten Kabbalah contained the very keys to the construction of the universe and so this was only communicated from teacher to student after a bond of trust had been long established.

The Tree of Life

Unwritten Kabbalah is based on an incredibly powerful and profound yet deceptively simple structure known as the Tree of Life, or in Hebrew, the *Etz-ha-Chayim*. The Tree of Life forms the framework for your personal development. By the time you have completed your journey through this book, you will know all the branches on this mystical tree very well. (You might want to bookmark the page with the illustration for easy reference.)

The Tree of Life first appears in the *Sefer Yetzirah,* one of the earliest Kabbalistic documents, as a series of descriptions of the way in which the universe emanated from the Divine. The stages of this process of emanation can be shown as a diagram consisting of 10 specific stages of development connected by 22 paths. Many Kabbalists believe the *Sefer Yetzirah* simply put into print what had been known secretly by generations of Kabbalists before.

There are, of course, many ways one could construct a diagram to represent these 10 stages joined together by 22 paths. However, almost all Kabbalists now use the arrangement of circles and paths shown in the following diagram, which was popularized by the seventeenth-century Kabbalist Athanasius Kircher. As you can see, the Tree of Life has an obvious and beautiful symmetry.

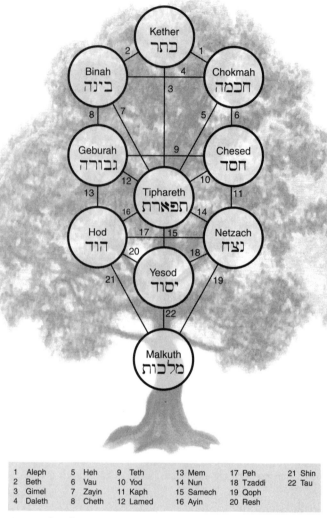

1	Aleph	5	Heh	9	Teth	13	Mem	17	Peh	21	Shin
2	Beth	6	Vau	10	Yod	14	Nun	18	Tzaddi	22	Tau
3	Gimel	7	Zayin	11	Kaph	15	Samech	19	Qoph		
4	Daleth	8	Cheth	12	Lamed	16	Ayin	20	Resh		

The Tree of Life.

Each of the 10 stages on the Tree of Life is shown in the diagram as a circle. Each of these stages is known as a Sephira, or Sephiroth when referred to in the plural. In keeping with the mysterious nature of the Tree of Life, there has been debate about the interpretation of these Hebrew terms. The root of the word from which Sephira and Sephiroth are derived can be linked to words meaning "book," "to tell a story," and "number."

Each of these possible origins is appropriate in its own way, and so perhaps it is right that the debate continues.

The words within each circle are the names of the Sephiroth. You'll learn more about them later in this chapter, and subsequent chapters explore the symbolic meaning of these Hebrew names in detail. However, let's first look at how this simple illustration can be the source of so much wisdom.

Reading the Tree of Life

One of the beauties of the Tree of Life is that it can be used to represent so many different fundamental aspects of both the spiritual and the physical universe. It makes very clear the way in which all aspects of the universe intrinsically link under the overriding and complex patterns created by the will of the Divine.

As mentioned previously, this book focuses on practical ways to apply the wisdom of Hermetic Kabbalah to reshape our lives. To fully appreciate the reasons and meaning of these practical applications, you need to understand some of the symbolism of this diagram of the Divine universe. It's no accident that there are 10 Sephiroth. In the ancient world, nearly all forms of mystical numerology used a base 10 counting system. One could even argue that our decimal system in use today derives from this ancient mystical heritage.

Each number from 1 to 10 has a very specific spiritual meaning, and the recognition of this is the first step toward an understanding of the Tree of Life. The secret meanings of each number are as follows:

1. Divine existence, consciousness
2. Duality, the possibility of creation
3. Creation through the union of opposites
4. Material existence
5. Physical life with potential for union with the Divine
6. Physical creation and choice
7. Independence and drive
8. Construction of forms, both mental and physical
9. The will and ability to create as an individual
10. Completion and union with the Divine

Before we consider how the meanings of these numbers begin to make sense when reading the Tree of Life, let's briefly look at the paths linking the 10 Sephiroth. Referring to the diagram, notice the 22 paths that connect the Sephiroth. This is important because the Hebrew alphabet also contains 22 letters. Each path on the Tree of Life is represented by a letter from the Hebrew alphabet, as shown in Appendix A.

The paths on the Tree of Life are also associated with either a sign of the zodiac, one of the seven ancient planets, or one of the elements of Fire, Water, or Air. (Earth is excluded because it is represented in the final Sephira.) When we add the number of planets (7), zodiac signs (12), and elements (in our case, 3) we get the number 22. The Major Arcana of the Tarot also contains 22 cards—that is, those cards that differ from the suits that one would find in a normal pack of playing cards.

For centuries, Kabbalists have passed down the story that the Divine created the universe by uttering the Hebrew alphabet letter by letter. This notion is now gaining indirect support from unexpected quarters. At the cutting edge of modern physics is a discipline known as string theory, and the very latest theories in this area suggest that the ultimate structure of the universe consists of—you guessed it—22 fundamental qualities or frequencies!

Many books would be required to document all the unexpected and compelling links between Kabbalistic wisdom and the latest discoveries in modern science. However, I hope that this brief look at the mysteries of the paths on the Tree of Life encourages you to go beyond the activities in this book and become entranced by the complexity, mystery, and beauty of Hermetic Kabbalah.

The Tree of Life as a Map of Creation

Returning to the Sephiroth, you can see how their arrangement represents not only the creation of the universe, but also our own physical body and the different stages that lead to a full realization of our link with the Divine.

In the creation of the universe, the Divine resides beyond the highest Sephira of *Kether,* shown at the top of the diagram, but Kether represents the closest we can come to an understanding of the Divine nature. Kether literally means "crown" and signifies the Divine consciousness.

Moving to the right, we come to the Sephira *Chokmah,* which represents the capacity for pure force or creative energy. This raw force then develops the capacity to take on a definite shape or form in the Sephirah *Binah,* directly across to the left. Binah is also known as the "Great Mother," and so we can relate to the notion of the capacity for form in terms of the way in which a fertilized egg represents a raw unformed energy but carries within it the capacity for form through its genetic code.

Moving down and to the right, we have *Chesed,* which is associated with Jupiter. In this Sephira, we see the capacity for form lead into the actual creation of the actual forms or "principles" that lead to the physical universe. Jupiter is especially appropriate because in Graeco-Roman mythology it is the planet linked with the actual creation of the world. *Geburah,* directly across to the left, represents the essential opposing force to Chesed. If we have the creation of forms, we must also have the destruction of forms, because it is only through mortality that new beginnings are possible.

Tiphareth, in the center, is the result of the combination of the two opposing forces of Chesed and Geburah. It represents the point at which the physical becomes actual rather than simply an "idea" in the mind of the Divine. Its name literally means "beauty," and this is an important label to remember if you are to gain a full understanding of the Kabbalistic worldview. In many religions, the physical is seen as something from which we should seek to escape; in Kabbalah, however, we learn that the physical universe is in some ways a positive completion of the will of the Divine.

If Tiphareth represents the beginnings of physical life, then *Netzach,* down and to the right, is the point at which life forms with the ability to act independently emerge. These life forms have the basic drives to eat and reproduce, for example, that can be associated as a physical version of the raw force represented by Chokmah. If we think purely in terms of human evolution, Tiphareth represents the emergence of humanity as a group of beings with consciousness, with Tiphareth functioning as a lower version of the consciousness of Kether. In this case, Netzach represents the early ages of mankind, which were driven by very basic needs.

Hod, straight across to the left, marks the development of higher life forms that have the ability to think at least to some basic degree or have the capacity for social organization. In purely human terms, Hod refers to the beginnings of order and communication. This is followed by

Yesod to the right, which we can see as the point at which animals that are genuinely self-conscious emerge. From a human perspective, Yesod indicates the emergence of spiritual consciousness.

The final stage in the emanation of the universe is the Sephira of *Malkuth,* at the bottom of the diagram. In general evolutionary terms, this marks the emergence of humanity. It is for this reason that Malkuth is known as the "bride." We are the only species with the potential ability to awaken the Divine spark that lies within us. So as people we can be seen as the bride of Kether, because when we make contact with our own inner spark we become spiritually wedded to the Divine. If we look at this Sephira in terms of human history, it indicates civilizations where the spiritual consciousness of Yesod has been replaced by a focus on material goods. Over time this leads to the establishment of well-ordered societies but also to a sense of separation from the Divine.

What is startling about this Kabbalistic model of the emanation of the universe is its closeness to contemporary models of physical evolution. Even the initial moment of "tzim tzum" can be favorably compared to the Big Bang theory. The Kabbalistic tzim tzum refers to the very first moment of creation, where the Divine contracts itself and creates a tiny space so that the universe can flow into that space. One thing that sets apart the Kabbalistic view of creation is that it considers the origin of the universe a gradual process of emanation. This is a surprisingly sophisticated view of the universe when compared to many other models of creation that emerged at a similar time to the earliest forms of Kabbalah.

The Tree of Life as a Map of the Body

Whereas science requires a number of different models to explain and describe a range of processes, the Tree of Life can be used to describe an almost infinite range of features of life at both the individual and the universal level. The Tree of Life diagram can be seen as a symbolic picture of a human being. At a visual level, one can immediately see the resemblance, particularly if one looks just at the Sephiroth themselves without the linking paths.

The first Sephira, Kether or the "crown," represents the top of the head and the seat of consciousness, sometimes associated by the ancients with the pineal gland or "third eye." The next two Sephiroth, Chokmah and Binah, also known as "wisdom" and "understanding," respectively, represent the two halves of the brain. We can see the association with our brains in terms of the titles of the two Sephiroth, and the titles also make sense given that one half of our brain is concerned with rational analytic order or form and the other with creativity or the pure outpouring of inner force.

We then move down from the head to the shoulders and the two Sephiroth of Chesed and Geburah. Geburah is the right shoulder, because when we look at the Tree of Life we are looking at a symbolic mirror image of ourselves. This means that our right arm is associated with the potentially destructive force of Geburah. Historically, it was the right hand that would have wielded a sword in combat.

The central Sephira of Tiphareth lies over the heart, the center of the body. At one level, it represents the heart itself as the source of physical life and as the symbol of our emotional and spiritual consciousness. Its central position also relates to our lungs. This is appropriate given Tiphareth's importance as representing the point of connection between the purely spiritual and the wholly physical worlds. This is especially so within Kabbalah because practical breathing exercises lie at the heart of all Kabbalistic exercises.

The next Sephirotic pair is located at the hips. Because Hod represents the intellect and communication, and Netzach refers to dynamic activity, this may seem an inappropriate location at first. However, remember that our hips enable us to be mobile, and that in early civilizations communication was dependent on the ability to travel. Additionally, in the ancient world, almost all forms of creative expression were dynamic and involved dance and drama to some degree. One translation of the next Sephira, Yesod, is "foundation." It should be no surprise then to learn that Yesod is located in the groin area. It is, of course, our ability to reproduce that is the foundation of our continuation as a species. In addition, the Sephira of Yesod is associated with the unconscious and the lower emotions. I think most of us can associate our lower emotions with often being driven by our desires.

Finally, we come to Malkuth. This Sephira is the realm of the purely physical; it is quite literally the ground on which we stand. It is quite appropriate then, that Malkuth is located at our feet. It is through our feet that we have the most direct contact with the physicality of the world. As we evolved into Homo sapiens, we began to stand up and walk erect. Consequently, our feet are the last reminder of the lower levels of consciousness from which we have emerged.

The Tree and the Worlds

When I was first introduced to the Tree of Life, I was reasonably cynical about the possibility of a single diagram being the product of a Divine revelation. Over a period of weeks, however, I was shown how the Tree of Life could be used to appropriately map any number of processes, from the separation of the physical universe into vegetable, animal, and mineral to the processes that we go through when we develop a relationship with another person.

The intricate detail that can be provided by the Tree of Life increases the more closely one explores it. For instance, each of the 22 paths and 10 Sephiroth can be brought into each new use for which one is exploring the Tree. If you read more widely on Kabbalah, you will find that very often the Sephiroth are also referred to as paths in their own right, and hence some books refer to 32 paths.

As we delve deeper into the symbolism of the Tree of Life, we find the added complexity of the four worlds of Kabbalah. This refers to the Divine, the Archangelic, the Angelic, and the Physical worlds. These four worlds can be attributed to certain sections of the Tree. Alternatively, one can consider each world as having its own Tree, so that the bottom of the Tree in the Divine world is the first Sephira of the Archangelic world. For the reader who really enjoys the sense of the infinitely complex, there is even a model that sees each Sephira as containing within itself an entire Tree of Life!

The four worlds have a particular impact when we are looking at the Tree of Life as a map of the spiritual evolution of the individual. In the Single Tree model, one begins in the Physical world and gradually progresses until, upon reaching Kether, one is effectively residing in the Divine world. In the Single Tree model, we move from the Physical to the Angelic world when we move from Malkuth to Yesod. The Archangelic world begins with Geburah, and the Divine world begins with Binah, although some versions of the Single Tree model have the Divine world restricted to Kether.

Some Kabbalists argue that because we are always a part of the Physical world until we die, it is not possible to achieve any kind of link with the level of spirituality represented by the higher Sephiroth. This concern is addressed by the Four Tree model, and it is this model that we will be using. In the Four Tree model, each of the worlds contains an entire Tree of Life. The Physical world begins in Malkuth and ends in Kether, but this Kether represents the sense of the Divine as it appears in the material world. This is followed by the Angelic world, which also contains a whole Tree of Life. In this tree, Malkuth represents the Physical world as seen through the eyes of an astral or angelic being, whereas the Kether of this world represents the energy of the Divine as experienced by angelic beings. Similarly, both the Archangelic and the Divine worlds contain a whole Tree of Life, and so it is only when we reach the Kether of the Divine world that we reach the Divine in its fullest sense. We begin and end the exercises in this book still firmly within the Physical world. However, in the Four Tree model, the Kether of the Physical world is still linked to the Kether of the Divine world, and so it is possible to attain an understanding of the Divine. It may even be possible for the advanced Kabbalist to move from the Kether of the Physical world into the Malkuth of the Angelic world, at least in terms of state of consciousness.

The Tree of Life as a Map of Spiritual Growth

In the two previous examples, we began our journey at the top of the Tree of Life, with the Sephira of Kether. When we consider the Tree as a diagram of the spiritual development of an individual, we have to start at the bottom, with the Sephira of Malkuth. This is because we all exist within the Sephira Malkuth, and so here must begin our spiritual journey. The downward path from Kether is known as "the lightning flash" or "the path of the Flaming Sword." The path upward touches all points on the Tree and is known as "the path of the Serpent" because it undulates along each of the paths.

In Malkuth, we are separated from the Divine because of our concentration on material concerns. Before we can move onward, however, we need to make sure that we have properly organized our material life in such a way that it no longer controls us. We then move into Yesod, where our spiritual development begins, primarily through the lower astral realms and dreams. The translation of Yesod as "foundation" makes as much sense here as in the view of the Tree as a map of creation, because the spiritual developments of Yesod act as a foundation for the rest of our inner journey.

When we reach the Sephira Hod, we learn to combine our physical understanding of the world with the spiritual awakening of Yesod. This helps us to understand our new spiritual level of consciousness. It is only when we have a clear mental concept of our spirituality that we can fully move across to the Sephira of Netzach, where we begin to express this spirituality in a dynamic and practical way.

The culmination of these first four stages occurs in Tiphareth, which is appropriately titled "beauty." It is in Tiphareth that we achieve a real connection with the Divine and/or our own Higher Self depending on the way in which the Kabbalist has conceived of this journey when in Hod. In the Single Tree version of the four worlds, this is the highest that can be achieved in a physical incarnation.

If we follow the Four Trees model of the Tree of Life, we can pass beyond Tiphareth. However, we have to remember that when we experience the next Sephira of Geburah, we are experiencing it in a diluted form because it manifests in the Physical world. One way of thinking of this is to compare it to the difference between looking directly at the sun and looking at a reflection of the sun in the water. Geburah is the Sephira associated with the destruction and severity of the universe. In terms of a spiritual evolution, it is here that we have to accept that the seemingly negative and cruel aspects of the universe are still part of the Divine.

In Chesed we have to understand at a deep level the sense of God as merciful. This is the opposing force to the severity of Geburah. It is not enough just to recognize the potential for mercy in the universe at this stage. Instead, the aim is to copy that same capacity for mercy and compassion in our own lives.

The next pair of Sephiroth is a higher reflection of the learning processes represented by Hod and Netzach. In Binah, we develop a deep understanding of the necessity of everything that exists and of the way in which it exists. This may sound like a passive acceptance, but when you experience this realization for yourself it is a very powerful moment. Binah again functions as a "Great Mother" because one passes out of the acceptance of Binah into the raw force and energy of Chokmah. This Sephira is the point in your journey where you actively engage with the Divine spark and could be seen as the ideal Sephira to represent the practical Kabbalist.

The final Sephira of Kether cannot be adequately described beyond its title of "the crown." It is here that one is filled with an understanding of the Divine. In that understanding, we are filled with a sense of being united with the light of the Divine as opposed to still having to reach up to that pure energy. This Sephira can be best described perhaps as a perfect peace that passes beyond all expectations.

The Importance of Order

Like so many other aspects of our lives, the way in which we practice our spiritual beliefs tends to adjust to changes in the general culture in which we live. As a result of living in a consumer society, we have reached a point where spirituality can be something of a hodge-podge of often contradictory belief systems. We can explore our spiritual side through New Age approaches such as crystal healing or aromatherapy. And although these may be beneficial, they don't offer a structure for developing an increasing level of spiritual awareness; instead, they tend to focus on specific issues. In aromatherapy, for instance, you can learn to cure or improve a whole range of ailments. In doing so, you will also feel more spiritually aware, but aromatherapy does not offer any system for increasing this level of spiritual awareness.

The Kabbalistic Tree of Life provides that system. The structure and order of the Tree of Life is an essential part of its spiritual power. If you were to try to start the journey at Tiphareth, for example, rather than the earthly Sephira of Malkuth, you would inevitably fail. It would be a bit like trying to drive away in your car without switching on the ignition.

The Tree of Life provides a stable and safe framework through which to work. It works on different aspects of your personality and your life in an order that has been established through centuries of practice and successful results. As you may have noticed, the Tree of Life can be seen as three vertical pillars consisting of three, four, and three Sephiroth, respectively. By following the Sephiroth in the correct order, you are constantly kept in a state of internal balance as you move from each pillar to the next in order. To approach the Tree in a different order could lead to an excess of severity or weakness depending on which pillar you focused on.

As you work through this book, you are setting out on the greatest journey of your life as you explore each Sephira in depth. Your voyage of discovery begins with the Sephira of Malkuth in Chapter 2.

According to the Western Mystery Tradition, four elements make up the universe: Earth, Air, Water, and Fire. In each chapter, practical exercises you perform will awaken the element of Earth in that particular Sephira, and the meditations will awaken the element of Air.

The element of Water is awakened by the special Kabbalistic techniques in each chapter, and the rituals in each chapter complete the balance by awakening the element of Fire. The sincerity with which you approach the work will guarantee that when the four elements in each Sephira are activated, the final element of Spirit bursts forth within you. As you awaken each of the elements, you will also be making direct changes in your daily life. Each Sephira impacts particularly on one area of your life. Netzach, for instance, will empower your creativity, whereas Malkuth helps you to resolve material concerns, and Geburah strengthens your will and character. Within each chapter, the Earth-based exercises will lead to obvious and material changes in the way you practically live your life. The Air-based meditations will improve your understanding of the spiritual importance of the work that you're doing in each chapter. The Water-based techniques will encourage positive emotional growth, and the Fire-based rituals will stimulate your inner spark of pure creativity. Each one of these activities is empowering in its own right, but the incredible power of Kabbalah as an empowering force in your life comes from the combination of all four elements—so that at every level your life is enhanced and improved.

Chapter 2

Malkuth: The Kingdom of Earth

Malkuth is the lowest Sephira on the Tree of Life. It is pronounced "Maal-Koot," and is made up of the Hebrew letters
Mem, Lamed, Kaph, Vau, and Tau. In Chapter 1 you learned
that in Literal Kabbalah, each Hebrew letter has a meaning and
a value. This means that we can analyze words and discover new
hidden meanings within them in a process known as gematria.

Turn to Appendix A to see the literal meaning of each letter
next to a representation of how the letter looks written in Hebrew. You need to remember two things about ancient Hebrew.
First, according to Kabbalistic tradition, the letters themselves
are holy symbols; so if you do choose to write them down for
any purpose, take care that you write them properly. Second,
Hebrew is written from right to left, and so Malkuth would
appear on the page in this order: Tau (Th), Vau (V), Kaph (K),
Lamed (L), Mem (M). You can see the Hebrew spelling of
Malkuth and the other Sephiroth in the Tree of Life diagram in
Chapter 1.

Using the literal meaning of the individual letters, we can
construct a Kabbalistic interpretation of the meaning of the title
of each Sephira, and each chapter includes such an interpretation.

(These interpretations are the result of my own meditations; you may want to meditate on each letter yourself and discover your own understanding.) When I look at the spelling of Malkuth, I find a message there encouraging us all to progress upward on the Tree of Life. It tells me that the great Mother (Mem) will spur us on (Lamed) to both practical (Kaph) and intellectual (Vau) activities that will take us on the first path out of Malkuth (Tau).

The value of the Hebrew word Malkuth is 496. This can be reduced to the number 10 (4 + 9 + 6 = 19, and 1 + 9 = 10). This number is hugely appropriate because Malkuth is the tenth Sephira. If we further reduce 10, we get the number 1 (1 + 0 = 1), which is significant because Malkuth is the first step on our journey toward a new and empowered life.

Being the lowest of the Sephiroth on the Tree of Life, Malkuth is linked with all things physical and is associated with the element of Earth. It is the symbolic representation not just of the world but also of the whole physical universe. All the Sephiroth have a number of esoteric titles, and one of the so-called Divine names of Malkuth is Adonai Ha Aretz (Aah-Doh-Nye Haa-Aah-Retz). This name translates as the "Lord of Earth" and emphasizes that when we are working with the energies of Malkuth we are concerned with all those aspects of our life that could be seen as having an "earthy" character.

Malkuth is associated with the way we look after our own physical body, and in the way in which we treat our environment. In the modern world, our physical lifestyle is greatly affected by our financial position; Malkuth also relates to our money and how well we organize our financial affairs. This Sephira is also linked with our own commitments and sense of stability because these reflect the solidity that we associate with the material world. In Kabbalah there is always a commitment to balance, and so in all things we find the positive balanced by the negative. Because Malkuth is all about the material world, the negative traits of Malkuth include stubbornness and avarice. Stubbornness is what we get if we become too solid and fixed, avarice and greed occur when we become too concerned with our material or financial situation at the expense of other concerns.

Despite its status as the symbol of the physical, we shouldn't underestimate the spiritual importance of Malkuth. One of Malkuth's many titles is "the gate"; this refers to its role as the way into the realms beyond the physical. Malkuth is also known as "the bride" in relation to the Sephira of Kether. At a mystical level, Malkuth is the completion and perfection of the desire of the Divine to manifest in the same way that Kether is the completion and perfection of our desire to understand the Divine. We could compare this to giving presents to our children on their birthdays. The child wants to receive the present, but as parents our joy is in the giving of the gift. Similarly, the joy of the Divine is in the gift of the physical universe.

Areas of Empowerment

When working with the energies of Malkuth, you will be concentrating on the more practical aspects of your life. When you consider that your goal in working through this book is to reinvigorate all areas of your life, it makes perfect sense to start here. It is far easier, for example, to restructure the way in which you approach your emotional life if you no longer have to worry about having a completely disorganized approach to your financial affairs.

It's up to you to decide how far you want to explore the energies of each Sephira. The resources listed in Appendix C offer you excellent access to a more detailed understanding of Kabbalah. However, it's best to focus on the Sephira that you are currently exploring to avoid any confusion of energies.

If you are physically healthy, you will increase your self-esteem and your self-confidence and thus will find it easier to believe that you are going to succeed with the empowerment tools provided in the chapters to come. It's a fact that financial issues cause more stress than any other problem. This is not restricted to serious financial crises. For most of us, it refers to the constant low-level nagging concern that we have spent a little bit too much again this month.

Empowering Your Life with Kabbalah has been designed to fit in with a busy lifestyle. However, no matter how much time you decide to set aside per week to work through the exercises, you will find that the results come much more quickly and powerfully if you stick to a definite routine. By developing an organized approach to your goals now, you will be in a much better position to reap the reward of the later Sephirotic energies.

As you make your way up the Tree of Life, you will experience many exciting insights and profound feelings. It's an excellent idea to keep a record of your progress in a journal. Write down any ideas, feelings, or impressions that you get from any of the activities that you complete. By the end of this book, when you'll have completed your journey up the Tree of Life, you will be able to look back and remind yourself of all the important steps and challenges that you conquered along the way.

Masters are under no cosmic compulsion to live on mountains only.
—Paramahansa Yogananda, *Autobiography of a Yogi* (1946)

Practical Activities

This section provides you with two exercises that will directly impact your health, financial control, and organization. You can do these exercises as many times as you think is useful, but don't move on to the next chapter until you feel comfortable with each of the activities.

Becoming Friends with Earth

Don't be put off by the title. It may sound rather "fluffy" in nature, but I can assure you that if you complete the steps you will feel invigorated and profoundly affected at a deep level—and physically worn out to boot!

A key point of *Empowering Your Life with Kabbalah* is that you should be able to undertake all the activities with as little preparation as possible. For this first exercise, all you need to do is put on some comfortable clothes that you don't mind getting messy.

At the end of this exercise, you should feel physically invigorated, calmer, and more centered in yourself. Repeating this practice once a week for a few weeks will develop a strong sense of your connection to the natural world.

1. Find a nice quiet spot, not too far from your home, that has all or most of the following: trees, inclines, a natural water source, an area of planted earth.

2. Slowly walk around your secluded area and try to feel the earth energy reaching up through your feet as you take each step.

3. As you walk around, try to find a particular spot where you feel especially calm and "at home." Take off your shoes and socks and just stand still, focusing on the feel of the ground against the soles of your feet. Close your eyes and direct all your awareness to your feet and the contact between them and the earth from which we all emerge.

4. When you feel ready, gently shake out all your arms and legs and begin to jog gently around your chosen circle of nature. Steadily increase your speed until you are running. If possible keep your shoes off for this part because the sensation of the grass brushing your feet as you run is remarkably intense.

5. Ideally, you are in a location with at least a slight incline, the steeper the better. Now run up this incline as fast as you can, being aware of the earth energies pulling you toward the earth and the inertia of the earth trying to slow your ascent.

6. When you reach the top of the incline, allow yourself to collapse, quite literally, in a heap. Now just lie against the earth and for a few moments feel the heat generated between your body and the soft ground.

7. As you feel that heat being generated, symbolizing the vigorous power that lies unseen within the stability of Malkuth, begin to roll back down the slope. (Remember how much fun you had doing that as a child?) You may feel foolish the first time you do this, but remember that true inner freedom begins to emerge when we no longer care what others think. Now matter how silly you feel, it will be hard not to feel wonderfully alive by the time you reach the bottom.

8. Repeat this cycle of walking, standing, running, and then rolling at least four times. Ideally, your total number of cycles should be a multiple of four because this will unconsciously emphasize the balanced and grounded self that you are trying to achieve.

9. Note how you feel during this exercise. Retain the physicality of the experience by finding a space of planted earth and taking some of the earth in your hands. Sit on the ground and try to feel the energy of the earth in your hands. Really take in all the details you would normally not notice.

10. Before leaving, thank the spirits of the earth for allowing you to access their energy, and ask that the stability and gradual growth that stems from the Earth element be present in your life. Say whatever feels natural to you; there are no prescribed words. The Kabbalistic name for the Divine in Malkuth is Adonai Ha Aretz, so you may wish to address your words or thoughts to this particular manifestation of the Divine. For example, you might say, "Spirits of Earth, thank you for giving me your energy, and I also give thanks to Adonai Ha Aretz for guiding me to the stability that lies in the heart of Malkuth."

The Life Inventory

Some of the most empowering and life-changing actions we can take can be incredibly simple. Often this simplicity both contains their power and is the reason why the actions keep being put off. The following exercise is an excellent example of such an activity.

Everything you need for this exercise you can find in your own home. Collect an assortment of favorite family photographs, souvenirs from vacations and trips, and personally significant ornaments (perhaps any degrees or awards that you have gained over the years). You also need a pad of paper and some pens (ideally with black, red, green, and blue ink).

The aim of this exercise is twofold. It is designed to increase the level of organization in your life. This is essential, because when we have a structured practical life we can properly focus on the deeper aspects of our lives. In addition, an organized approach can make profound changes to the quality of your life.

1. Sit at a table with plenty of space so that you can set out your collection of photos and mementos around you. List on a piece of paper everything you do on a daily basis. Beneath this, list things that you do on a weekly basis, then on a monthly basis, and finally those things that you do once a year.

2. Create four lists, using the black pen, that neatly lay out in order all of these activities into a daily list, a weekly list, a monthly list, and an annual list.

28

3. Review each list and, using the red pen, add anything that you should be doing but aren't. This might include working out a proper budget or spending a definite amount of time each day solely with your children or partner.

4. Using the green pen, write in all those things that you don't have on your list but that you would like to make time for in your life. As you are working in the Sephira of Malkuth and trying to organize your life in a realistic manner, it is very important that the green-ink activities be realistic. Some examples might be learning a new hobby or going back to school for your degree.

5. At this point, you probably have a rather colorful set of lists in front of you! Now cross out anything on your lists that is neither essential nor enjoyable. Focus equally hard on both these factors. You may *think* you like doing many things, but they may only be the result of habit rather than actual enjoyment. For example, it is hard to believe that the average person really actively wants to watch so many hours of television every week. We watch so much television because it is an easy form of relaxation and we haven't organized our lives enough to plan activities that will enrich our day-to-day experience of the world.

6. If you have been suitably strict with yourself, you will now have a much more manageable set of lists. The final stage is to convert those lists into plans. The trick here is to not be too specific. You want to allocate a rough amount of time for each activity and a rough time when it will take place. However, you do not need to specify the exact day that you will complete your tax return, for example.

7. This completes the first stage. If you have been thorough, you will find that you immediately free up many, many hours a year. Ideally, keep your lists under a piece of clear quartz because quartz is associated with clarity of thought and action.

8. Malkuth is also about understanding what aspects of your physical life are truly important. Take a few moments now to read through your lists and write down on a fresh sheet of paper, using the black pen again, what seem to be the most important items on your list.

9. You have been probably been wondering why you needed to collect all those photos and souvenirs. Well, first of all they were there to

remind you of why it is that these lists are so important; these lists will allow you more time for the areas of life that bring you happiness. They also have another purpose. Write down, using the green pen, what it is that is most important about each of the items that you have selected. This should be a description of an activity rather than a feeling.

10. Now compare the list you produced at Step 8 with the list you produced at Step 9. You will be probably be quite surprised at the differences. What this exercise helps to bring home is that what we think we believe is important is often very different from what deep down we know to be important. With that in mind, return to your task lists and underline those activities that really are fundamentally important.

The trouble is the narrowness of consciousness. It is as if you tried to see a panoramic scene through cracks in a high fence, but were never allowed to look over the fence and see it as a whole ... But in moods of deep serenity ... Suddenly I am aware of vast inner spaces, of strange significances inside me. I am no longer a puny twentieth-century human being trapped in his life-world and personality. Once again I am at the center of a web, feeling vibrations of meaning ... I am like a tree that suddenly becomes aware that its roots go down deep, deep into the earth.
—Colin Wilson, *The Occult* (1987)

Meditations

The two meditations in this section will help to embed the positive energies associated with Malkuth within your consciousness. The meditations build on the practical activities but function at a deeper level. Their impact is more subtle, but if you perform one meditation per week you will gradually notice a very definite shift in the way that you approach your life.

The essence of meditation is that it takes place in a quiet space. Therefore, you need to set aside a small part of your home for undertaking the meditation exercises. When meditating, you need uninterrupted "you-time," so make sure the phones are off or unplugged, the TV is off, and that no one else (including the family pet) is in the room. Evening is a great time for meditation because there tends to be less noise from outside and we are often calmest toward the end of the day. Above all, the key to good meditation is relaxation. You can never force results in a meditation—just relax and the results will come to you. A bedroom is an ideal meditation space because some meditations are best performed lying on a bed. Put on some comfortable loose-fitting clothes that don't restrict your breathing in any way.

Earth Meditation

This meditation is the main meditation of Malkuth. It awakens your own inner associations with the element of Earth.

1. Before you begin, recite a short affirmation to yourself. This may be spoken out loud or just in your head. Ask the force of Adonai Ha Aretz to assist you in your meditation and to help you achieve the solidity and stability of the element of Earth in your life. For example, you might say, "I call upon Adonai Ha Aretz to guide me in my search for the power of the element of Earth in my life."

2. Lie down in a comfortable position, ideally on the floor (because you are seeking to make contact with the element of Earth). Don't cross your arms or legs; your meditation will be more effective if you do not create blockages in the way that the energy flows round your body.

3. Begin to breathe in a slow and steady rhythm. (Breathing techniques are discussed in more depth in Chapter 3.) For these meditations, concentrate on breathing slowly and regularly.

4. As you breathe in, be aware of the ground supporting you and holding you up. Focus on the strength of the ground and begin to feel any built-up stress in your muscles fading away and seeping into the ground beneath you.

5. The more relaxed you feel, the lighter you will feel. With your eyes closed, begin to visualize yourself sinking into the earth. You can feel the warm support of the soil holding you, almost as though you were returning to the great womb of the earth.

6. Now that you are protectively encased deep within the earth, focus inward. As you breathe in, try to sense those parts of your body that feel heavy and solid. As you breathe out, feel them increasing in density. Don't worry about thinking at this point; you will feel these sensations without having to create them in your mind.

7. What you are doing at this point is awakening the solidity of Earth and embedding this within your psyche. Allow the feeling of heaviness to seep into every part of your body. The feeling should not be unpleasant but warmly reassuring, like the sensation experienced after a good meal.

8. The final part of this visualization involves becoming completely one with the earth. Feel the contours of your body blurring as you merge with the living entity that is the material universe.

9. You can stay in this final state for as long as it feels comfortable. When you are ready to leave, thank the spirits of Earth for their support and then slowly visualize yourself detaching from the earth and ascending to the surface. Allow yourself some time to readjust before opening your eyes and returning to a wakeful state.

Building an Astral Kingdom in Malkuth

This meditation is designed to assist you in building a personal sacred space that you can return to whenever you need to focus on or resolve any matter that relates to the Sephira of Malkuth. You will be building an astral kingdom for each of the Sephira on the Tree of Life.

1. To prepare your senses for this exercise, hold and smell some fresh earth before you begin. If you can obtain a quartz crystal, lay this over your chest in the position of your heart. If not, you can also use salt as a symbol of Earth. If possible, obtain some Dittany of Crete or sage incense (available at many New Age shops and online; see Appendix C).

2. When you've prepared your senses and lit your incense, if you have some, lie down on the bed and position your quartz or salt. When you are lying in a comfortable position, begin to establish your breathing rhythm.

3. Imagine yourself walking through a wooded area. The time period should be either medieval or more ancient. Notice evidence of the

historical period as you walk through the woods. For example, you might see peasants in the fields, people riding past on horseback, a castle on the horizon through the trees, or chimney smoke curling up into the sky. These will all give you clues as to the time period that you are in.

4. You will see a door in front of you. This door is made of some natural material, but the specific details will present themselves to you from your unconscious. Stand in front of this door and declare, "In the name of Adonai Ha Aretz, may my temple in Malkuth be open to me."

5. The door opens and before you is a series of stairs leading downward. The temple is lit by some form of natural illumination, either luminescent crystals or torches.

6. As you walk down, feel the walls and notice the deep energy of the earth filling you. You arrive at another doorway. Stand in front of this door and declare, "In the name of Adonai Ha Aretz, may my secret inner sanctum be open to me."

7. You enter a room that is constructed entirely of natural materials. There may be plants or grasses inside this room. This inner sanctum can be of any size. This is your own inner understanding of Malkuth, and you should allow its design to be guided by your unconscious will.

8. There is an altar within your inner sanctum. This may be wooden or stone or even a large piece of quartz. Stand before your altar and utter a brief prayer, in your own words, to the Divine essence associated with Malkuth. Repeat this prayer four times. Now reflect on whatever the matter is that you are seeking to resolve. Ask for the assistance of Adonai in finding the resolution. After you have determined your course of action, retrace your steps until you find yourself lying on your bed again.

Empowerment Technique for Malkuth: Physical Stillness

Over the centuries, Hermetic Kabbalists and ceremonial magicians within the Western Mystery Tradition have developed a vast range of powerful esoteric practices. These secret techniques can take many months to perfect, but their positive empowering effects will be felt within the first few days.

Every Sephira on the Tree of Life is associated with a particular element and with a particular aspect of the process of inner development. Another name for this personal evolution is the "Great Work." The aim of the Great Work is total individual transformation, and the techniques provided in the "Empowerment Technique" section of each chapter will help you to progress with more confidence toward the completion of the Great Work.

> Buddhists have conceived an object as an event and not as a thing of substance ... Buddhists understand our experience in terms of time and movement.
> —Fritjof Capra, *The Tao of Physics* (1976)

The Kabbalistic technique that we are going to explore is the skill of achieving physical stillness. This is much more difficult than you might think.

For this special Kabbalistic technique, wear comfortable, loose-fitting clothing. You also need a small hardcover book and a set of prayer beads. If you cannot locate a supplier of prayer or meditation beads, make your own from household thread and some beads. Make sure there is room to slide the beads along the thread, for reasons I'll discuss a little later.

In the Western Mystery Tradition, there are said to be four key skills that must be mastered. They are referred to as a series of instructional commands: to know, to dare, to will, and to be silent. These are also known as the four powers of the Sphinx. This particular exercise relates to the last command, to be silent. To progress within Hermetic Kabbalah, you must be able to perform the various exercises without distraction. Silence in this sense does not just mean the ability to be verbally quiet; it also refers to the ability to achieve a sense of total stillness. When you first try this, you may be reminded of trying to get a toddler to sit still for five minutes—a significant challenge! As you train your "inner toddler," however, pretty soon you'll be able to still yourself whenever you want to.

1. Without any preparation, sit down and try to be absolutely still. You may notice that the very decision not to move makes you suddenly aware of your body and you find it extremely difficult not to move.

2. Realizing that this is not so simple as it seems, perform the Earth Meditation (described earlier in this chapter). Now try being still again; you will find that you feel much calmer and relaxed. You will also discover that you can remain still for a longer period of time if you meditate first.

3. When attempting inner stillness, you will probably find that you suffer from sudden itchiness in various parts of your body. Hold the prayer beads in your hand. Every time you feel an itch, move a bead along the string. You can do this easily with your thumb by draping the string over your hand so that the beads sit in your palm and the empty string runs along the back of your hand. This will allow you to track your progress. If you do move your position (moving the beads is allowed), restart the exercise.

4. Remember, this is *very* difficult, so don't feel bad if you can achieve only a couple of minutes of real stillness. It is still well worth the effort. By being physically still, we calm our mind and our unconscious. This allows us to be far more receptive to the spiritual and promotes a healthier and more positive outlook on life.

5. When you are able to sit still for a few minutes without any significant limb movement, move on to the next stage. You must now learn to control those distracting itches. When you feel an itch, focus your concentration on that area and visualize a warm energy at the point of the itchiness dissipating the distracting feeling. With practice, this will make the itch disappear without you having to move.

6. When we talk of physical stillness, we need to think about outward and inner stillness. You can help this by focusing on your breathing and making it as slow and deep as you can.

7. The next phase of this exercise is perhaps the most difficult, but is also the most important in terms of developing a firm foundation for success in the Great Work: Try to shift your consciousness away from your body—that is, actively forget your control of your arms and legs, for instance.

8. You can help this process by actively visualizing the consciousness of your body as a yellow network of lines connecting your brain to your body. Then visualize this network of veins as lines retreating toward your brain until they have entirely disappeared.

9. You will now be approaching a state of authentic physical stillness, and your consciousness will be focused only on the mind and on the spiritual aspect of your existence. This is an essential part of the work of Malkuth because it ensures that you really are building a stable material vessel in which to progress your inner development.

Kabbalistic Ritual: Rite of Protection

As mentioned in Chapter 1, one of the four broad headings of Kabbalah is the discipline of Practical Kabbalah. Originally this only included talismanic magic (magic using special symbols and images) and the visionary practices developed by the Merkabah mystics.

However, Hermetic Kabbalah introduced many of the practices and theories of the ancient Greek and Egyptian spiritual traditions. Over time, a whole range of physical activities was developed. This is the basis of the Western Mystery Tradition.

For this ritual, wear loose-fitting clothes and have a black or white candle handy. If you find that external atmosphere helps you to focus, you may want to burn some Dittany of Crete or sage incense.

This ritual is designed to gradually build up an aura of protection around you. You must work on this aura before you progress to any of the higher Sephiroth. If you practice the Rite of Protection at least once a week, you will find that you are open only to positive energies.

1. Prepare a space in which to perform your ritual. Ideally, use the same space for all your ritual work. This should be a part of your home that you can keep relatively private. If you use incense, light it and place it in the east; if you want, place a candle in the center of your working space.

2. While seated, perform the Building an Astral Kingdom in Malkuth meditation described earlier in this chapter. This ensures that when performing the ritual your consciousness is in an enlivened state and in touch with the energies of Malkuth.

3. You may act out the ritual itself literally, or you may choose to visualize yourself carrying out the required actions while remaining seated.

4. All the actions that follow can be carried out literally or in visualization. Stand up and deliver a prayer in your own words to the Divine force of Malkuth. Make it from the heart, but address it to Adonai Ha Aretz and request his support in ensuring that all negative influences depart and that the protective force of Adonai surrounds you.

5. Face east and visualize a large black cube about three feet in front of you. This cube symbolizes the solid reality of materiality. This cube is going to absorb all the negative energy within you and act as a barrier to any negative energy seeking to attach itself to you. As you focus on the cube, say the Divine name "Adonai Ha Aretz."

6. Turn to face south and visualize another cube. Again while focusing on this cube, say "Adonai Ha Aretz."

7. Repeat this action first facing west and then facing north. Then turn so that you are again facing east. Stand still and feel the cubes at each of the compass points as powerful and solid energy. See a line of white-gold light linking all of the cubes so that you are standing in the middle of a diamond of light.

8. Visualize a bright point of white-gold light above your head and intone, "Above me the power of Adonai Ha Aretz." Visualize a bright point of white-gold light below you and intone, "Below me the power of Adonai Ha Aretz." Visualize that same point at shoulder level to your right and intone, "On my right the power of Adonai Ha Aretz." Now do same on your left side but intone, "On my left the power of Adonai Ha Aretz."

9. The white-gold light now emanates from each of these four points until it merges forming a sphere of light with you at the center. This sphere forms a protective barrier against any negative energy, and the cubes of Malkuth absorb the negativity that you already have within you.

10. Remain in this position as long as you are comfortable. When ready, give thanks to Adonai Ha Aretz for offering you protection. You may then sit down and continue with your rhythmic breathing until you are ready to leave your working space.

Signs and Symbols of Malkuth

This section lists symbols, colors, and other associations with Malkuth. These are interesting in their own right and can be meditated on to arrive at your own deep understanding of their meanings. Additionally, while you are working with the energies of Malkuth or when you want to attract positive energies relating to a matter governed by Malkuth, you may want to wear or carry with you something that relates to Malkuth. If you want a raise at work, for example, you may want to wear a quartz necklace, or keep a square-shaped ornament on your desk.

Appendix A shows the pathway correspondences at a glance, and Appendix B lists more symbols, including easy-to-copy planetary and elemental symbols.

- **Symbols:** Cube, square, equal-armed cross
- **Colors:** Dark green, black, brown
- **Numbers and letters:** 4, 10, 55, Nun (N), Heh (H)
- **Crystals and stones:** Rock crystal, quartz, salt
- **Plants and incense:** Sage, oak, Dittany of Crete
- **Archangel:** Sandalphon
- **Direction:** North
- **Element:** Earth, whose archangel is Uriel and whose spirits are the gnomes
- **Planet:** Earth, whose archangel is Sandalphon

Chapter 3

Yesod: The Kingdom of Dreams

Yesod is the first Sephira on the Tree of Life that we reach after we leave the realm of Malkuth. It is pronounced "Yes-od," with the "o" sound elongated and is made up of the Hebrew letters Yod, Samech, Vau, and Daleth. The Sephira of Yesod is reached by passing along the path of Tau on the Tree of Life. Turn to the Tree of Life diagram in Chapter 1 to see the Hebrew spelling of Yesod and the path of Tau that leads into it. This path is associated with self-sacrifice and so indicates the attitude that we must carry with us if we are to pass beyond the purely material view of the world.

Appendix A shows the literal meaning of each letter next to a representation of how the letter looks written in Hebrew. When you meditate on the meaning and associations of each letter, you might like to use the following interpretation as a guide. When I look at the spelling of Yesod, I find a message regarding the importance of commitment to the Great Work. It tells me that the flame of our enthusiasm (Yod) will support us (Samech) in our mental efforts (Vau) and open the door (Daleth) to the higher realms.

The value of the Hebrew word Yesod is 80. This can be reduced to the number 8 by reductive addition (8 + 0 = 8). The number 8 is the value of the Hebrew letter Cheth. This letter literally means "fence" or "wall" and is associated with forces of protection. This is appropriate because it refers to the fact that we should not enter Yesod until we have built up a protective force through our activities in Malkuth. Additionally, the number 80 has the same value as the letter Peh, meaning "mouth." Because Yesod is the Sephira in which we begin to communicate with our Higher Self through dreams, this is very appropriate. It also fits in terms of the association of Yesod with the moon and emotional relationships because communication is the key to all positive relationships.

Although Yesod lies beyond the purely physical, it is not fully within the realm of the spiritual. When we are in Yesod, we begin to access the higher realms through the medium of our dreams. Because the Sephira of Yesod is linked with the moon, we also have to work through our lower emotions in this section of the Great Work. The phrase *lower emotions* should not be taken to mean that these emotions are inferior but that they are the emotions driven by our ego self. As a result, Yesod tends to have an impact on our romantic relationships.

The key Divine name of Yesod is Shaddai Al Chai, which is pronounced "Shah-Die Al Ky." If possible, the *K* should be pronounced in a guttural manner. This name translates as "the almighty and living one" and emphasizes that when we are working with the energies of the Sephira Yesod we are focusing on those aspects that really make us feel alive. It also tells us that the Divine character of this Sephira is both creative and expressive as well as powerful.

Yesod is associated with the way we relate to ourselves emotionally, but also with the way in which we communicate our emotions and indeed our more intimate sensual feelings to our partners in relationships. Yesod is associated with the element of Air, and along with Yesod's links to the Moon, this explains why dreams are a focus when working with the energy of Yesod. At a spiritual level, Yesod is concerned with the first forays into the astral level of existence. The astral is the numinous layer between the purely material and the purely spiritual. In Kabbalah, there is always a commitment to balance, and so Yesod is also connected to the negative qualities of inconsistency and melancholy because they reflect certain qualities of the moon and the element of Air taken to an unhealthful extreme.

In the Kabbalistic text the *Sefer Yetzirah,* Yesod is called the "purifying intelligence"; this tells us that the role of Yesod is to act as a cleansing and preparation of the self for further advancement. The meaning of the title Yesod is "foundation," which emphasizes the role of Yesod in your personal development. Whereas Malkuth helped us to sort out our material life, Yesod provides us with the foundation on which we can build our spiritual development. We should also not forget that the path leading into Yesod is the path of Tau. The letter Tau is linked with notions of self-sacrifice, and so although you are working on your emotions, it is a process of purification rather than indulgence.

Areas of Empowerment

In Chapter 2 I made the bold claim that the Tree of Life is the ideal framework for self-development because of the way in which it is structured. As you move from Malkuth into Yesod, this should become clearer to you.

In Malkuth you worked on the purely physical and material aspects of your life. This was crucial because it is difficult to focus on the spiritual when you are worried about paying the bills and other distractions. Chapter 4 focuses on the more purely mental aspects of your life. After all, you cannot usefully work on your romantic emotions and your ability to relate to the world in a sensual way until you have your life organized on a day-to-day operational level. This is why we have to journey through Malkuth first. It is also difficult to develop your mental concepts and ideas before you have achieved a level of inner emotional balance. Hopefully, you are beginning to see the innate sense in the order in which the Tree of Life seeks to help you to empower aspects of your life.

The exercises in this chapter encourage a greater level of calm and self-understanding, especially in terms of your desires and sexuality. This self-knowledge will prove hugely helpful as you continue to travel upward on the Tree of Life. The exercises focus on your sensuality, your self-image, your romantic attachments, and most important, on building on your mystical abilities.

If you are sexually and romantically balanced, you will inevitably be calmer because you will find that inner tensions and conflicts that may have been present since an early age fade away. As these tensions are removed, they will no longer create feelings of frustration and confusion within you. Additionally, the more comfortable you are with your body, the easier you will find it to successfully meditate. This emotional calm increases the power of the empowerment tools that you will use later because emotional conflicts will not be blocking their energy.

Practical Activities

This section covers two exercises that directly impact your self-image, sensuality, and imagination. You can do these exercises as many times as you feel is useful, but don't move on to Chapter 4 until you feel comfortable with each of the exercises.

The Mirror Exercise

Many people find this exercise difficult at first because it requires a proper level of honesty. When people persist with the exercise, however, they find that it becomes surprisingly reassuring and self-affirming. All you need for this exercise is a full-length mirror, a piece of paper, and a pencil or pen.

At the end of the first stage of this exercise, you are likely to feel slightly uncomfortable about your appearance. By the time you have completed the Mirror exercise, however, you will feel much better about your physical attractiveness. What's more, this exercise will make you feel significantly more comfortable with yourself and as a result more relaxed at a holistic level.

1. Stand fully clothed in front of a full-length mirror. As you look at your reflection, remind yourself of the sense of solidity that you achieved in the Earth Meditation from Chapter 2. This will increase the chance that you are able to see yourself as you truly are as opposed to the slightly distorted view that we all tend to have when we see ourselves in the mirror.

2 When you feel centered in yourself, imagine that you are looking at someone else for the first time. What do you think of the person you see? What do you assume about his or her character? Is he a happy person? Is she a thoughtful person?

3. Write down your thoughts from this exercise. Read through your thoughts and think about whether they coincide with how you would normally see yourself. Chances are there will be some differences, especially if you have been really honest with yourself. Most

of those assumptions that you will have made will have been based on slight changes in expression that we are often not conscious of making. If you have been really honest, you will have focused on the expressions and not on what you usually assume about your own character.

4. Stand in front of the mirror again. This time think of what you feel are your key characteristics. Again imagine that you are looking at a stranger in the mirror and simply experiment with your posture and expression until the person looking at you from the mirror matches the characteristics that you recognize within yourself.

5. Repeat Steps 1 through 4 until you begin to feel a sense of self-assurance when you look in the mirror. After you reach this point, you will find that when you meet new people you feel a lot more self-confident. This is because you are aware that the image you present is the image that properly reflects the way you feel about yourself.

6. Remove your clothes and stand naked in front of the mirror for a few minutes. This may make you feel uncomfortable at first, but to feel fully comfortable with yourself and your body it's important to accept yourself as you truly are. This means that you have to accept yourself as you are naked.

7. The next stage is more difficult; it requires you to actually examine yourself while naked. Of course we have all seen ourselves naked, but we tend to find ways to avoid really looking at ourselves. So, first of all, just spend a few minutes looking as closely as you can at yourself—starting at your feet and working up to your head. Make a mental note not only of those aspects that you are unhappy with, but also those points that you can see as attractive.

8. Write down in one list those aspects of your body that you do not like. Create a second list of those aspects of your body that you do feel are attractive. After you have your lists, read through each item that you don't feel happy about and try and decide whether your decision is an objective one or is based on feelings of insecurity. If you feel that your friends have better-looking legs or wrists or what-ever part of your body it is you don't like, chances are your feelings are due to your own insecurities.

9. Look at those parts of your body that you feel happy about and try to focus on the feeling that you get when you look at those parts of your body. It's important to remember that our sensual or aesthetic

appeal comes as much from our personality as it does from our outer appearance.

10. Finally, look at those parts that you are less happy with. Again, try to imagine that this is someone else's body because this will help to reduce the impact of years of negative feeling. Then try to find that feeling you discovered in Step 9. When you can hold that feeling in your mind consciously, focus on it while looking at the parts of your body that you currently dislike. If you perform this exercise over a period of time, you will find that you do come to see your whole body in a much more positive light.

Self-Massage

The Sephira of Yesod is associated with the moon, which is traditionally associated with romance. This exercise begins to awaken those romantic lunar energies within you. In a sense, you could see this exercise as working on a Yesod-level energy but through the practical sphere of Malkuth. You need a soft-bristled body brush, a feather, and some jasmine or ylang-ylang massage oil.

When working with Yesod, you are exploring energies that are linked to all things sensual. One of the great things about achieving the goals of this particular chapter is that not only should you find yourself feeling much more comfortable with your body, you will also begin to enjoy experiencing your body. This is not only a great boost for your love life, it will also make you feel much more self-confident.

1. Create an atmosphere of sensuality by taking a long, relaxing bath. Light the bathroom with candles to really get yourself in the right frame of mind.

2. After your bath, gently dab yourself dry with the biggest and fluffiest towel that you have. What's more, make sure that your whole house or apartment is nice and cozy and warm; after all, the idea is for you to get in touch with that relaxed and languid aspect of yourself.

3. When you are dry, lie down on your bed. Light your bedroom with candles or drape some scarves or silk squares over the top of your lampshades to create a candle-lit atmosphere. Make sure that the body brush, feather, and massage oil are within easy reach.

4. Begin to brush your body with the body brush, using long steady strokes. Brush in one direction all the time to encourage the energy to flow round your body. Begin at your feet and work your way up your whole body. The brushing will awaken and sensitize your skin.

5. With the feather, begin at your feet and gently stroke your body in circular patterns, working your way up gradually toward your neck. This is meant to be enjoyable, so don't worry if you decide that you spend longer on your legs than your arms, for instance. The crucial thing is that you begin to realize how alive your whole body can feel. Whereas the brushing will have brought your skin to life, the feather will make every single hair stand on end.

6. By the time you finish with the feather, you should feel very aware of every part of your body as enjoyable and ready to communicate with your mind. Spend a few minutes feeling deeply relaxed and aware of your body.

7. We all enjoy being sensual in our lives, and so you've probably been reading this wondering when I'm ever going to get around to the massage oil! Of course, one key element of sensuality is that anticipation is in itself hugely sensual. The first thing to do with the massage oil is to pour some on your hands and just enjoy the warm, soft feeling of your hands rubbing against each other.

8. After the brushing and the feather, you will probably be quite eager to begin to feel the oil on your whole body. This time, begin with your arms. The idea is to caress your arms softly but with a definite pressure. Be sure to cover your whole arm and to go as slowly as you can manage.

9. Continue stroking your feet and legs and then the rest of your body, making sure to end with the back of your neck and your temples. You need only a little oil, just enough to create a silky sheen over your body.

10. This final step is designed to really connect you with your inner sensuality and to lock this into your self-image. With the very tip of your finger, stroke as gently as possible in a vertical direction the back of your neck above the spine, the very base of your spine, the inside of your arm at the elbow, the back of your knee, and finally from the base of your wrist to the top of your palm. The sensations this produces will be surprising, to say the least. Before you carry on with the rest of the day, make a point of telling yourself that you are as beautiful and sensual as you feel.

Thy elements do screen my Soul again,
I can undress my Self by thy bright Glass,
And then resume the Inclosure, as I was.
Now I am Earth, and now a Star, and then
A Spirit; now a Star, and Earth again ...

—From "For Agrippa," a poem by Henry Vaughan, a celebrated fifteenth-century Hermetic Kabbalist

Meditations

The three meditations in this section help to embed the positive energies associated with Yesod within your consciousness. The meditations build on the practical activities but function at a deeper level.

As you progress along the Tree of Life, you will be able to add more elements to your empowerment activities. For the Yesod meditations, burn some incense while meditating. The ideal incense to burn for these meditations is jasmine, which has traditionally been used in Hermetic Kabbalah for all ceremonies associated with Yesod.

Moon Meditation

This is the main meditation of Yesod. It awakens your own inner associations with the moon. You might want to perform this meditation after the Self-Massage exercise earlier in this chapter to enhance your connection with the sensual energies of the moon.

1. Before starting, recite a short affirmation to yourself. This may be spoken out loud or just in your head. Ask the force of Shaddai Al Chai to assist you in your meditation and to help you bring the imagination and sensuality of the moon into your life. It might be something like, "I ask that the power of Shaddai Al Chai be with me now as I bring the energies of the lunar sphere into my life."

2. Lie down in a comfortable position. Don't cross your arms or legs. Your meditation will be more effective if you do not create blockages in the way that the energy flows round your body.

3. Begin to breathe in a slow and steady rhythm. Your meditation will be more successful if you also try to achieve the physical stillness that you learned in Chapter 2.

4. As you breathe in, be aware of all the thoughts in your mind swirling around in your consciousness. Focus not on the thoughts themselves but on the sensation of random thoughts drifting in and out of your mind.

5. One effect of focusing on your thoughts is that you become less and less aware of your own body. You may find that you feel slightly disorientated and possibly even a little dizzy.

6. Now that you are protectively encased deep within the earth, focus inward. As you inhale, try to sense those parts of your body that feel heavy and solid. As you exhale, feel them increasing in density. Do not worry about thinking at this point; you will feel these sensations without having to create them in your mind.

7. Visualize a full moon above your head. It is bright and shining with a milky-white glow. At the moment, it is very distant, but you can see tiny flecks of white light floating down toward you. These tiny moonbeams travel down toward you in groups of nine, and you sense them circling around your head.

8. As the moonbeams float down toward you, a desire grows within you to float upward to the moon. Within the moon, you can see a female figure who is tall and athletic and surrounded by animals. She is beckoning to you. Concentrate on this image and say inwardly, "May the energies of Levanah (the moon) empower my life."

9. As you repeat this affirmation, feel yourself floating upward on the moonbeams until you are immersed in the milky-white glow of the moon. Stay in the presence of the feminine spirit of Levanah until you feel ready to return to a normal waking state.

Meditation to Empower Your Inner Sensuality

This meditation takes your awareness of your inner beauty and sensuality to a deeper and more powerful level. If you have some pearls, even cultured pearls, hold these in your hands throughout this meditation. Pearls are linked with the energy of the moon.

1. For this meditation, you should be lying down. It is important that you feel very warm and relaxed for this meditation, so either lie under a soft throw or rug. You can also do this meditation in the bath. (Make sure you have plenty of luxurious bubbles and candlelight.)

2. As with any meditation, be as physically still as possible. Because you are empowering your sensuality, however, you need to feel physically relaxed, so don't hold yourself still in a tense or stiff manner. Begin to establish a steady breathing rhythm, as deep and languorous as possible.

3. After you have established your breathing, begin to imagine yourself going through the Self-Massage exercise described earlier in the chapter. This time, however, all the sensations are being imagined.

4. You can now feel a warm breeze in your hair. The element of Air is linked strongly with Yesod, and its presence in this meditation ensures its deeper purpose. As the breeze caresses you, say internally, "I welcome the sylphs of Air."

5. The gentle breeze now takes on a personal form. You are aware of a number of slight fairylike creatures flitting around you. They are graceful and elegant, and the beat of their wings is both calming and invigorating.

6. You are now lying in a pool of silver liquid. This liquid is almost like mercury in appearance, and it supports you so that you are able just to lie back in its receptive warmth. This pool is in a large room reminiscent of the Greek or Roman era. The tiles are in vibrant yellow, and a scent of almonds hangs in the air.

7. On your left side stands a young man dressed in a yellow robe playing a small harp or lyre. The music is soothing and beautiful. On your right side stands a young woman in a long lilac dress holding a fan in one hand and an incense censer in the other.

8. You look up and see that on the ceiling the night sky has been meticulously reproduced. As you gaze at the stars and the moon, you hear the spirit of the moon whispering in your ear. She tells you that you have an inner beauty that shines like the silver pool in which you are reclining.

9. You may stay in this moon pool for as long as you wish, but remember that as you return to your waking state, you should do so gradually and gently.

Building an Astral Kingdom in Yesod

The following meditation is designed to assist you in building a personal sacred space that you can return to whenever you need to focus on or resolve any matter that relates to the Sephira of Yesod.

1. Prepare your senses for this meditation. Yesod is linked with the element of Air, and so you need to awaken your sense of smell. Burn some jasmine and essence-of-almond incense. Also have some fragrant flowers with you. If you have a wind chime or even a simple bell, ring it nine times while asking Shaddai Al Chai to watch over your journey into Yesod. You may want to say, "As I enter the kingdom of Yesod, may the power of Shaddai Al Chai watch over me."

2. Lie down and establish your breathing rhythm. Lie with your arms outstretched because the path from Malkuth into Yesod is the path of Tau. The path of Tau literally means "cross" and is associated with self-sacrifice. The shape that you form with your body acts as a living symbol of the mystical journey that you are taking.

3. You see a violet ray of light coming down and illuminating the room. This light brings with it the faint sound of lyres being played, and in the distance you can hear the tinkle of tambourines and finger cymbals. You become aware of your astral body standing and walking into the ray of violet light.

4. You are approaching a circular door made of a pearlescent material. As you look down, you notice that you are now dressed in a yellow toga-style outfit and are wearing lilac-colored sandals. Stand in front of this door and declare, "In the name of the archangel Raphael, may my kingdom in Yesod be open to me."

5. The door will open and before you will be a slope of some glasslike or crystalline substance. This slope leads into an open area filled with the light, with a refreshing scent of various herbs and incenses. Although you can't see them, you can also hear the sounds of innumerable wind chimes.

6. You walk through this area, which is dedicated to the element of Air, and arrive at doorway covered with a heavy violet silk drape. This doorway is the entrance from the region of Air to the region of the moon. Stand in front of this door and declare, "In the name of Selachiel, may the region of the moon be open to me."

7. You enter a room that is full of soft drapes and cushions, almost Arabian in appearance. Around the room are poppies and lotus flowers. In the center of the room is a silver bowl in which burns an almond-oil incense. When you are ready, you pass to the west wall of this room. Before you is a tall archway with carvings of peacocks on each side. A lavender-colored curtain covers the entrance. Stand before this entrance and declare, "In the name of Shaddai Al Chai, may my temple in Yesod be open to me."

8. The inside of the temple reflects the nature of your inner imagination. You will find that as you look around, the temple forms before your eyes. One feature that you will find is a central altar. This is a nine-sided altar made of silver with almond-bark details. On the top of the altar is a large pearl or moonstone. Stand before your altar and utter a brief prayer to the Divine essence associated with Yesod. Repeat this prayer, wholly in your own words, nine times. Now reflect on whatever the matter is that you are seeking to resolve and ask for the assistance of Shaddai Al Chai in finding the resolution. After you have determined your course of action, retrace your steps until you find yourself lying on your bed again.

You have the ability to see and connect with realities beyond the visible and known Universe.

—Sanaya Roman and Duane Packer, *Opening to Channel* (1987)

Empowerment Technique for Yesod: Ritual Breathing

Chapter 2 discussed the way the Hermetic Kabbalah has developed within the Western Mystery Tradition, and the way in which certain key techniques have been passed down over the centuries. The first principle to perfect is that of physical stillness. When we can be still, we can begin to concentrate on what happens inside us as we work with our empowerment exercises.

The Kabbalistic technique that we are going to explore is the skill of correct breathing patterns. Breath is the source of life, and so if we want to empower our lives on a mystical level it is important that we know how to control this most important of activities.

For this technique, wear comfortable, loose-fitting clothing. If you like, you can use a metronome to regulate the rhythm of your breathing, although I find it can interfere with the flow of inner energies and so prevent a proper state of relaxation.

As you learned in Chapter 2, in the Western Mystery Tradition there are said to be four key skills that must be mastered: to know, to dare, to will, and to be silent. By learning to control our breathing, we can begin to exert control over our bodily processes. This is the first step toward mastering our own will, and it is by getting in touch with our inner will that we will truly empower our lives. In our normal waking state, our sensory organs are constantly feeding us information. The overwhelming data of smells, sights, and sensations allow us to construct the reality in which we operate. To enter a different level of reality, it is necessary to silence this data. Controlling our breathing helps to slow down the rate at which this information is received and makes it much easier to enter a different level of reality.

1. Sit comfortably on a chair with your back straight. Breathe slowly and easily; do not attempt to hold your breath or to extend any part of the breathing cycle. Breathe in, hold, and breathe out.

2. Repeat the exercise, but this time breathe in, hold, breathe out, and then breathe in again. After you have established a comfortable rhythm, count the number of beats that each stage of the cycle lasts. To create a sustainable pattern, take the beats of the smallest cycle as your base unit. In most cases, this will be the gap between exhalation and inhalation. Double this unit for breathing in and out and use this unit as the time for which you hold the breath in your body and wait before the next inhalation. For example, I wait three seconds between exhaling and inhaling, and so my breathing rhythm should be as follows:

Inhale	Hold	Exhale	Hold
6	3	6	3

   This pattern works very well for ritual preparation, but for meditation, working a 6, 6, 6, 6 pattern is better. For a beginner, however, it is difficult to hold the breath and the lungs empty for sufficient lengths of time to make this pattern workable at first.

Many people try to use counting as a way to keep the pattern. However, I strongly advise against this because you will find that it is incredibly hard to drop the counting when you start to use the breathing in your ritual work. It is hard to be effective in a ritual when your head is repeating "and 1 and 2 and 3 and breathe" constantly!

3. After you set your breathing rhythm, practice breathing in this pattern while sitting comfortably with your back straight.

4. Having established a rhythm, make sure you are breathing properly. Lie on your back on a hard surface and breathe in. You will no doubt feel your chest rising—and this is where you need to change your breathing. Effective breathing needs to be total breathing and involves the whole of the lung cavity.

5. Lying on your back, pull in your breath with your diaphragm—holding your hand over your stomach will help you know when you are doing it right—so that your lungs begin to fill and your belly rises. After your diaphragm has finished, you can now continue to pull air into your body by breathing with your chest, allowing it to fully expand.

6. When exhaling, begin by contracting the chest in the normal way. When the chest has fully contracted, use the diaphragm again to push any remaining air away from your body. This form of breathing takes practice. When you have mastered it, you will find it highly effective in creating the meditative stillness of mind that you are looking for as a preparation for ritual working.

7. When you are comfortable with this style of breathing while lying down, practice breathing in this same way while standing up. This is an important skill to perfect because many of the empowerment rituals require you to be standing up.

8. When you can breathe fully in a standing position, you need to gradually extend the length of each element of the breath cycle. This allows enough time in a breath cycle to perform an action or visualize an image. I suggest that you aim at a breath cycle in seconds of roughly 8, 4, 8, 4.

9. Facing east, begin to breathe in the rhythm you have learned. Imagine that as you breathe the sound of your slow and steady heartbeat is all you can hear; it should be as if the universe is breathing and

beating in time with your own body. As the sound fills your ears, become aware of your whole body expanding and contracting with your breath, as though your whole body were solely engaged in the act of pulsating with your breath.

10. Visualize yourself within a perfect sphere of white. As you continue to breathe, your consciousness is insulated from the outside and you are able to enter the focus of any ritual with far greater success.

Kabbalistic Rituals

Practice the special breathing technique just described before you try out the two rituals provided in this section. Having balanced your Earth energies in Chapter 2, you are now ready to begin to make changes on a more internal level.

Relaxation Ritual

This ritual creates a deep sense of relaxation within you. This is more than a mere feeling of calm or contentment. The feeling generated by this ritual is more akin to a return to the womb; in addition, the Relaxation Ritual enables you to absorb the positive energies of Yesod and allow them to begin to impact your daily life.

For this ritual, wear comfortable, loose-fitting clothes. In addition, you need a yellow candle, some jasmine incense, a bell or tambourine, and some almond massage oil.

1. Prepare your ritual space. Place the yellow candle and incense in the eastern quarter, the incense in the western quarter, the bell or tambourine in the south, and the massage oil in the north.

2. Perform the Rite of Protection (described in Chapter 2) to ensure that only positive energies can be awakened during the Relaxation Ritual.

3. After you have created a protective space, enter your temple in Yesod by performing the Building an Astral Kingdom in Yesod meditation described earlier in this chapter. You perform this meditation so that your Higher Self is in contact with the particular forces related to Yesod. Although you will be performing actions within your actual ritual space, you should feel yourself in your personal astral temple of Yesod.

4. Walk toward the east and light the yellow candle while announcing, "May the light of Shaddai Al Chai shine down upon this work." Now move to the south and strike the tambourine or bell nine times and declare, "May the rushing spirits of the Air be present in my working." Move to the west and light the incense and announce, "Let Shaddai Al Chai be present in this working." Finally move to the north and dab yourself with the massage oil on your forehead, temples, chest, wrists, abdomen, and the backs of your knees and then say, "May the power of Shaddai Al Chai enliven the energies of Levanah within me."

5. Lie down with your head facing west and your feet pointing to the east. Ensure that you are physically still and that you are breathing according to the instructions earlier in this chapter. As you breathe, allow yourself to sense the scent of the incense behind you and the light of the candle in front of you.

6. Visualize a pale yellow, pulsating ball of light in the east. Say, "This is the light of Shaddai Al Chai—may it make me whole." The light moves to the south and again you hear the chiming of your bell or tambourine nine times. At this point, you are imagining the sound of the bell or tambourine; you don't need to get up and go and strike it again.

7. The ball of light now moves to the west, just behind your head. Visualize the smoke from the incense coating the ball of light so that it now has a milky-white appearance with a yellow glow deep within. Visualize it moving to the north where the vapor from the almond oil coats it again so that as well as a warm glow the ball of light now gives off the scent of almonds.

8. Visualize the ball returning to the east. From this position, it moves toward your feet. It is only a few inches above your feet, and you can feel its soothing warmth.

9. Again intone, "Let the power of Shaddai Al Chai make me whole." The ball of light delivers a deep, soothing warmth to your feet, and you feel all tension falling away from you. Visualize it slowly work- ing its way up your legs and over your whole body. As it moves, a whitish yellow glow is left surrounding the part of your body that it is leaving.

10. This process can take as long as needed for you to feel utterly relaxed.
    When you feel completely and deeply relaxed in every pore of your
    body, give thanks to the Divine for sending its soothing light. When
    you are ready to stand, extinguish the candle and the incense in that
    order. Finally, thank the sylphs of Air and the spirit of Levanah
    before leaving your ritual space.

Ritual to Bring Insightful Dreams

Humanity has always been fascinated by dreams. According to Kabbalists,
dreams should be treated as oracles. Dreams can tell us many things
about ourselves, our relationships, and even hint at what may happen in
the future. The following ritual increases the chances of you having
dreams that will be informative and helpful in some way.

Perform this ritual last thing at night when you are already in bed.
You need two lavender-colored candles, some jasmine massage oil, and a
precious stone (ideally moonstone or pearl, but even a piece of rose
quartz will work). Also, have your journal and a pen by your bedside so
that you can record your dream when you awake.

1. Light the two candles; ideally, one should be on either side of your
   bed. Lie back in your bed and establish a steady breathing rhythm.
   Then declare, "It is my will that my dreams shall bring me true
   signs of what is and what is yet to be."
2. Take a drop of the jasmine massage oil and rub it into your forehead and temples. Declare, "Let the powers of intuition ruled by the
   spirits of Levanah be with me this night."
3. Place the stone that you have chosen on your chest. Visualize a violet ray of light penetrating the stone. See the stone glow from within
   with this violet light.
4. The light from your stone spreads out over your whole body. This is
   a warming and relaxing light. Announce, "I invoke the guidance of
   Shaddai Al Chai, and the intuition of Levanah, to inspire my dreaming this night."
5. Place the stone under your pillow and extinguish the two candles.
   Before you go to sleep, enter your temple of Yesod using the Building
   an Astral Kingdom in Yesod meditation described earlier in this
   chapter.

6. As you are drifting off to sleep, you should be seated in your astral kingdom of Yesod looking into the moonstone or pearl on your altar. It is in this precious stone that you will see the events of your dream.

7. As you sleep, it is highly likely that you will have a very insightful dream. When you awake, write down all the details of your dream in your journal.

8. Later that same day, review your journal notes and try to understand the significance of your dream's detail. Before doing so, say a short prayer to Shaddai Al Chai and the spirits of the moon to help you contact your intuitive understanding of your dream.

Signs and Symbols of Yesod

This section lists symbols, colors, and other associations with Yesod. These are interesting in their own right and can be meditated on to arrive at your own deep understanding of their meaning. Additionally, while you are working with the energies of Yesod or when you want to attract positive energies relating to a matter governed by Yesod, you may want to wear or carry with you something that relates to Yesod. If you are hoping to find a new relationship, for example, you may wear a pearl necklace or keep a peacock feather on your bedside table.

Appendix A shows the pathway correspondences at a glance and Appendix B lists more symbols, including easy-to-copy planetary and elemental symbols.

- **Symbols:** Nine-sided figures, crescent, two pillars
- **Colors:** Violet, yellow
- **Numbers and letters:** 8, 9, 21, 32, 45, Mem (M), Tau (Th)
- **Crystals and stones:** Moonstone, pearl, rose quartz
- **Plants and incense:** Willow, almond, jasmine
- **Archangel:** Gabriel
- **Direction:** East
- **Element:** Air, whose archangel is Raphael and whose spirits are the sylphs
- **Planet:** Moon (Levanah), whose archangel is Gabriel

Chapter 4

Hod: The Kingdom of Intellect

Looking at the Tree of Life diagram in Chapter 1, you'll notice that Hod is the first Sephira that takes us away from the central pillar that leads directly into Kether. This central pillar is known as the pillar of Mildness, and the other two pillars are known as the pillar of Severity (on the left) and the pillar of Mercy (on the right). In general, the Sephiroth on the pillar of Severity are concerned with form rather than force—form is concerned with shaping, whereas force is concerned with raw energy. This is certainly the case with Hod, the lowest Sephira on the pillar of Severity.

Hod is pronounced with an elongated "o" sound like the "o" in poke. It is spelled using the Hebrew letters Heh, Vau, and Daleth. The Sephira of Hod can be reached by passing along the paths of Shin and Resh on the Tree of Life. The path of Shin is linked with the element of Fire and refers to the need for vigorous determination to succeed in the Great Work. The path of Resh is linked to the energy of the sun, and because the sun has always been associated with intelligence, this is a very appropriate path for the areas of our life that we will be exploring in Hod.

If you look back at the Tree of Life diagram, you can see how the Sephira Hod would be written in Hebrew. You could look at the shapes of the three letters as variations of the final Daleth letter shape. Daleth literally means "door," and so we can look at the Sephira of Hod as being a doorway in our lives. Specifically it offers us a doorway into our mental processes. As we have done in earlier chapters, we can also find messages within the spelling of the Sephira itself. When I consider the spelling of Hod, I find a message regarding the importance of mental clarity. It tells me that every opportunity (Heh) to clearly define (Vau) our thoughts and perceptions is an opportunity to further open the doorway (Daleth) to higher levels of perception and consciousness.

The value of the Hebrew word Hod is 15. This can be reduced to the number 6 by reductive addition (1 + 5 = 6). The number 6 is the value of the Hebrew letter Vau. This letter literally means "nail" and is associated with the element of Air. This is appropriate for the Sephira of Hod because the element of Air is primarily associated with mental processes. Additionally, the number 6 is regarded by the Western Mystery Tradition as a number linked with solar energies, which connects the spelling of Hod to the path of Resh.

Each Sephira on the Tree of Life is associated with certain aspects of life and qualities of behavior. The Sephira of Hod is mainly concerned with rationality and our intellect. Although it may not seem immediately spiritual, the energies of Hod provide us with a much needed clarity in our mental processes. It will continue to help us as we progress up the Tree of Life. Hod is traditionally linked with the planet Mercury. You may be aware of Mercury as the wing-footed messenger of the gods and so will not be surprised to learn that much of the work that we will be doing in Hod will be to improve our communication skills.

The key Divine name of Hod is Elohim Tzabaoth, which is pronounced "El-Oh-Heem Za-Ba-Oht." This name translates as "the lords of the hosts." Note that the name is plural; this reflects the fact that in Kabbalah the Divine is seen as both a single and a plural spiritual force. The title is important because it refers to the "hosts," which are a particular level of angel in the hierarchy of heaven. In Kabbalah, the order of spiritual beings is very clearly ordered, rather like ranks in the army or within the priesthood. At a much lower level, what we are doing in Hod is constructing a clearly defined structure through which to mentally understand the world, and the sense of order in this Divine name reminds us of this.

Hod is not only concerned with our mental processes but also with the ways in which we make choices in life. Mercury is linked to quick wits and the ability to choose in a positive way. When we have internalized the energies of Hod, we find that we can make those key choices in life with much greater ease. In general terms, the Sephira Hod is linked with the element of Water. This may seem strange at first because the element of Water is often thought of as being associated with our emotions. However, the aim of Kabbalistic empowerment is to re-create ourselves according to a spiritual framework, and so even our intellect should be guided by a deep emotional sense of the interconnectedness of the universe.

Many positive qualities are associated with Hod, such as the ability to think and communicate clearly. If we take the energy of Hod to an extreme, however, we are in danger of becoming rather cold and pedantic in our dealings with others. We may also become too reliant on what we see as a logical or scientific explanation of the universe. Because Hod is positioned away from the central pillar of the Tree of Life, this danger for excess is increased. However, the Kabbalistic technique that you learn later in this chapter is ideal for ensuring a balanced approach to the energies of this Sephira.

Areas of Empowerment

Before we can look fully inside ourselves, we must first be properly grounded, and this is what we achieved in Malkuth. Similarly before we begin to work on the mental choices that we make in life, we must first ensure that we are open to the influence of the Divine, and this is what we achieved in Yesod.

By the time you have practiced all the rituals and techniques within this chapter, you should find that you are a much better communicator and are far more comfortable in social settings. In addition, you will be able to think with greater clarity. The energies of Hod often act as an encouragement for people to rediscover interests in learning and education.

As you make your way through the empowerment exercises in this chapter, remember the experiences you encountered in Yesod. Your intuition will now be more sensitive, and so listen to it when it speaks. You may, for instance, have a definite sense that you should enroll in a course at your local college or perhaps start reading books in a particular area of knowledge. These sorts of activities are in tune with the energy of Hod, and they will enhance the impact of the empowerment tools provided here.

The key focus of Kabbalistic self-development is inner and outer balance. Each Sephira you work through will bring about a state of balance in its own area. However, we also need to maintain a healthful balance between these different aspects of our life. We do not want to totally focus on our emotions at the expense of our career, for example.

Because it sits on the left pillar of the Tree of Life, the Sephira of Hod is balanced by the Sephira that faces it on the right pillar of the Tree of Life. This is the Sephira of Netzach, which is explored in Chapter 5. You can help to avoid feelings of imbalance by setting some time aside each week to perform the Earth Meditation (see Chapter 2). This will give you a strong sense of being grounded and stable as you absorb the energies of Hod.

I belong neither to any century to any particular place; my spiritual being lives its eternal existence outside time and space. When I immerse myself in thought I go back through the Ages. When I extend my spirit to a world existing far from anything you perceive, I can change myself into whatever I wish. Participating consciously in absolute being, I regulate my action according to my surroundings. My country is wherever I happen to set foot at the moment. I am that which is free and Master of Life.

—Cagliostro, famous eighteenth-century occultist and Kabbalist

Practical Activities

The two exercises in this section will directly impact your social skills and your ability to think quickly and clearly. You can do these exercises as many times as you like, but don't move on to the next chapter until you are comfortable with each exercise.

Word Games

No one should see self-development as just hard work. There is absolutely no reason at all why it shouldn't be fun. This particular empowerment tool is intended to be both fun and somewhat frustrating, all at the same time! The more often you practice, of course, the more you will benefit.

There is very little needed for this activity. You need a thesaurus, or a dictionary if you don't have a thesaurus. Other than that, all you need is to keep your wits about you!

This exercise stimulates your ability to think quickly and make speedy decisions. In addition, it should have the side benefit of increasing your vocabulary and your confidence with exploring new words and concepts.

1. Randomly flipping through your dictionary or thesaurus, find one word that particularly appeals to you. It should be a fairly uncommon word and one which you would not normally use in conversation.

2. This is the point where you may wish that you had chosen a more obvious word! Use this word at least once in every conversation that you have for the next day. One of the key rules of this game is that the word has to be used in a proper sentence.

3. If that was all there was to the game, it would be far too easy, so let's make it a little more challenging. Decide on a trigger word. This should be a word that is reasonably common. For the following day, every time anyone says the trigger word you have to fit your chosen word into your next sentence.

4. Select another word. This will probably come as something of a relief. However, if you want the game to work as well as possible, it is important that you still pick a relatively unusual word.

5. Write as many sentences as you can using this new word in a slightly different context each time. This is an effective way to increase your mental agility, and you may like to try this with a number of different words.

6. This next step helps your powers of recall and mental organization. List as many words as you can that have the same or very similar meaning to your chosen word. You may like to use a thesaurus to both check your list and give you even more word ideas.

7. Now we get to the really tricky part! Pick no more than eight words from your list and memorize them. The reason you should pick no more than eight is that you also have to remember the words in order.

8. Having memorized your list of words, use them in your conversations that you have the following day. To make it even more challenging, you have to use the words in order. So your first word must be used in your first conversation of the day and so on.

9. After you master that, pick one word from each letter of the alphabet and construct a paragraph that uses all 26 words (in order would be great, if you can manage it). What you are not allowed to do, however, is to make a paragraph with sentences that go like this, "I found the word such-and-such in my dictionary today."

10. Write another paragraph, this time using a word that is the opposite of the meaning of each of your 26 chosen words.

Water Exercise

The Sephira of Hod is connected to the element of Water. The four elements of Earth, Air, Water, and Fire were used by the ancients to represent a whole range of different qualities from the spiritual to the physical realms. The element of Water is linked to our deep emotions, which are also those emotions most suited to personal development. It is only when we have acquired a sensitivity to the fluidity of Water that we can fully enhance our intellect. This is partly because our intellect needs to be emotionally grounded to prevent it from being too harsh or unfeeling.

Before you begin, you need some blue bath oil, a nose clip, some earplugs, a plant sprayer, kettle, some ice cubes, a bowl, and access to a swimming pool or open body of water such as a lake or the ocean.

One of the key concepts within Kabbalah is "As above, so below." This can be explained as a belief that the Divine level of existence is reflected within the physical universe. Within the *Sefer Yetzirah,* we are told that "Kether is in Malkuth and Malkuth is in Kether." We can take this notion of connectedness and apply it to other aspects of life. So, for instance, if we are trying to bring the Divine energies of the element of Water into our lives, we can help to make this occur by immersing ourselves in the qualities of the physical element of Water.

1. Water seems to be very simple, in part because it is so essential to all life on the planet. If we are really going to bring the energy of Water into our lives, it is essential that we begin to appreciate water in all its many forms and temperaments. Start making friends with water by visiting a local art museum or gallery and spending some time experiencing the wide range of emotions that are expressed by artists through their use of water within their art.

2. When you return from the museum/gallery, run yourself a bath and add some of the blue bath oil to the water. It's important that the bath water be tepid. By having tepid water, you will not slip into the usual feelings that you have when bathing. Have your nose clip and earplugs handy.

3. While lying in the bath, set up the steady breathing rhythm that you developed in previous chapters and focus on the feel of water on your body. As you look at the deep blue of the water, visualize the calming energy of that color seeping into your body. See all the different tones of blue that you remember from the art reflected in the water.

4. Put on your nose clip and earplugs. Take a deep breath and close your eyes. Then slowly sink into the bath until you are completely submerged under the water. Allow the water to support and surround you; just enjoy the sensation and note the feelings that arise.

5. After your bath, don't immediately get dressed. Instead, fill your plant sprayer with cold water. Now comes the invigorating part of the exercise! Spray your whole body with a fine mist of cold water. Having just experienced water as supportive, it's important that you also experience the element of emotions as a surprising and somewhat shocking force.

6. Like all the elements, Water acts on us through our imaginations and minds, but also through its literal physical manifestation. Water is unique in being familiar to us in a range of states. Boil a kettle full of water and fill a bowl with water from the tap. Take some ice cubes from your freezer and stand so that you can see the steam rising from the kettle while one hand is in the bowl of water and the other holds the ice cubes. (Hold this hand over the sink or another bowl to avoid drips as the ice cubes begin to melt.)

7. Stay like this until the ice cubes have almost entirely melted in your hand. One purpose of this section is that it embeds certain notions into your unconscious. Most important is the fact that although water occupies a number of different states, ultimately it returns to being water. This has profound significance for how we experience our own emotions.

8. Up to now, you have been experiencing water in a fairly passive way. Now go to a swimming pool and experience water as a passive force itself. The key thing when you go swimming is not the amount of time that you spend in the water. What is important is that you swim with as much vigor as you can muster. This makes it clear to your Higher Self that you are not at the mercy of your emotions but can navigate your way through them. As you are swimming, imagine all your emotional worries are in front of you and you are slicing through them as you speed through the water.

9. We are at the mercy of the weather for the next part of the exercise. You need to wait until it's raining before you can finish this set of steps. When it is raining, go out for a walk without an umbrella or raincoat. Doing so will reinforce your openness to new emotions.

10. While you are out in the rain, there is one last element of fun to be had. You have probably not jumped in puddles for many years. There are any number of reasons why this is an excellent thing to do, and it's exactly what you need to do to finish this stage of your emotional empowerment. It's easy to feel terribly self-conscious while doing this, but it is hugely important that you keep going until you reach a point where you no longer mind what other people might be thinking.

Meditations

The three meditations in this section help to embed the positive energies associated with Hod within your consciousness. The meditations build on the practical activities but function at a deeper level. Their impact is more subtle; if you perform one meditation per week, however, you will gradually notice a very definite shift in the way that you approach your life.

The breathing skills learned in Chapter 2 will do wonders for the depth of your meditative experience, and so the key thing you need in your Hod meditations is to maintain the physical stillness and proper breathing that you have begun to perfect. Because the Sephira of Hod relates to the intellect, you will also write down a short phrase before each meditation. For this you need some blue paper and a pen with orange ink or an orange crayon.

Mercury Meditation

This meditation awakens your inner connections with the energy associated with Mercury. Before you begin, light a lavender-colored candle and burn some sandalwood incense. Place the incense and candle in the east.

1. While the scent of the incense fills the air, write the following on your blue paper: "May the energies of Kokab (Mercury) empower my life under the agency of the archangel Raphael." Beneath this, write the number 2080 and beneath that the number 88. The numbers 2080 and 88 have been seen as "power" numbers linked with the planet Mercury. According to the Western Mystery Tradition, writing down these numbers helps to activate the power of Mercury.

2. Sit in a high-backed chair with the paper laying on your lap. Tilt your head so that you can see the paper, but otherwise try to keep your back as straight as possible. Remember to keep your arms and legs uncrossed.

3. When you achieve proper physical stillness and are breathing in a regular and deep rhythm, imagine that superimposed on your body is a blue and orange caduceus. A caduceus is a staff with two serpents entwined round it—exactly the same as the well-known medical symbol. (Appendix B includes a picture of a caduceus.) This is the symbol of Mercury, so hold it in your mind throughout the meditation.

4. As you breathe in, visualize a capital letter *A* in brilliant blue. As you exhale, allow the letter to become a word beginning with an *A*. See this word as orange in color. On your next inhalation, visualize the letter *B* and again when you exhale allow this letter to become a word.

5. Repeat this process until you have worked your way through the whole alphabet. As far as possible, try to keep all the words circling around you. Do not be discouraged by the fact that many of the words dissipate or become vague. This is entirely to be expected.

6. When you reach the end of the alphabet, continue breathing and watch the words that remain. Allow them to form into a phrase. You may well find that some of the words change. This is not something that you need to force, but will happen of its own accord. Note the phrase that appears and make a promise to yourself to achieve an understanding of its significance for you.

7. Strongly concentrate on the caduceus superimposed on your body. Visualize a pair of winged sandals on your feet and a winged helmet on your head. Say to yourself, "In the name of Taphthartharath (Taf-Tar-Ta-rath), I embody the spirit of Kokab (Koh-Kahb)."

8. Above you shines a small sphere about the size of a golf ball. It is milky-white in color, but as it spins you can see bright flecks and shimmers of orange, gold, and purple beneath the surface. As you inhale, the sphere expands slightly; as you exhale, the flecks of color increase in intensity.

9. Visualize a concentrated ray of silver light emanating from this sphere. The ray of light touches the very crown of your head. Visualize this silver ray becoming liquid and penetrating your head. This liquid forms a network of silver filaments within your head. As this network spreads, you feel yourself becoming more and more alert. Continue to breathe steadily as the ray retracts into the sphere. When you are ready, the sphere gradually fades and you return to a normal waking state.

Meditation to Increase Problem-Solving Skills

This meditation also involves working with the energy of Mercury. Before beginning, obtain a piece of opal or agate; these stones are associated with the positive energies of Mercury. Your meditation will be assisted if you burn some lavender-colored candles and storax incense. Storax is a strong-smelling incense, so you may want to use sandalwood instead.

1. On a piece of blue paper, write the following in orange: "May the energies of Kokab bring to me the wit and wisdom of Tahuti (Ta-Hoot-Ee)." Beneath this write the number 8, which is one of the key numbers for mercurial powers, and below this, two squares drawn to form an octagon. (See Appendix B for an example of this symbol.)

2. Perform this meditation lying down. Place the paper beneath your head and hold the opal or agate in your hands, which should rest on your chest. When you are comfortable, establish a deep-breathing rhythm. Although this is not usually advisable, the nature of this meditation is such that it can improve the results to count the rhythm of your breathing.

3. Throughout this meditation, be aware of the glowing sphere that you visualized hovering over you in the previous Mercury Meditation. A silver ray shines into the crystal that you hold in your hands and causes a silvery light to spread upward over your chest and head.

4. As you breathe, think of a problem you have had recently. This should not be primarily an emotional problem, but one that can be solved with clear and logical thinking. Visualize this problem as a ball of heavy rope. As you look closer, you can see that the rope is tied in a series of complex knots.

5. The knotted rope moves farther away from you, and two paths of colored light appear leading to the ball of rope. The left path is amber, and the right path is crimson. These are the paths of Resh and Shin, respectively. In Kabbalah each path on the Tree of Life can be colored in four different ways depending on in which of the four worlds we are using the path in question. The colors that we use in the meditations relate to the Physical world and are known as the "empress scale" of colors.

6. Visualize yourself traveling along the amber path. When you arrive at the knotted rope, you can see how to untie each knot. For every knot that you undo, however, another knot forms. This is not frustrating to you because you are immersed in calculating how to untie the knots.

7. Retrace your steps and then approach the knot by the crimson path. When you arrive at the rope, you find that you are holding a flaming sword and the knotted rope is now surrounded by a heavy metal chain. You cut through each of the links one by one but are unable to cut through the rope.

8. Retrace your steps. As you stand in front of the two paths, they begin to move closer to each other until you are able to stand on both paths at the same time. The space between the two paths is filled with a silvery glow.

9. Carefully, you walk up this double path and arrive at the knotted ball of rope. As you look at the complex pattern of knots, you realize that in all this complexity there is still a solution if you know how to look. You hold one free end of the rope in your hand and the ball in the other. As you gently pull, the rope unravels until it is in a neat flat coil. You may now return down the double path of Resh and Shin and return to a waking state.

Building an Astral Kingdom in Hod

This meditation assists you in building a personal sacred space that you can return to whenever you need to focus on or resolve any matter that relates to the Sephira of Hod. You will use this astral space for all the ritual work associated with the Sephira of Hod.

1. To prepare for this meditation, take a tepid bath and then, while you are drying, spend some time attempting a crossword puzzle or a similar brain teaser. When you are dry, burn some orange-colored candles and some storax or sandalwood incense. On the table where you are burning the incense, also place a bowl of water.

2. Sit comfortably on the floor or an a large floor cushion, preferably one with a blue or orange cover. With your hands, make the shape of a downward-pointing triangle, your thumbs making the two diagonal sides of the triangle, and bring your hands up so they are resting against your forehead. As you do this, say, "In the name of Elohim Tzabaoth (El-Oh-Heem Za-Ba-Oht), I shall find my way to my kingdom of Hod."

3. Having established your breathing and physical stillness, visualize a maze before you. It is made of a silvery metal, and its walls tower over your head. You enter the maze and begin making your way through.

4. Despite its complexity, you reach the end of the maze and before you is a wide river on the other side of which stands a mountain of opal. Looking down, you see that you are wearing winged sandals. Stand on the edge of the riverbank and declare, "In the name of the archangel Michael, may my kingdom in Hod be open to me."

5. A bridge of amber and crimson light will appear over the river. You cross the bridge and can now see an eight-sided opening in the mountain of opal flanked by two tall birch trees. In front of this opening is a pool of water that you must swim through. You swim to the other side of the pool and stand in front of the opening to the mountain.

6. As you walk into the mountain, you look around at the walls of pure opal. Etched into the walls are strange hieroglyphic carvings that you feel as though you recognize without being able to translate them. Certain images seem to evoke a definite meaning. You

walk toward a silver-colored door and declare, "In the name of the Beni Elohim (Ben-Eye El-Oh-Heem), may the region of Kokab be open to me."

7. You enter an eight-sided room. Various geometric carvings are on the walls, and on silver plinths stand exotic puzzle boxes. Against one wall is a bookcase and opposite that a shelf full of colored inks and quill pens. At the far end is a small door made of pale wood. The door handle is carved in the shape of an ibis head. Stand before this door and declare, "In the name of Elohim Tzabaoth, may my temple in Hod be open to me."

8. The inside of the temple reflects your own intellectual strengths. Some of us think very analytically, others think more laterally and reflectively. Look around this temple area and allow its shapes and furnishings to appear. What you will find is an octagonal altar made of fire opal. On the altar, burn eight orange candles, which burn with a blue flame. Stand at the altar and make the sign of a downward-pointed triangle with your hands while uttering a brief prayer to Elohim Tzabaoth. Repeat this prayer eight times. When you have competed any work you wish to perform in your temple of Hod, thank the Divine and retrace your steps to your normal conscious state.

Empowerment Technique for Hod: Mental Focusing

One of the things that you will have noticed in your visualizations is that it can sometimes be difficult to hold on to an image. The next key technique that you need to develop is clear mental focus. This is important for spiritual empowerment, but also useful for developing your mental skills in general.

Because Hod is linked with the planet Mercury, it seems appropriate that we should be looking at a technique associated with mental alacrity and clarity. All spiritual traditions place a huge emphasis on mental focus or "one-pointedness" as it is sometimes known. Although it is not well known, there is a strong tradition of creating tools for mental focusing in the West. Spanish soldier and ecclesiastic Ignatius Loyola developed a whole series of mystical meditations that are still used by Western Mystery Schools today.

For this technique, wear comfortable, loose-fitting clothing. You also need eight orange-colored candles, two sheets of paper, a pen, and a straight edge or ruler. Other than that, all you need is a strong sense of determination!

In previous chapters I briefly referred to the four powers of the Sphinx: "to know, to dare, to will, and to be silent." The empowerment tool of one-pointedness both increases our ability to actively control our inner will and to increase our inner knowledge. When we are urged "to know," this does not just mean the sort of knowledge that we can get through book learning. If we wish to truly know things, we must also experience them on a deep level. The following steps will greatly increase your ability to achieve the right level of control over your thoughts. A practical benefit of proper mental focus is that it significantly increases your ability to keep a balanced view of all sorts of difficult issues in your life.

1. Before you begin, arrange the eight candles in a circle on a table in front of you and light them. Sit down in front of the candles and place the sheets of paper, pen, and the ruler or straight edge on the table.

2. Establish your breathing rhythm and perform the Mercury Meditation described earlier in this chapter. This will help to create a high level of receptivity in your mind for the abilities that you are seeking to develop. Having completed the Mercury Meditation, mark eight dots on one of the sheets of paper. The dots should form a rough circle. The easy way to do this is to mark four points as you would the corners of a square and place the remaining four points in the middle of each set of two dots.

3. Place your pen on the top dot. Using a ruler or straight edge, join this dot to the one that is three dots away. Continue in this way joining every third dot. What you will have drawn is an eight-pointed star with an octagon at its center (see Appendix B). Holding the paper at a comfortable distance, focus on the overall pattern. You will find that your eyes are drawn to specific angles in the pattern; using your breathing techniques while focusing will help you to avoid this.

4. A key aspect of one-pointedness is being able to ignore distractions to your concentration. Try to focus only on the octagon that sits in the middle of your eight-pointed star. Every time your attention

wanders away to any of the points, put the paper down for a moment before trying again. When you can focus on the whole pattern without visual distraction, you are ready to move on.

5. Don't be discouraged by the difficulty of this—it's meant to be tough! If you can achieve a minute of pure focus, you are doing really well. You can now allow yourself to focus on the whole pattern again. You will find that your eyes are attracted to certain patterns of lines in the diagram. When this happens, see how long you can continue to focus on those particular lines without shifting to another point of interest.

6. Take another piece of paper and draw a large neat square on it. Mark a point in the middle of each line, but outside the border of the square. Using your straight edge, join these four points so that you have a diamond superimposed on your square. You have now drawn the symbol referred to in the Meditation to Increase Problem-Solving Skills section earlier in this chapter. (The symbol is also pictured in Appendix B.) Concentrate on this image for a minute or so, remembering your breathing and stillness skills while you do so.

7. Now turn the paper over, close your eyes, and try to picture the image. This will probably take a lot of practice, because what usually happens is that you can see only one of the squares clearly and the other tends to come in and out of focus. It is important that you keep trying because the ability to hold an image is crucial for the development of your focusing ability.

8. When you can see this image clearly with your eyes closed, the next stage is to mentally "see" it with your eyes open. You may find it easier to begin with one square and then mentally see the next square laid over the first.

9. As you have been focusing on these images, you will have no doubt been distracted not only by the images changing as you try to concentrate on them, but also by various random thoughts popping into your head. Now repeat Steps 1 through 8. When random thoughts appear, remove them by visualizing a blank white screen in front of you. This screen wipes away all intrusive thoughts. You can then allow your image to reform on the front of this screen.

10. Up to now, we have been using fairly simple geometric images. These are relatively easy to work with because we can think of them in an abstract way. After you have mastered the art of focusing on these images and in removing intrusive thoughts, move on to something more complex. The ideal subjects for one-pointedness are those that occur in nature, such as a single tree or a hill.

Kabbalistic Rituals

Progress with the mental-focusing technique just described before trying the two rituals in this section. Remember that whereas the energy of Hod is very mercurial, it is also linked to the element of Water. By remembering the importance of deep emotions when carrying out these rituals, you will ensure that they have more than a merely superficial impact in your life.

Confidence Ritual

Unusually, for this ritual dress in your nicest clothes. This will help to instill a sense of social confidence. You also need some sandalwood incense, a bowl of water, one red and one orange candle, some blue paper, and a pen with orange ink.

You will find that you are a better communicator and feel much more relaxed in social situations after you have performed this ritual a few times. One of the dangers of confidence is that we can become rather vain and arrogant. This ritual is carried out under the influences of the two paths of Shin and Resh, which work together to ensure that your confidence does not become misdirected. The path of Shin is quite fierce and forceful and so prevents any vanity, while the path of Resh helps to keep your benevolent nature at the front of your mind.

1. Prepare your ritual space by lighting the incense and placing it in the east. Place the bowl of water in the west. Light the red candle in the south and the orange candle in the north. Place the paper and pen in the east in front of your incense.

2. Perform the Rite of Protection (see Chapter 2). This will ensure that only positive energies can be awakened during the Confidence Ritual. After you have created a protective space, enter your temple in Hod by performing the Building an Astral Kingdom in Hod meditation

described earlier in this chapter. Although you will be performing actions within your actual ritual space, feel yourself in your personal astral temple of Hod.

3. On the piece of paper, write, "I invoke the power of the sphere of Kokab to empower me with confidence under the agency and guidance of Elohim Tzabaoth." Read this declaration aloud while facing east.

4. Walk toward the west, passing through the south, and stop in front of the bowl of water. Dip your finger into the water and trace a downward-pointing triangle on your forehead. While facing west, declare, "With this symbol of the element of Water, I invoke the protection and steadfastness of Nesher (the kerub of Water) in my dealings."

5. Return to the east via the northern point in your ritual space. As you stand facing east, see the glow of the red and amber paths of Shin and Resh on either side of you. Breathe the incense in deeply and declare, "As I breathe in this incense, I draw into myself the wit and wisdom of Thoth-Hermes." As you say this, see the caduceus symbol shining before you in the east.

6. Walk around, passing the south and west quarters, until you arrive in the north. Here declare, "The light of the path of Resh guides me under the power of Elohim Tzabaoth." As you say this, you feel the warmth of the sun shining with a warm orange glow above you. Before you are two small children smiling and playing in the grass.

7. Begin moving in a clockwise direction again until you reach the south and are standing in front of the red candle of the path of Shin. The sun over your head has moved with you, and you can still feel its warmth filling you. You now declare, "The determination of the path of Shin moves me on under the power of Elohim Tzabaoth." As you say this, you hear the blast of a trumpet and the sun overhead begins to glow with a crimson light.

8. Walk around to the west and then turn so that you are facing east. Walk forward until you are standing in the middle of your ritual space. Now ask, "How shall I find my confidence in this dark world, oh Elohim Tzabaoth?"

9. You feel yourself bathed in a clear light and in your ears you hear the response, "Trust in the Divine and keep right by the paths of Resh and Shin." In front of you on the floor appear two glowing pathways, one in crimson and one in amber. Walk forward to the east declaring, "I walk the paths of Resh and Shin with perfect trust and perfect confidence."

10. As you stand in the east, two figures approach you. They are male and female but with birds' heads. The male has the head of an ibis, and the female has the head of an eagle. They stretch their hands out over your head and you feel yourself filled with a calm sense of inner confidence. You hear them say in unison, "May the blessings of Tahuti and Nesher (deities of Hod and Water) be upon you." When the two figures fade, give thanks to Elohim Tzabaoth and declare the ritual closed.

Absolute knowledge is thus an entirely nonintellectual experience of reality, an experience arising in a nonordinary state of consciousness which may be called a meditative or mystical state.

—Fritjof Capra, *The Tao of Physics* (1976)

Ritual to Increase Memory

For this ritual, you need eight blue candles, a bowl of water, some storax or frankincense incense, a glass filled with water, and a fire opal or piece of agate.

The Sephira of Hod rules our intellect, including our memory. When we are able to fully recover memories, we achieve two positive results. First, we are able to better understand ourselves. Second, by using this ritual we can regain the feelings and attitudes that we associate with that memory which may have been lost over time.

1. Arrange the eight candles in an octagon shape, marking your ritual space. Place the bowl of water in the west and light the incense in the east. The glass of water should be in the west and the piece of fire opal or agate in the east.

2. Perform the Rite of Protection and then say the following, "May I regain the memories that I seek under the guidance and protection

of Elohim Tzabaoth." Move to the west in a clockwise direction and repeat this declaration.

3. While standing in the west, take up the glass of water and trace a downward-pointing triangle in front of your forehead and say, "May Gabriel the archangel of the element of Water bring me the memories that I seek."

4. Move to the north and repeat this action and declaration. Do the same in the east and the south until you arrive back in the west. Hold the glass above your head and declare, "Let the power of Elohim Tzabaoth fill this water with the power of true recollection."

5. Walk toward the center of your ritual space still holding the glass above your head. In the center of the room, you look up and see an amber/orange ray of light that covers the glass. You inwardly give thanks to the Divine as the ray of light recedes.

6. Now approach the east and set the glass down. Take the fire opal or agate in your hands and say, "May the Divine powers make this stone open to their influence." Now move to the south and repeat this statement while holding the stone. Repeat this again at the western and northern quarters.

7. Return to the east and place the stone next to the glass of water. Extend your arms outwards horizontally from the shoulder and intone, "Above me the power of Elohim Tzabaoth, before me the force of Michael, behind me the depth of Gabriel."

8. Pick up the glass in your left hand and the stone in your right hand. As you place the stone into the glass of water you declare, "May the powers awakened in this ritual and held in the element of pure Water be absorbed by this stone that I may recover the memories I seek."

9. You can now set down the glass with the stone inside, and give thanks in your own way to Elohim Tzabaoth. After a day, take the stone out of the glass. Dispense with the water and keep the stone somewhere safe.

10. Whenever you want to recover a lost memory, just go into your temple in Hod while holding this charged stone. When you are in your astral space, begin to focus on the lost memory while holding the stone in your lap. You will find that your lost memories come flowing back to you.

Signs and Symbols of Hod

This section lists symbols, colors, and associations with Hod. These are interesting in their own right and can be meditated on to arrive at your own deep understanding of their meaning. Additionally, while you are working with the energies of Hod or when you want to attract positive energies relating to a matter governed by Hod, you may want to wear or carry with you something that relates to Hod. If you are hoping to do well on an exam, for example, you might wear an opal on a silver chain.

Appendix A shows the pathway correspondences at a glance, and Appendix B lists more symbols, including easy-to-copy planetary and elemental symbols.

- **Symbols:** Eight-sided figures, caduceus, downward-pointing triangle, cross of 13 squares, bowls, and cups
- **Colors:** Orange, blue, silver
- **Numbers and letters:** 6, 8, 36, 64, 2080, Mem (M), Resh (R), Shin (Sh), Tau (Th)
- **Crystals and stones:** Fire opal, agate
- **Plants and incense:** Sandalwood, storax, birch, lavender
- **Archangel:** Michael
- **Direction:** West
- **Element:** Water, whose archangel is Gabriel and whose spirits are the undines
- **Planet:** Mercury, whose archangel is Raphael

Chapter 5

Netzach: The Kingdom of Fire

As you can see from the Tree of Life diagram in Chapter 1, Netzach sits directly opposite Hod on the Tree of Life. Like Hod, the Sephira of Netzach sits away from the central pillar on the Tree of Life and is the first Sephira on the pillar of Mercy. Netzach fits the general definition of Sephiroth on the pillar of Mercy because it is concerned with force rather than form. Specifically, Netzach is concerned with our emotional state.

We pronounce Netzach "Net-Sack"; if possible, try to make the final "ck" sound rather guttural. It is spelled using the Hebrew letters Nun, Tzaddi, and Cheth, as you can see on the Tree of Life diagram. We can reach Netzach by three paths. From Malkuth we follow the path of Qoph, from Yesod the path of Tzaddi, and from Hod the path of Peh. The path of Qoph is linked to the moon and mirrors the experience of Yesod (see Chapter 3) to a degree. It is also concerned with emotional anxiety, which is fitting because Netzach is very much concerned with our more powerful emotions. The path of Tzaddi is connected to the Tarot card the Star and is a very hopeful path associated with commitment and optimism, which links with the creative aspect of Netzach. The letter Peh means "mouth," and as we might expect it is connected with issues of communication. It is our experience of Hod that allows us to pass into the Sephira of Netzach with our enhanced communication skills.

When I consider the spelling of Netzach, I find a message regarding the importance of emotional change and self-expression. It tells me that emotional expression (Nun) will act as a route to greater hope (Tzaddi) and as a means of self-protection (Cheth). In the Western Mystery Tradition, the letter Cheth has been regarded as a glyph of the holy grail and so we can see our expressive ability as a route to our own personal holy grail.

The value of the Hebrew word Netzach is 148. This can be reduced to the number 13 by reductive addition (1 + 4 + 8 = 13). This is highly significant because the number 13 is traditionally associated with great changes in our life. We would normally keep reducing until we arrive at a single number, but 13 is significant in its own right. This reminds us that Netzach lies on the pillar of Force and that we should expect significant changes as a result of working with its energies. When we further reduce the value of Netzach to the number 4 (1 + 3 = 4), we are reminded that Netzach is the final Sephira that is primarily linked to the material world.

The Sephira of Netzach is mainly concerned with our emotions as they are expressed. Specifically, we embody the energies of Netzach when we are being creative, so all forms of visual art and dance fall under the influence of Netzach. At a spiritual level, the experience of Netzach allows us to know our inner feelings and to begin fully expressing them. This in turn helps us to be empowered as a whole person. Netzach is associated with the planet Venus, or *Nogah* as it is known in Hebrew. Venus governs our affections and is linked with passion, physical poise, and grace.

The key Divine name of Netzach is YHVH Tzabaoth, which is pronounced "Yod-Hay-Vow-Hay Za-Ba-Oht." This name translates as "Lord of the hosts." This title is similar to the Divine name of Hod—the word Tzabaoth meaning "hosts" is the same, but the word for the Divine is changed (see Chapter 4). The only difference is that whereas the prefix Elohim is feminine and plural meaning "lords" or "gods," the prefix YHVH is male and singular and means simply "Lord" or "God." The name YHVH is often translated into English as Jehovah or Yahweh. In Kabbalah, however, because its true pronunciation is said to be unknowable, we just write the letters YHVH, and when speaking the name we pronounce each of the letters separately without any vowel sounds in between. The singular nature of the Divine name in Netzach also emphasizes the focus on emotional force rather than mental form within this Sephira.

It's easy to misunderstand the role of Netzach when we consider it from a modern perspective. We know that Venus is the planet ruled by Netzach, and we are used to thinking about Venus in a fairly sentimental manner. However, the real energy of Venus and Netzach is that strong and single-minded passionate emotion that we only feel from time to time. It is because of the emotional power that is revealed in Netzach that we must first balance ourselves mentally in Hod before we attempt to master the energies of Netzach.

When we think of Venus, we need to have in mind the sort of mysterious and awesome power that was attributed to the ancient goddesses such as Ishtar and Isis. The translation of Netzach is "victory," and as a title for the Sephira this gives a strong hint at the innate force that lies within Netzach.

Netzach is attributed to the element of Fire. Fire is unpredictable and dangerous, of course, but it is also life-giving in that new life springs from the ashes. On a mythical level, you might think of the phoenix, the bird that rises from its funeral ashes to live again. In the natural world, forest fires, while devastating, also create wonderfully fertile soil that in the long term yields an abundance of life. This makes fire an excellent symbol of our passions and potential for unfettered self-expression. On the spiritual level, the element of Fire is a lower reflection of the creative force that first brought the universe into being.

The energies of Netzach can help us to develop the positive qualities of creativity, honesty, and passion. Against this we have as always the potential dangers of Netzach, including anger, self-absorption, and rash behavior.

The paths that lead into Netzach offer additional protection from the dangers of taking the energies of this Sephira to an extreme. The path of Qoph reinforces the sensitivity and intuition we developed in Yesod and softens the flames of Netzach when they burn too harshly. The path of Tzaddi brings in the element of Air through its association with the zodiac sign Aquarius. The thoughtful and committed nature of the path of Tzaddi ensures that your fiery energies remain focused on your own empowerment. Finally the path of Peh carries with it the balance and distance that we learned in Hod. The path of Peh is linked with the Tarot's Tower card, which teaches that before we can build ourselves anew we must first be willing to destroy the claims of our ego.

Areas of Empowerment

Having read of the power that resides within the Sephira of Netzach, you can see the importance of a proper route when exploring the Sephiroth. If we followed our personal preferences, we would focus on the one Sephira that would most inflate our ego and do the least to truly empower our lives.

When you have completed your journey through Netzach, you will be ready to move on to a level where you begin to make direct contact with you own Higher Self. Before we can attempt this, it's important that our passions are brought under the control of our true will. The aim of the work with Netzach is not to repress your emotions, but to make them more alive than ever. You will find that when you have completed this chapter, you will be able to express yourself with greater vigor and sincerity without the danger of those positive feelings boiling over into something destructive.

If the key lesson from Hod was mental balance and social communication, the key lessons of Netzach can be seen as a mirror of those qualities. You will develop emotional balance and the ability to communicate at a deep emotional level. The exercises in Netzach will awaken your ability to deal with the complexity of your feelings.

When you are experiencing the energies of Netzach or just thinking about the qualities of this Sephira, also reflect on how this might develop your spirituality. One of the key points of Kabbalah is that the Divine wants us to be joyful whole people expressing our love for the Divine through our love of life.

In Chapter 4 I recommended that you perform the Earth Meditation at least once a week to help ground the energies of Hod. Because we are again dealing with a Sephira that does not sit on the middle pillar, it's a good idea to continue with this practice.

> The Goddess is always with me whenever I perform my rituals ... She is the fire inside me and the beauty that I find around me every day.
> —From a female member of a modern-day Western Mystery Tradition group

Practical Activities

The two exercises in this section will directly impact your creativity and ability to express yourself. You can do these exercises as many times as you feel is useful, but don't move on to the next chapter until you feel comfortable with each of the exercises.

Free Dancing

Here's another empowerment exercise intended to be both fun and maybe a little frustrating! One thing you need for this experience is a sense of rhythm. However, you already have this, even if you don't realize it yet. You also need some kind of exercise tape or video and a full-length mirror.

By the time you have worked through all the steps, you should have found that you are back in touch with your inner rhythm. At the practical level, Netzach is concerned with the full expression of ourselves, and dancing is one of the best ways of achieving that sort of emotional release.

1. Follow your workout tape for a few days. There are a couple of reasons for this. Most important, it will give your body a renewed sense of energy and will mean that you will realize the benefit of properly warming up before any physical exertion. It will also get you used to moving in a coordinated way.

2. After you have followed your workout tape for a few days, exercise to your tape in front of a mirror. Don't worry about whether you think that you look good; the point of this step is to increase your latent understanding of the ways in which your body moves.

3. Now that you have made a start on the physical side of dancing, spend some time with your emotions. Sitting in front of the mirror, think of something very happy and watch how your face reacts to that memory. Now think of something upsetting and watch the reaction again. Repeat this with a number of different emotions.

4. Play some music that you like and see what facial expression you can make that seems to suit the mood of the music. Many people forget that when we are dancing, our faces are as much a part of how we express ourselves as the more obvious movements that we make.

5. Now try a different piece of music, and this time change your expression slightly as the mood of the piece shifts in tempo and mood. You can now begin to extend your expression to your whole body.

81

Make a physical shape using as much of your body as possible that seems to express the feeling of the music. Trust me, you will feel silly doing this, but when you get past that feeling the whole process becomes wonderfully liberating.

6. The next stage is to fit in movements between your shapes. You may be tempted to try to mimic the way you would dance if you were out at a club or the way in which you have seen other people dancing to your chosen style of music. The dancing you are doing now is for you alone. That is why it's important that the way you move is how you want to and not how you think that you are supposed to.

7. If we are going to learn to express ourselves fully, we need to be able to access all our emotions. So now find some music that you wouldn't normally listen to and repeat Steps 5 and 6. It is even worthwhile trying to do this with music that you don't really like because it forces you to reach deep inside yourself to find fitting emotions.

8. Turn the music off and begin to move in a rhythmic manner. This need not be very vigorous or complicated; the main thing is that you allow yourself to move freely.

9. The longer you move, the easier you will find it to feel the music that is already in your head. As you move around, allow whatever emotions are inside you to come to the surface. Express how you feel not just with your face but with your whole body and really let go. You may find that you end up jumping around quite wildly or just slowly rocking back and forth; if you just allow your feelings to guide you, however, the experience will be very cathartic.

The Power of Honesty

The Sephira of Netzach will help you to develop your creative talents. Any artist will tell you that to express yourself you also need to be honest about what you are expressing.

For this exercise, you need some paper and a pen, a mirror, and, oh yes, a good friend. You also need to be able to contact someone who has annoyed you or hurt you, but you'll be pleased to hear that you need that person only briefly!

The Power of Honesty exercise encourages and develops a naturally honest response to the world. When we use the word *honesty* in the context of Netzach, we are less concerned with the idea of facts than we are with the way things feel to us as individuals. This is because the key factor in Netzach is how the world "seems" to us, how we as individuals feel about the world, and our reality is what counts when we are working with this Sephira.

1. Like so many other things in life, the best place to start with being honest is with ourselves. Write down a list of all your positive traits. This can be more difficult than you might think because what you are doing is making a list of what you actually think, which may not be the same as what you are told by your friends.

2. After you have made your list of positive qualities, make a list of negative traits that you believe you have. Read through both lists and try to decide how true they actually are and whether their truth has any impact on the way you actually feel.

3. Putting your feelings on paper is difficult, but when you are facing yourself in the mirror, an extra level of immediacy is added to the situation. Select seven negative and seven positive traits from your list. Then while looking yourself right in the eye in the mirror, tell yourself what these qualities are. It is best if you alternate the positive and negative comments.

4. Now that you have been equally harsh and encouraging to yourself, take this same level of honesty out into the world. This is where you need a friend to help you. Ask your friend to tell you four positive traits and three negative traits he or she feels you have. Encourage your friend to be blunt.

5. When your friend has told you how he or she feels about you, don't immediately make any response. Go home and spend half an hour or so reflecting on what your friend has said, using the breathing techniques that you have learned to ensure a deep level of reflection.

6. It only seems fair now that you should get to be honest about other people. The emotional honesty of Netzach is very unstructured in its raw form because it comes from the pillar of Force rather than the pillar of Form. To avoid losing the sense of structure that you gained in Hod, now engage in some fairly distanced honesty. Write

a review of a film that you have recently seen and submit it to your local newspaper for consideration.

7. Now write a poem to yourself about a subject that you really feel passionate about. Don't worry too much about rhyming schemes for this—what matters is the amount of emotion that you put into both the words and the writing of the poem itself.

8. Find that friend again. Instead of asking your friend to be honest with you, it's your turn to be honest with him or her. Don't plan what you are going to say before you meet your friend. Instead, try to hang on to the feelings that you experienced when you were writing your poem. What you should do is simply tell your friend exactly how you feel about him or her, including how much he or she means to you.

9. Emotional honesty does not always feel comfortable, but it is always beneficial. We all have moments in life when someone has been cruel or hurtful to us in some way and after the event we sit and go over in our head what we wished we had said to that person at the time. What you need to do is contact somebody who at some time in your life has been hurtful in some way. Tell that person exactly how it made you feel and indeed how it still makes you feel today. Don't get angry when doing this; instead, put all your energy into being direct and honest about how you feel.

10. You may have seen the film *Liar, Liar* starring Jim Carrey and laughed at his awkward position. Now it's your turn! Spend a whole day being entirely honest with everyone that you speak to. The only exception is where being emotionally honest would cause an undeserved degree of distress to a person. If such a situation occurs, reflect on why you would feel such thoughts toward that person.

Meditations

The three meditations in this section help to embed the positive energies associated with Netzach within your consciousness. The meditations build on the practical activities but function at a deeper level. Their impact is more subtle; if you perform one meditation per week, however, you will gradually notice a very definite shift in the way that you approach your life.

Netzach is about being fully yourself in emotional and creative terms, while seeking the guidance of your Higher Self and the Divine to ensure that this expression operates in a wholly positive way. To emphasize the fact that you are stripping away all emotional repressions, these meditations work best if you perform them without clothes. As you are also seeking to enliven your creativity, play some relaxing classical music in the background while working through these meditations.

Venus Meditation

This meditation awakens your inner connections with the energy associated with Venus. Before you begin, light a green candle and burn some sandalwood or ylang-ylang incense. Place this incense in the west and place the candle in the east.

1. Begin playing the music as soon as your candle is lit. While the music plays and the rich scent of sandalwood or ylang-ylang fills your senses, sit in a high-backed chair and establish a deep-breathing rhythm. The high-backed chair will help to keep your back straight. When we are meditating on emotional issues, it's easy for our back to slump a little, which interferes with our breathing technique.

2. As you breathe, allow the images of past and current friends, family members, and, in particular, past and current relationships to drift across your mind. Allow yourself to feel all the emotions that you associate with those different people.

3. As the images shift in your consciousness, notice that it becomes more and more difficult to separate how you feel about each person. You are left with something akin to a rich broth of emotions with no single emotion more prominent than another. You realize that what is valuable is the nature of the emotion itself, not the quality of any particular emotion.

4. These images now all fade, and as you breathe, focus directly on your heart. You can feel it beating, and with every beat you become more aware of the heat within your body. As the heat increases, you can visualize almost a heat haze surrounding your body.

5. Instead of just dissipating, this heat haze begins to coalesce and the droplets of liquid heat drift gently upward. As the droplets collect, they form a glowing emerald sphere, which slowly spins within a milky-white mist.

6. As you watch the spinning emerald sphere, you become aware of the scent of fruit trees in the air and the soft, low buzzing of bees. As you inhale, the scent of fruit trees fill your senses; as you exhale, the emerald sphere above your head glows an ever brighter shade of emerald.

7. Before you stands a tall and beautiful woman with olive skin. In her navel is a polished piece of lapis lazuli. She holds an ancient tambourine in one hand and a sculpture in brass in the other. Her eyes look straight into yours, and you feel the energy passing from her emerald eyes into your body.

8. As your body and mind fills with creative energy, you say to yourself, "Spirit of Nogah (No-Gar), goddess of the morning and of the evening, I thank you for your gifts." The woman slowly retreats and is replaced by a scene of green-cloaked figures wearing copper anklets and bracelets dancing in a glade.

9. You may watch this scene for as long as you wish; their energy will in turn energize you. When you are ready again, give thanks to the spirits of Nogah (Venus) before returning to your normal waking state.

Meditation to Discover Your Inner Talents

For this meditation, you will some green paper and a pen with red ink, an emerald stone or a piece of jade, and some rose incense. These stones and incense are all associated with the power of Netzach.

1. On your piece of green paper, write the following: "May Haniel under the authority of YHVH Tzabaoth help me discover my inner talents." Beneath this draw the symbol of Venus and the upward-pointing triangle of Fire. (These symbols are shown in Appendix B.)

2. Perform this meditation lying down. Ensure that you have started your chosen piece of music and lit your incense in the east before you lie down to meditate. Place your precious stone on your chest resting on top of the paper on which you have just written. When you are comfortable, begin to establish a deep-breathing rhythm.

3. When your breathing rhythm is established, visualize a large, upright triangle. Within this triangle is a bright emerald flame that flickers as you watch it. Focus on the flames and be aware of what you most

notice. Is it the colors, the sound of the crackling fire, or even the movement of the flames that most draws your attention?

4. You pass through the triangle of Fire and are standing in a meadow full of lush grass filled with roses. As you bend to smell them, a cat passes by and sits within easy reach of you. You may now either bend to stroke the cat or to smell the roses. Note which of these things you do.

5. A lamp lies before you in the grass, and as you pick it up, the sky grows dark and cloudy. You have to use the light of the lamp to find your way through the field. As you follow the lamp, focus on what most attracted you about the flames and what you did in the meadow of roses.

6. You can see a woman in an ancient Greek costume at the side of the dark path. She tells you that you are just in time for the festival. She points toward the east, but as yet you can see nothing.

7. You continue walking toward the east and as you draw nearer you notice evidence of a festival. It may be that the sounds of music reach your ears, or perhaps you see the brightly colored tents and banners.

8. You are now at the entrance to the festival. Unfortunately, your way is blocked by the same beautiful woman from Step 6 (a type of Venus symbol). She says that only those who contribute to the festival may enter. She then asks what you will bring to the festival.

9. When you reply that you do not know, you are asked a number of questions. She asks you what you noticed at the doorway of flame, what you did in the field of roses, and finally, how you came to know where her festival was located. As you reflect on the answers to these questions, you will find that you become aware of which area of the arts is best for you. You may then give her your answer and seek further inspiration within her festival of creativity.

Building an Astral Kingdom in Netzach

This meditation assists you in building a personal sacred space that you can return to whenever you need to focus on or resolve any matter that relates to the Sephira of Netzach.

1. To prepare for this meditation, light a green candle and have some rousing classical music playing in the background. Prepare yourself physically and emotionally by spending a few minutes free dancing (described earlier in this chapter). If you are feeling quite warm and invigorated when you start to establish your breathing rhythm, you will find that the meditation itself has a much more powerful impact.

2. Lie down on some comfortable floor cushions, which should ideally have bright green or pink covers. With your hands, make the shape of an upward-pointing triangle, your two forefingers making the two diagonal sides of the triangle, and bring your hands up so that they are resting against your forehead. As you do this, say, "In the name of YHVH Tzabaoth (Yod-Hay-Vow-Hay Za-Ba-Oht), I shall find my way to my kingdom of Netzach."

3. Having established your breathing and physical stillness, visualize an immense brass door before you. On either side of the door are two large brass cauldrons filled with a greenish yellow flame. You knock loudly on the door and declare, "In the name of the archangel Haniel (Han-Ee-El), may my kingdom in Netzach be open to me."

4. The door opens, and before you stretches a lake of fire. There are three paths across the lake. One is a translucent flesh color, one a bluish-purple color, and one a deep red color. You begin to walk across the flesh-colored path. Above you the light of the moon gives only a weak light, and soon you have to return back to the brass doorway.

5. Now you try the bluish-purple path. Ahead you see a bright star. This fills you with hope, and you begin to walk faster. You fail to notice that this path is not as solid as it seems, and you trip. The burning lake of fire beneath you convinces you to try the last path.

6. The final deep red path is the path of Peh, whereas the first was the path of Qoph, and the second the path of Tzaddi. The path of Qoph carries with it a sense of anxiety, and the path of Tzaddi can lead to undue optimism. However, the path of Peh leads out of Hod and represents effective communication. As you cross the path of Peh, you are met by seven salamanders (the spirits of Fire) that lead you to a doorway of lapis lazuli, at which you declare, "In the name of the Elohim (El-Oh-Heem), may the region of Nogah be open to me."

7. The door slides back revealing a seven-sided room that is brightly furnished and filled with sculptures and artwork of every kind. On small raised daises around the room, people are dancing or performing plays or singing. A dove flies over your head and you follow it to the back of the room where you see a doorway of rose quartz on which has been carved a large seven-pointed star. Stand before this door and declare, "In the name of YHVH Tzabaoth, may my temple in Netzach be open to me."

8. The inside of the temple reflects your personal creative talents as discovered in the previous meditation. Generally speaking, however, the temple is filled with symbols of whatever this form of expression might be. So, for instance, if you warmed to the idea of creative writing, this temple may be filled with images of quills and scrolls. In the center of your temple stands an altar made of brass. On top of the altar is a large emerald cut in the shape of a rose, which floats in a bowl of greenish-yellow flame. Stand at the altar and make the sign of an upward-pointing triangle with your hands while uttering a brief prayer to YHVH Tzabaoth. This can be as simple as, "I give thanks to YHVH Tzabaoth for delivering me safely into the heart of my astral kingdom in Netzach." Repeat this prayer seven times. After you have completed any work you want to perform in your temple of Netzach, thank the Divine and retrace your steps back to your normal conscious state.

Empowerment Technique for Netzach: Energized Imagination

When you can hold a single image in your mind, you can begin to make those mental images work for you. This is the essence of pure creativity, and so is hugely appropriate to the Sephira of Netzach.

Some schools of Kabbalah focus on the imagination for its mystical applications, others focus on its potential for theurgy. Hermetic Kabbalah sees theurgy or "holy magic" as having just as much importance as the mystical aspects of Kabbalah. You will probably remember the idea of "as above, so below" that tells us that the world of the Divine is reflected in the material universe. In Kabbalah the universe is created out of the mind of the Divine. Similarly, by empowering our imagination, we can gradually learn to create material reality through the power of our own minds.

For this technique, wear comfortable, loose-fitting clothing. You need a piece of paper and a pen with red ink. If you progressed well with the empowerment techniques detailed in earlier chapters, you will find these skills have a profound impact on your rituals. The Energized Imagination technique enhances and awakens our latent powers of positive visualization.

What you will do in the following steps may seem similar to the visualizations you've already experienced, but there is a big difference. In the visualizations, it doesn't matter whether the key images you are given are accompanied by other sights and sounds. In this process, the only things that you can allow to be in your mind are those that you have actively put there through your own imagination.

1. Stimulate your higher consciousness by briefly returning to the Mental Focusing technique in Chapter 4. Draw a large red triangle (the symbol of elemental Fire) on a piece of paper. On the reverse side, write, "May the power of YHVH Tzabaoth enliven and awaken my true creative powers."

2. Establish your breathing rhythm and physical stillness while staring fixedly at the red triangle. Feel its shape seeping into your consciousness as you stare at it. Use the techniques of Chapter 4 to ensure that no distracting thoughts disturb your concentration.

3. Turn the paper over and while retaining the image of the red upright triangle in your mind's eye, read the declaration on the reverse side that is now facing you in a loud and confident voice. As you read this pronouncement, the red triangle in your mind's eye should begin to expand and then begin to spin. Remind yourself as this happens that it is your will that is making this happen.

4. You are now going to go beyond simply moving or expanding your image. The single triangle is now going to replicate itself in your mind's eye. After you have four of these triangles, form them into a four-sided triangular pyramid. This is the three-dimensional symbol of the element of Fire. (Refer to Appendix B to see the symbol for Fire, an upright triangle. What you are now doing is making that symbol a real object by giving it three dimensions.) Allow this symbol to be absorbed by your consciousness by seeing it gradually sink into your mind.

5. This is where you start to take the latent power of your imagination and creativity and really put it to work for you. Think of something that you would like to occur in the next week or so. This should be something simple and something that is feasible. So it's no good thinking that you would like to win a million dollars! You need, at this stage, to be thinking in terms of not having to fight for 20 minutes to find a parking space, or to be bought something small but thoughtful by a loved one, for instance.

6. After you have selected the event that you would like to occur, write it down. Imagine the event like a scene from a film or drama and write down what will happen. Focus on the specific events. If you are thinking of receiving a gift from a friend at work, for instance, you don't need to imagine at what time this will happen; instead, imagine what the expression on your friend's face will be like and what he or she will say to you.

7. Now that you have the scene written down, visualize it happening. The most important thing here is that you focus strongly on the main event that you wish to occur. Visualize it with an absolute certainty that it will happen.

8. As soon as you have created this scene vividly in your mind and watched it happen, stop thinking about it. The key to effective positive visualization is moving beyond hoping that something will happen to being certain that it *will* happen.

9. There is no limit to the number of times you can try this exercise. It may well take a few attempts before you have any real success. However, when you start getting results, you can try positive visualization as you go about your daily life.

Kabbalistic Rituals

You can enhance the experience of your rituals by visualizing the result of the ritual before you carry it out, using the technique described in the previous section.

Creativity Ritual

For this ritual, you need some rose incense, seven green candles, a tambourine or bell, an example of your creative work (something you produced in the Meditation to Discover Your Inner Talents section earlier in this chapter), a painting, and a small sculpture or piece of craftwork.

The purpose of this ritual is to empower the creative aspects of your life. This ritual opens you up to the influences of your Higher Self, which helps you to see the potential for creativity in all aspects of your life.

1. Prepare your ritual space by lighting the rose incense in the east. Arrange the candles on a table in the south, making the shape of a triangle within a square. Place the tambourine or bell in the east, and place your own piece of creative work in the center of your ritual space. The painting sits in the west, and the sculpture or craftwork belongs in the north.

2. Enter your temple by performing the Building an Astral Kingdom in Netzach meditation described earlier in this chapter. Having done so, walk from the east of your ritual space, past the south, and then into the center so that you are standing behind your own piece of creative work. This can be a painting or even a tape recording of some singing. While holding your own piece above your head, you declare, "In the name of YHVH Tzabaoth, I dedicate all my creative acts to the Divine force. In the name of the unknowable Divine, I ask that the energies of Netzach enliven and awaken my creative powers."

3. Walk toward the east, still holding your creative work. Hold the piece over the incense smoke and repeat the Divine name YHVH Tzabaoth in a sonorous tone seven times. Now place the creative work on the ground and take up the tambourine or bell, which you should strike seven times while visualizing a green cone of energy surrounding you.

4. Walk toward the south, and while focusing on the arrangement of candles, form an upward-pointing triangle with your hands, which you then place on your forehead. Spin around (not too speedily) in a clockwise direction while declaring, "May the power of YHVH Tzabaoth free my creative imagination."

5. Move to the west and focus on the picture before you. While focusing, try to emotionally connect with the painting and declare, "May the power of YHVH Tzabaoth inspire my relationship to all created things." As you say this, you should feel the cone of green light that surrounds take on a liquid quality momentarily.

6. When you are ready, move to the north and take up the sculpture or piece of craftwork. Close your eyes and just feel its texture and shape. Now open your eyes, and while focusing on this piece declare, "May the power of YHVH Tzabaoth aid me in the manifestation of my creative abilities that I may add to the beauty in the world."

7. Return to the east and again strike your bell or tambourine seven times. Then, with your arms outstretched, declare, "In the name of YHVH Tzabaoth, I call upon the power of the holy archangel of Netzach. In the name of YHVH Tzabaoth, I call upon Haniel." As you say this, a young, tall angelic figure appears bathed in an emerald light.

8. Bring your hands back to your forehead in the shape of an upward-pointing triangle as a salute to the archangel Haniel. Declare, "In the name of YHVH Tzabaoth, I call upon Haniel to bring forth the choirs of the Elohim." The reason for this section of the ritual is that each lower level of angelic being can only be called by the authority of a higher being.

9. You are aware of an almost static electricity buzzing in the air as the Elohim enter your sphere of sensation. You now address these angelic beings: "Elohim, I ask you in the name of Haniel, under the authority of YHVH Tzabaoth, to place me in the path of Peh that I may learn." You will immediately be bathed in a deep red light. This is the light of the path of Peh, the path that is associated with communication and links the Sephiroth of Hod and Netzach.

10. As you stand bathed in this light, reflect on the nature of the energy that you are feeling and why it should be that the path of Peh will encourage your true creativity to shine through. Declare, "May the energy of the path of Peh teach me to build anew on that which is destroyed and learn the secrets of true communication. In the name of YHVH Tzabaoth, may it be so." Give thanks to the spirits before leaving your temple in Netzach and returning to a normal state of consciousness.

Ritual to Improve Relationships

For this ritual, you need seven green candles, some benzoin or rose incense, a photograph or photographs of your loved ones, and an emerald or jade stone.

It is in our relationships that emotional expression is most important. This ritual opens you up to being more expressive and improves your ability to understand the emotional needs of those whom you love and care about.

1. Arrange the seven candles in the east so that four of them form the compass points of a circle, with the remaining three below the circle so that if you were to join them with a line you would form a circle with a cross beneath it (which symbolizes Venus; see Appendix B). Place the incense also in the east, and place the pictures of your loved ones in the west. Place your emerald or jade in the center of the circle of candles.

2. Having entered your temple in Netzach, face east and declare, "Let the power of YHVH Tzabaoth be present in this ritual and guide it to conform with my inner will and that of the Divine."

3. With arms outstretched, look upward and see a glowing red triangle above your head. Now look straight ahead and say the following while being aware of the glowing symbol of the element of Fire above you. "In the name of the victorious power of YHVH Tzabaoth, I invoke the energies of the spirits of Nogah."

4. Pass to the south, then the west, and then the east, and at each point repeat the declaration you made in Step 3. Return to the east and visualize a glowing emerald sphere in front of you, which grows and grows until it fills your field of vision.

5. Focus on this glowing sphere and say, "Under the authority of YHVH Tzabaoth, let Anael the archangel of Nogah come forth so that I may learn." After you say this, an angelic figure approaches you.

6. The angel indicates with its hand three paths in front of you: the paths of Qoph, Tzaddi, and Peh. The paths are colored pink, flecked with silver, sky blue, and red, respectively. You hear a voice that comes from outside yourself, saying, "First you must learn the lesson of the path of Qoph." You walk round to the west and are bathed in a stone-colored glow as above you shines the crescent of

the moon. You declare, "May Anael instill within me the sensitivity and intuition of the path of Qoph."

7. Move to the north. Again hear the voice of Anael tell you, "Now you must learn the lesson of Tzaddi." You are now surrounded by a purplish white glow and above you is a seven-pointed star. You declare, "May Anael grant me the optimism and determination to persevere in my relationships."

8. Move back to the east. As you face the east, you hear the voice tell you, "And finally you must accept the lesson of the path of Peh." The aura surrounding you changes to a emerald color and you declare, "May Anael help me accept that communication is in all things and that as each tower falls, it provides the bricks by which we build the next."

9. Take the emerald or jade and hold it aloft. Above you a bright and deep emerald glow forms a cloudlike shape. Declare, "In the name of YHVH Tzabaoth, may this stone receive the energies of Netzach and Nogah." A ray now emerges from the cloud and surrounds the stone in your hand.

10. When you are ready, replace the emerald or jade and leave your temple in Netzach. As always, offer a prayer of thanks to the Divine before leaving. Keep the emerald or jade in a safe place in your home.

Signs and Symbols of Netzach

This section lists symbols, colors, and other associations with Netzach. These are interesting in their own right and can be meditated on to arrive at your own deep understanding of their meaning. Additionally, while you are working with the energies of Netzach or when you want to attract positive energies relating to a matter governed by Netzach, you may want to wear or carry with you something that relates to Netzach. If you are hoping to bring some passion into your relationship, for example, you might make a drawing of a Venus symbol with a red Fire triangle inside and keep this in your pocket.

Appendix A shows the pathway correspondences at a glance, and Appendix B lists more symbols, including easy-to-copy planetary and elemental symbols.

- **Symbols:** Seven-sided figures, Venus symbol, upward-pointing triangle, candlesticks, lamps
- **Colors:** Red, green, brass
- **Numbers and letters:** 7, 8, 13, 28, 49, 1225, Kaph (K), Cheth (Ch), Qoph (Q), Tzaddi (Tz), Peh (Ph)
- **Crystals and stones:** Emerald, jade
- **Plants and incense:** Rose, benzoin, laurel, myrtle
- **Archangel:** Haniel
- **Direction:** South
- **Element:** Fire, whose archangel is Michael and whose spirits are the salamanders
- **Planet:** Venus, whose archangel is Anael

Chapter 6

Tiphareth: The Kingdom of the Sun

When we move into the Sephira of Tiphareth, we return once again to the central pillar on the Tree of Life. Not only is Tiphareth in the so-called pillar of Mildness, it is also the central Sephira on the Tree of Life as a whole, and so, not surprisingly, Tiphareth occupies a significant position within the Kabbalistic model of inner development. Tiphareth's location on the pillar of Mildness indicates that Tiphareth is concerned with the balanced and harmonious union of force and form.

We pronounce Tiphareth "Tiff-A-Ret" with the final "T" sound pronounced very clearly and sharply. Tiphareth is spelled Tau, Peh, Aleph, Resh, Tau. We can reach Tiphareth by three paths. From Yesod we follow the path of Samech, from Hod the path of Ayin, and from Netzach the path of Nun. The path of Samech is also known as "the Tentative One," and this points to its association with harmonious balance, which is exemplified by its function as a link between the moon (Yesod) and the sun (Tiphareth). The path of Ayin, or "the Renovating Intelligence," is linked with the zodiac sign Capricorn and represents the need to positively integrate the material with the spiritual to achieve a genuine inner balance. The path of Nun is very complex. On the one hand, it connects with the creative powers associated with Netzach from which it links into Tiphareth. However, Nun is also associated with emotional changes that may be quite traumatic. Again, we are reminded that in many ways it is our emotional life that is most significant and most difficult to balance. In Hermetic Kabbalah, the path of Nun is associated with the Tarot card Death, which is itself symbolic of difficult but positive new beginnings and experiences.

If you turn back to the diagram of the Tree of Life in Chapter 1, you will see how Tiphareth appears when written in Hebrew. The central letter Aleph is very different in shape from the four surrounding letters. This is further emphasized by the fact that the first and last letters are the same. The letter Aleph represents perfect unity, not the least because it is the very first path to emanate from the Divine. It is ideally situated at the heart of this Sephira's name because Tiphareth is strongly associated with ideas of unity at the level of the individual. The shape of the letter Aleph is quite similar to many ancient symbols of the solar force, and Kabbalah has traditionally linked Tiphareth with the sun.

When I consider the spelling of Tiphareth, I find a message regarding the importance of self-sacrifice, and a willingness to recognize the importance of balance as the source of all true happiness. It tells me that self-sacrifice (Tau) will enhance my ability to communicate with those around me (Peh), and that self-sacrifice (Tau) in terms of following my Higher Self rather than my ego will lead to the benevolence of the Divine (Resh). By fulfilling these two sides of the Great Work, I will come to a state of harmonious unity (Aleph). Another more directly mystical interpretation would be that through ego-silence (Tau) we can communicate (Peh) with the perfect unity (Aleph), from which comes all benevolence and life (Resh) and gives voice to the soul (Tau). (By ego-silence, I mean the ability to listen to our Higher Self and not always be guided by the desires of our conscious self or ego.)

The value of the Hebrew word Tiphareth is 1081. This can be reduced to the number 10 (1 + 0 + 8 + 1 = 10). You'll recall from Chapter 2 that the value of Malkuth can also be reduced to 10. This points to a relationship between Malkuth and Tiphareth. Malkuth represents the completion of the creative will of the Divine through the creation of the physical universe. When we look at the Single Tree model of the Tree of Life, Tiphareth represents the highest level of spiritual development that an individual can achieve. So the number 10 points to Tiphareth as being in one sense the completion of the spiritual quest.

In Chapter 1 you learned how the Tree of Life can be used as a diagram of many different aspects of the creation. Because we are looking at the Tree of Life as representing the spiritual development of an individual, Tiphareth is not the highest that we can reach, but represents the point where we begin to truly interact with our spiritual self. In this sense, the number 10 is still very symbolic because we have completed a major stage of our journey of empowerment, and now the key focus is on inner rather than outer development.

Remember, the Tree of Life for all its uses is still a diagram. We should not say, "I am in Tiphareth," for instance, unless we have clarified exactly what is meant by that. In some versions of Christianized Kabbalah, for example, Tiphareth symbolizes the self-sacrifice and balance of Jesus Christ. It is really only as we complete our explorations of each Sephira that we can say what it is to be "in" that particular Sephira.

If we return to the value of the word *Tiphareth,* we can see that 10 represents the completion of the primarily physical or elemental aspect of our development. When we reduce the value further to 1 (1 + 0 = 1), we are representing the first step on the mainly spiritual stage of our life journey. The full value of Tiphareth is also very interesting. The numbers 1, 0, 8, and 1 tell something of an appropriate story themselves, when we learn that the number 8 has long been a symbol of eternity: The individual ego (1) must be removed (0) so that the power of the eternal (8) may lead us to a new balanced self (1).

The Sephira of Tiphareth is linked with balance and harmony—the pure joy of living in a fully balanced state. It is a particularly mystical Sephira because this sense of balance comes not just from within but from a recognition and trust in the Divine power emanating from beyond Kether. Remember that the number 6 is linked with responsibility and choices, and because Tiphareth is the sixth Sephira as you move from the top down on the Tree of Life, it is here that we have to make the most difficult choice and begin to place our trust in our inner will as guided by the Divine.

While spiritually focused, your work with Tiphareth will impact your day-to-day life in a hugely positive way. You will become more aware of your own life goals and in general will begin to take a much more relaxed and trusting approach to life's obstacles and challenges.

Tiphareth is associated with the sun, or as it is known in Hebrew, *Shemesh* (She-Mesh, the initial *e* short as in "pet"). The sun is responsible for all the life on Earth and with its awesome power and life-giving properties, it is the ideal planet to be associated with Tiphareth. The sun is regarded as a positive symbol of the Divine because it is so central and crucial to our solar system. Tiphareth is the first point where a direct appreciation of the presence of the spiritual becomes fully possible. This is partly because when we reach Tiphareth, we have balanced the four elemental energies of Earth, Air, Water, and Fire and are able to begin working with the fifth element of Spirit.

The key Divine name of Tiphareth is YHVH Eloah Ve-Daath, which is pronounced "Yod-Hay-Vow-Hay El-Oh-Aah Vee-De-Aht." The "De" is short like the *de* in "detective," whereas the final *t* should be pronounced clearly and sharply. This name translates as "the Lord God of Knowledge." The emphasis on inner balance is again shown in this Divine name because we have the male and female Hebrew words meaning God side by side.

We are now dealing with a Sephira that requires us to accept some kind of Divine being. However, that does not have to be an understanding of the Divine that is recognized by any particular religion. The tree on which the fruit of Jewish Kabbalah grew had its roots in the mysteries of Egypt, Babylon, and even the earliest civilizations of Sumer. Hermetic Kabbalah recognizes this rich variety and requires only that you accept the existence of a Divine being, whose will is revealed in the unfolding of the universe.

Areas of Empowerment

Tiphareth affects us on all levels of our existence and will tend to change every aspect of our practical lives. However, it is quite specific in terms of what it does to our attitudes and perceptions of our lives. The title Tiphareth translates as "beauty," which wonderfully sums up the shift in consciousness that will emerge as you progress through this chapter.

The energy of Tiphareth encourages a full awakening of the spiritual within us. As a result, we are able to see the innate beauty in all things. When we accept the beauty of the Divinely willed universe, we can begin to develop a deep sense of trust in our own futures, and even approach the perfect innocence of a child tempered by the wisdom of a spiritually aware adult. You will probably find that people who know you will be struck by the new sense of direction and inner balance that you possess if you learn the lessons of Tiphareth.

Practical Activities

The two exercises in this section will directly impact your levels of trust and connection to the Divine. You can do these exercises as many times as you like, but don't move on to the next chapter until you feel comfortable with each exercise.

Learning to Trust

Trust is possibly the most precious quality that we can possess. Real trust is unconditional and does not ask questions of the people or situations that we are trusting. After we have a genuine level of trust, it can greatly enrich our lives.

For the following exercise, you need to have a trusted friend or member of the family to help you. In addition, you need access to a shop that sells crystals, a piece of cloth that can be used as a blindfold, and some paper and a pen.

Tiphareth is in part about the development of our latent psychic abilities and also the removal of anxieties. The development of trust in yourself and others will help lead to a deep sense of trust in the Divine and your own ability to tune in to your own Higher Self.

1. Trust is a quality that is best shared. When we learn to trust in the Divine, there is still a two-way bond of trust in operation, but this is less immediately obvious than the trust that we can share with another person. Choose a close friend or family member and tell that person a secret that you have never told anybody before. This need not be terribly important; it could be something that you just feel embarrassed about. What counts is that you trust someone else with this piece of information.

2. The next step may seem a little bizarre. However, by now you are probably getting used to the fact that what seem like quite strange activities can be very useful. Stand in front of a mirror and tell yourself a secret. This could be a secret that you have been told by someone else, or a secret about yourself. Also promise yourself that you are not going to share this particular secret with anyone else, and then make sure that you honor this promise.

3. It's important that you are also able to demonstrate to those who are close to you that you are highly trustworthy. Ask a close friend

to write down a secret on a piece of paper and then seal it in an envelope and give it to you with the understanding that you will never actually open the envelope and read its contents. You will be tempted to read it, but you must resist!

4. This next step is likely to be harder than you might think. You need your close friend again, whom you should ask to blindfold you. Once blindfolded, your friend should sit you in the middle of a room. Ask your friend to intermittently open and close the door, but not actually leave until after he or she has removed your blindfold. As time goes on, you will really have to work to trust in the fact that when the door closes your friend has not left.

5. Have your friend blindfold you again. This time your friend gives you directions around your own house and all you have to do is follow the instructions. Sound easy? It may not be in practice, but it will be quite useful.

6. Part of your exploration of Tiphareth is to begin to accept your own intuitive abilities, or your ability to know the world from a higher level. You can start this with a very easy and mundane exercise. Instead of deciding in advance what you are going to watch on television, just press the first numbers that come into your head on your remote control. You will be surprised at how often you will find something appropriate, if you are able to trust in your intuition.

7. A slightly harder but very practical way of encouraging a trusting approach to life needs to take place at your place of work. Like all of us, you will have certain tasks that you don't feel comfortable letting other people complete. For one week, delegate at least one of those tasks to someone else and then do your best not to keep checking on whether that person has completed it.

8. This next step is slightly harder again. Choose an activity that makes you feel very nervous or anxious. This might be riding a roller coaster or being near spiders, for instance. You then have to spend at least 20 minutes involved in this activity. You are not allowed to take a friend along to support you because it is important that you trust in the Divine to make sure that you are okay.

9. Having completed Step 8, you deserve some kind of treat! Visit a shop that sells nice crystals. Buy yourself a crystal, but don't choose it. Let it choose you! Look at all the crystals and wait until you see one that you feel drawn toward. This may take some time, but persevere.

10. The final part of this exercise is something that you should try to maintain in your life on a permanent basis. From now on, whenever you feel your instincts speaking to you, try to listen to them. This may be something silly like a feeling that you really should wear a blue shirt today, or something more potentially serious, such as a feeling that you need to slow down when driving.

Learning to Play Again

Almost all religious traditions recognize an association of spiritual insight with the innocence of a child's view of the world. Specifically, the aspects of childhood that link into a spiritualized world view are an unfettered imagination, a willingness to trust, and an untainted optimism. Childhood is also linked with the exuberance of feeling completely and dynamically alive. The Sephira of Tiphareth is linked to the sun, and Tarot's Sun card is represented by two small children playing in a walled garden with the sun overhead.

The main requirement for this stage of your self-development is a willingness to make friends with that part of you that is still a young child. In addition, you need some children's books, access to a toy store, some paint, a large bag of candy, and access to a zoo or theme park.

The different steps in this exercise help you to first empathize with the way in which children see the world and themselves. You then begin to get in touch with the childlike side of your own personality. Ultimately this helps you to see the world and your life in a way that is more innately spiritual and much more rewarding.

1. The best way to begin getting in touch with children is to develop a greater understanding of how adults who work with children see them. Spend a week watching at least half an hour of children's television each day.

2. After you have spent some time immersing yourself in children's television, you may well find that certain aspects of the programming appear to not fully understand a child's point of view. It is now time to read some children's books. These tend to be much more in tune with the way in which children understand the world, because books have to stimulate their imagination much more than a television.

3. The next stage involves spending some time with children yourself. There is almost certainly a local playgroup or nursery in your area that would be very grateful for some volunteer assistance. When you are there, pay attention to how the children interact when they are playing with each other rather than when they are talking to the adults in the group.

4. Now you are ready to start bringing out the child within yourself! Spend a couple of hours visiting your local toy store. Look at the toys from the point of view of a child. In other words, look at the packaging, imagine what the toy might be able to do as well as what it is supposed to be able to do according to the box. Buy at least one toy and take it home with you.

5. When you get home, make sure you have the place to yourself—because you probably don't want your friends around when you are playing with toys, which is exactly what you are going to do. Forget that you are a responsible adult with a career and bills to pay and just allow yourself to enjoy playing with your new toy.

6. Being a child is a very creative stage in our development as a person, because our imaginations are unrestricted by experience. As an adult, it's hard to recapture this unstructured imagination, but we can do this by removing any sense of design or planning in what we are doing. Take the paints that you have had ready and spend an hour or so finger painting. Finger painting is ideal because it makes it extremely difficult to impose any sense of adult order on what you are making.

7. After your shopping and painting, you might be feeling hungry. This is where the bag of candy comes into play. You are allowed to eat as much candy as you like. Don't just eat the candy, though; look at the candy and enjoy all the different colors and textures. Of course, you are also responsible for deciding when to stop, and this emphasizes the fact that when we allow ourselves to be more child-like, we still retain the fact that we have responsibility for ourselves.

8. You will probably want to set aside another day for the next step, although there is no reason why you shouldn't do all this in one adult-free weekend! Spend a few hours at a zoo or a theme park. It's not enough just to go though, you need to actually go on the rides or spend time really looking at the animals. True spiritual

innocence is reliant on a sense of wonder. We all have the ability to feel this wonder in our lives, but we need to find ways to let it out.

9. On the way back, spend part of the journey walking. While you are walking, either make sure that you avoid stepping on any cracks in the sidewalk or, if there are square paving slabs, you can play hop-scotch with yourself as you walk along.

10. When you get home, make yourself whatever you most liked as a meal when you were a child. Reflect on the different experiences you have had so far with this book, but try to consider them with the viewpoint of your newly discovered inner child.

Your inner child never takes anyone or anything for granted and finds exploring and learning about life and other people to be most fun when done experientially.

—Amorah Quan Yin, *The Pleidian Workbook* (1996)

Meditations

The three meditations in this section help to embed the positive energies associated with Tiphareth within your consciousness. The meditations build on the practical activities but function at a deeper level. Their impact is more subtle; if you perform one meditation per week, however, you will gradually notice a very definite shift in the way that you approach your life.

Tiphareth marks the boundary line between a life that is primarily driven by the needs of your ego and a life that is much more guided by the Divine as expressed through your Higher Self. To recognize this and to help establish a different level of self-perception, perform these meditations while wearing loose-fitting yellow or white clothes. If this is not possible, attach a yellow or white ribbon to the clothes that you wear when meditating. White and yellow are colors traditionally associated with the energies of the Divine.

Solar Meditation

This meditation awakens your inner connections with the energy associated with the sun. Before you begin, light six yellow candles and burn some frankincense. Place this incense in the south and place the candles in the east. Place the candles at the six points of two interlocking triangles. (See this figure in Appendix B.)

1. Begin the meditation by standing up facing east. Walk slowly around the area you have established for your meditation, breathing deeply and regularly as you walk. Move in the direction of the sun, from east to the south and then to the west. Then walk from the west to the east and sit down on a large floor cushion that you have placed in front of the candles.

2. When you are seated, be physically still. When you are visualizing in this and all future meditations, employ the Mental Focusing (see Chapter 4) and Energized Imagination (see Chapter 5) techniques. This will help your meditations to be much more powerful and the images within them feel more solid and real. The first thing that you should visualize is complete darkness. This darkness is absolute. Be aware of a lack of any sound, any smells, and even any movement in the air around you.

3. You then see a small pin-prick–sized point of light in the distance. As you see this light, you are aware of a sense of palpable relief.

4. As you focus on this light, you hear the sound of trumpets sounding as though announcing the arrival of a medieval king or a ancient pharaoh. The speck of light begins to grow and rapidly expands, forming an enormous glowing ball of golden light.

5. As you watch this ball of golden light, you feel a warmth on your face and a hot breeze blowing from the south. Rays of yellow light begin to emanate from this sphere, which only at this point do you recognize as a symbol of the sun.

6. The sun lifts in your field of vision and you see beneath it an arid landscape with a narrow river running through the middle. As the sun's rays touch the river, it begins to swell and burst its banks with great vigor. The water flows over the dry landscape and then recedes, leaving black and rich silt behind it.

7. Plants begin to grow in the fertile earth and soon there are waving fields of wheat before you. In the fields, you see two children playing happily together. Herds of grazing animals stand in the fields, and you can see the sails of boats moving along the river in the distance.

8. This scene begins to fade, and once again you are looking at the vibrant ball of the sun. Out of the center of the sun comes a tall and powerfully built man. He wears a crown and is dressed in clothes and a robe that seems to be spun of pure gold.

9. This kingly figure grows and grows in stature until you can no longer make out any details of his form. Instead, your eyes are just filled with a warm gold glow that stretches as far as you can see. You may sit and be bathed in this golden light for as long as you wish before returning to your normal waking state.

Meditation to Banish Worries

You need some paper and a pen with gold ink ready for this meditation. Also, have a piece of topaz or yellow citrine. If you wish to burn incense, use either frankincense or benzoin.

1. With your gold pen, write the following, "May Michael under the authority of YHVH Eloah Ve-Daath assist me in trusting to my Higher Self and the Divine." Underneath this draw a circle with a dot in its center, which is the symbol of the sun (see Appendix B).

2. You should be seated in a high-backed chair for the duration of this ritual. Ideally, place a gold or yellow cushion on the seat. It is important that you sit with a straight back and with one hand resting on your leg while the other hand rests palm upward on your leg holding the piece of topaz.

3. When your breathing rhythm is established, visualize an upward-pointing red triangle and a downward-pointing blue triangle in the distance. Watch as they interlock with each other to form a red and blue hexagram.

4. The hexagram now turns to a golden yellow. Construct in your mind a circle of yellow with a yellow dot at its center. This sun symbol should be positioned in the middle of the yellow hexagram. This will unite in your mind the images of the sun and the Sephira of Tiphareth.

5. The symbol of the sun and Tiphareth moves away from you, and in front of you are three paths colored in dark brown, dark blue, and gray. These are the paths of Nun, Samech, and Ayin, respectively.

Although all the colors are quite earthy, they are suffused with a yellowish sheen.

6. The path of Nun turns to a darker and richer shade of brown, and the symbol of Tiphareth and the sun hover above this path. You begin to walk along this path, which as soon as you step onto it is surrounded by deep blue water on all sides.

7. The path itself begins to change as you walk along it. You realize that its brown color is actually earth. Plants grow out of the earth, but as soon as they flower, they wilt and die. The path of Nun is linked with the Death card in Tarot and rules the changing nature of emotional life. As each plant dies, a new one springs up more beautiful than the last, thus illustrating the illusory nature of all loss.

8. The surrounding water begins to boil as if in a heavy storm. Thunder-clouds appear overhead, and flashes of lightning fill the sky. You stand in the middle of this maelstrom, unconcerned by the seething waters or the storm.

9. As soon as you are completely calm, the storm begins to die down. The symbol of Tiphareth and the sun then sinks down from the sky until it is level with your chest. A pinkish ray of light emanates from this symbol and envelops your heart center, filling you with a deep sense of calm trust in the Divine force. You may remain on the path for as long as you wish, feeling yourself being filled with the light of Tiphareth.

Building an Astral Kingdom in Tiphareth

This meditation assists you in building a personal sacred space that you can return to whenever you need to focus on or resolve any matter that relates to the Sephira of Tiphareth. You use this astral space for all the ritual work associated with the Sephira of Tiphareth. You may also want to try out the other meditations in this chapter when you are in this space. Whenever you feel that your life is out of balance or find it diffi-cult to see the positive aspect of any situation, you can spend some time in your kingdom of Tiphareth.

1. To prepare for this meditation, light a yellow candle, take some yel-low washable paint, and with your finger draw a circle with a dot

in its center on your forehead. On an index card, draw two inter-locking triangles in gold.

2. It is best to perform this meditation sitting on a large floor cushion. Lay the hexagram card on your lap so that it is pointing at the sun symbol on your forehead. Tiphareth is all about mediating and bal-ance, it is known as the "mediating intelligence" in the *Sefer Yetzirah,* and this sitting arrangement will allow the energies of the Sephira to be balanced within you. Declare in a loud and assured voice, "In the name of YHVH Eloah Ve-Daath (Yod-Hay-Vow-Hay El-Oh-Aah Vee-De-Aht), I shall find my way to my kingdom of Tiphareth."

3. Having established your breathing and physical stillness, visualize a towering castle before you. It is made of rose-colored stone that glows in the sunlight. On either side of the circular door stand two golden sculptures of lions, each of which carries a small child on its back. Stand in front of the door and declare, "In the name of the archangel Michael (Mee-Ky-Al), may my kingdom in Tiphareth be open to me."

4. The door opens and you step into what appears to be a vast cathe-dral. There are high, vaulted ceilings and stained-glass windows with a range of religious figures represented, including Moses, Jesus, and the Buddha. At one end of the cathedral is a large stained-glass window depicting a large cross with a blood-red rose at its center.

5. Three aisles run the length of the cathedral. The left path is a bluish-black color, and on each floor tile is inscribed the Hebrew letter Ayin. The right path is very dark brown, and on each floor tile is inscribed the Hebrew letter Nun. The central path is grass green in color, and on each floor tile is inscribed the Hebrew letter Samech. The first tile on this path consists of an interlocking blue and red triangle.

6. You walk along the path of Samech. When you reach the far end of the cathedral, you come face-to-face with a female angelic figure. She is the embodiment of the Tarot card Temperance, the representative of the path of Samech, or the "Tentative Intelligence" as it is referred to in the *Sefer Yetzirah.* She holds a red bottle in one hand and a blue bottle in the other, and as you watch, she pours them into each other, mixing their contents. She then empties both bottles into a crystal or diamond bowl on the cathedral altar. You now stand at the altar and declare, "In the name of the Malachim (Mal-A-Keem), may the region of Shemesh be open to me." *Shemesh* is the Hebrew

name of the sun, and the *Malachim* are the choir of angels belonging to Tiphareth.

7. The veil behind the altar parts and you walk into a room filled with gold and diamonds. It looks like a throne room of some description, and in the middle is a circular pool filled with the clearest and brightest water that you have ever seen. You walk beyond the pool to the rear of this room where there is a small wooden door. The only unusual feature is the handle, which is in the shape of a laurel wreath. You turn the door handle and declare, "In the name of YHVH Eloah Ve-Daath, may my temple in Tiphareth be open to me."

8. The door opens and inside you find a small inner sanctum. This is furnished in a style that most suits your own religious views and feelings. It may be like a small church, a Buddhist temple, or even a Wiccan ceremonial space. Spend some time noticing all the details in your temple. There will definitely be a central altar of some sort. This is six-sided, and on the top of this altar is a phoenix carved from gold that holds in its beak a six-sided piece of topaz. On either side of the altar grow vines. Stand at this altar and give a brief prayer to YHVE Eloah Ve-Daath, repeating the prayer six times. After you have completed any work you wish to perform in your temple of Tiphareth, thank the Divine and retrace your steps back to your normal conscious state.

Empowerment Technique for Tiphareth: Inner Listening

Tiphareth heralds the beginning of the more mystical aspect of our journey of self-empowerment. The specific techniques that you have learned in previous chapters have in a sense all been leading up to this next empowerment tool. When you have stilled your body and your mind and brought both under your control, you are in a position to awaken your Higher Self. Our Higher Self is always there in the background, but until we are properly balanced there is just too much "noise" in our internal systems for us to be able to listen to it clearly.

The open mind recognizes that which cannot be measured as real.
—Melody, *Love Is in the Earth* (1999)

For most of our lives we tend only to listen to our conscious mind. Inevitably, this often means that we are listening to the views of others, especially when it comes to reflecting on our own personality and nature. The aim of all mystical practice is to learn to listen to that part of us that is linked with the Divine. This "inner listening" can appear in many forms. It might be the development of latent psychic or clairvoyant abilities; it could be the honing of our intuitive senses, for instance. In all forms of Kabbalah, great emphasis has been placed on dreaming and on dream interpretation because when we sleep, our conscious mind is less able to act as an obstacle to our Higher Self communicating with the Divine.

For this technique, wear comfortable, loose-fitting clothing. You also need a deck of playing cards, a pair of dice, and some paper and a pen.

In terms of the four powers of the Sphinx, this Kabbalistic technique relates to the ability "to be silent." This may seem like the least spiritual of the four powers, but that is because we often misunderstood the power of true silence. This empowerment technique will allow you to take your skills of physical stillness and mental one-pointedness to a new level. You will be working for the first time not with your conscious mind, but through your Higher Self. Although it will take some time to get strongly positive results, you will find that when you do have a sense of "making contact" with your Higher Self, you will be able to move forward in all sorts of unexpected ways in your life.

1. To prepare yourself for awakening your Higher Self, accept a state of passivity. This may seem strange to you if you have spent a lot of time in the past few months developing an active and dynamic approach to life. However, the connection with our Higher Self only comes to us under the grace of the Divine, and this requires us to still the voice of our conscious mind. Sit on a comfortable floor cushion and perform the Earth Meditation (see Chapter 2) to ground yourself, and then just focus on your breathing.

2. After you establish a breathing rhythm, visualize a golden hexagram above your head and intone in a loud and sonorous voice, "In the name of YHVH Eloah Ve-Daath, I call upon the archangel Raphael (Rah-Fie-Al) to guide me in my quest for my connection to the Divine will." You perform these two steps every time you are planning on working through any of the exercises in this section.

3. Place the deck of cards on a table in front of you. Next to the cards place the paper and pen. Take a card and hold it up in front of you with the back of the card toward you. Without thinking, say out loud the suit that this card belongs to. It's important that you just say Spades, Hearts, Clubs, or Diamonds as soon as one of them comes into your head and that you don't try to "guess" the card.

4. Don't look at the card to see whether you were right or wrong, but write down your suit on the piece of paper. Place the card face down, and take up the next card. Repeat the procedure until you have worked your way through the whole deck. Only when you have completed the whole deck should you check how many cards you guessed accurately. The more you try this, the more cards you will be able to guess correctly.

5. Another good way to develop your latent psychic ability and to learn to trust in your intuition is to use dice. As you roll the dice, say the first number that comes into your head. You will probably feel pretty silly at first, but the more you relax and focus on your breathing techniques and keep a clear mind, the more success you will have.

6. When you begin to have a degree of success with numbers and cards, move on to more visual imagery. This tends to be slightly more difficult because you have to see the shape in your head rather than just speaking without your conscious mind getting in the way. Draw a circle, a square, and a triangle on equal-sized pieces of paper. Place them in a drawer or box and take them out in turn. As you take each one out, use the Mental Focusing technique (see Chapter 4) to clear your mind and then allow a shape to form in your mind.

7. Note the shape that you think it is and then move on to the next piece of paper. After a while, try this in reverse. You decide on a shape by seeing which one forms in your mind and then take out one of the pieces of paper and see whether it is the shape that you were visualizing.

8. Inner listening is about more than just predictive or clairvoyant skill. It also enables us to respond to our environment in a much more sensitive and deep way. Look at a favorite piece of art or read a poem while listening to your inner voice. As you read the poem or look at the art, allow your mind to become empty. Then visualize a large pool of water. In this pool of water, you will see images that

represent your deeper understanding of the poem or art. Allow these images to form and let yourself feel the associated emotions. You can apply this technique to pretty much anything from landscapes to people.

9. If you practice these techniques, you will become quite adept at tuning in to your inner voice, which is the expression of your Higher Self. This can be extremely useful at those points in your life when you are confused as to the best way to act. Find a quiet place and establish your breathing rhythm while focusing on the subject of the problem.

10. Then say inside yourself, "YHVH Eloah Ve-Daath, I ask that you send your archangel Raphael to show me the right course of action." Repeat this request in your head until you begin to see a scene in your mind's eye that shows the best way to resolve your situation.

Kabbalistic Ritual: Balancing

Tiphareth is translated as "beauty," and in terms of Kabbalah beauty is found in perfect balance and harmony. When we have balance and live in a harmonious way, our lives quite literally become more beautiful as a result. The following ritual is designed to increase the beauty in your life from a Kabbalistic perspective.

You need some frankincense, three red candles, three blue candles, six yellow candles, a small saucer of salt, a bowl of water, a bell or tambourine, a piece of yellow cotton fabric or silk ribbon, and a pin with which to attach it to your clothes.

When we have internalized the energies of Tiphareth, we feel more harmonious with others and with our surroundings. This ritual is designed to permanently fix the balance of the four elements in your soul. Because you have now mastered the elements through the four lower Sephiroth, the ritual ends with a pledge from you to the Divine. This is because now that you are moving into a state of consciousness that is governed by Spirit, it's fitting that you begin to actively make a commitment to taking responsibility for your inner development.

1. Prepare your ritual space by lighting the frankincense in the east. Place the three red candles in the south, and place the three blue

candles in the north. Place the six yellow candles in the east. The salt also belongs in the north, and the bowl of water goes to the west. The bell or tambourine and the fabric or ribbon go in the east.

2. Enter your temple in Tiphareth by performing the Building an Astral Kingdom in Tiphareth meditation earlier in this chapter. Having done so, you declare, "In the name of YHVH Eloah Ve-Daath, I declare this temple open." Strike the bell or tambourine six times and utter the following prayer to the Divine, "May YHVH Eloah Ve-Daath be with me as I enter the path of self-balancing. I call upon the energies of the eternal Spirit to guide me in my search for harmony."

3. Walk to the north and pick up the saucer of salt. Declare, "In the name of YHVH Eloah Ve-Daath, may I enter the path of Ayin." See yourself bathed in black shadow as you enter the path of Ayin, which is linked with the achievement of material goals. As you stand in the shadows, state, "I walk the path of the Renovating Intelligence, which leads me to my material desires, and yet my soul is still hungry."

4. Walk toward the west and pick up the bowl of water. Declare, "In the name of YHVH Eloah Ve-Daath, may I enter the path of Nun." See yourself bathed in dull brown shadow as you enter the path of Nun, which is linked with the experience of momentous emotional change. As you stand in the dull brown shadow, state, "I walk the path of the Imaginative Intelligence, which leads me to emotional understanding, and yet my soul is still hungry."

5. Move to the south and stretch out both your arms upward from the shoulder so that they reach above your head, not vertically, but in a curved shape with your palms facing inward. Declare, "In the name of YHVH Eloah Ve-Daath, may I enter the path of Samech." See yourself bathed in a yellow light as you enter the path of Samech, which is linked with harmonious balance. As you stand in the yellow light, state, "I walk the path of the Tentative Intelligence and my soul is at peace."

6. Walk around your ritual area clockwise until you come to the east. In the east, stretch out your arms again and give the following prayer to the Divine, "In the name of YHVE Eloah Ve-Daath, the Divine heart of the Sephira of beauty, I ask that Raphael your archangel instruct the Malachim to assist me in constructing an elemental harmony in the heart of my temple of Tiphareth."

7. Place one red candle from the south in the center of your ritual space. Place the water bowl from the west and the saucer of salt from the north in the center of your ritual space. Arrange them so that they face their appropriate directions and with room for you to stand in the center.

8. Stand in the space that you have just created facing east. There should be no items in front of you. Visualize a deep blue path running from where you stand to the east. Declare, "The Melachim have assisted me in the building of harmony and balance; now I may walk the Divine path of Samech to the heart of Tiphareth."

9. Walk along the path of Samech to the east with your arms outstretched. Above your head is a seven-pointed star, and from your hands you visualize blue and red light streaming behind you. When you arrive at the east, take the bell or tambourine and strike it six times.

10. Kneel on the floor and pin the yellow fabric or ribbon to your chest. As you do this, make the following pledge to the Divine, "I have crossed the path of Samech and found beauty in the heart of the Mediating Intelligence. I wear this ribbon as a token of my commitment to seek balance and harmony in all things. As I stand in the Sephira of Tiphareth, I promise with my whole soul that I will be harmonious in all my dealings with others and work toward a greater understanding of the Divine in all that I do. This I swear in the name of YHVH Eloah Ve-Daath."

Signs and Symbols of Tiphareth

This section lists symbols, colors, and other associations with Tiphareth. These are interesting in their own right and can be meditated on to arrive at your own deep understanding of their meaning. Additionally, while you are working with the energies of Tiphareth or when you want to attract positive energies relating to a matter governed by Tiphareth, you may want to wear or carry with you something that relates to Tiphareth. If you are hoping to ease tensions between people at work or are hoping to boost your connection with your inner self, for example, you could keep some laurel sprigs on your desk or keep sunflowers by your bed.

Appendix A shows the pathway correspondences at a glance, and Appendix B lists more symbols, including easy-to-copy planetary and elemental symbols.

- **Symbols:** Six-sided figures, sun symbol, blue and red hexagram, cross with a rose at its center, children
- **Colors:** Gold, rose, yellow
- **Numbers and letters:** 6, 10, 13, 180, 640, 7, 8, 28, 49, 1225, Nun (N), Ayin (A'A), Samech (S), Vau (V)
- **Crystals and stones:** Topaz, yellow diamond, yellow citrine
- **Plants and incense:** Frankincense, laurel, vines, bay, sunflower
- **Archangel:** Raphael
- **Direction:** East
- **Element:** Fire, whose archangel is Michael and whose spirits are the salamanders
- **Planet:** Sun (Shemesh), whose archangel is Michael

Chapter 7

Geburah: The Kingdom of Severity

You have now reached a point in your inner development where you will be beginning to sense a definite connection with the more spiritual aspect of your personality. Because you will now be dealing with energies that are primarily spiritual in nature, it is likely that you will feel the effects of each new Sephira even more strongly.

We pronounce Geburah "Ge-Boo-Rah," with the initial "Ge" sound pronounced like "get." Geburah is spelled Gimel, Beth, Vau, Resh, Heh. We can reach Geburah by two paths. From Hod we follow the path of Mem, and from Tiphareth we follow the path of Lamed. The path of Mem also goes by the name of "the Stable Intelligence." This title links to the notion of Mem as a symbol of maternal watery energy; it is a binding and stabilizing force in the world. As a link between Geburah and Hod, it also refers to the mediating energy that balances the severity of Geburah with the rationality of Hod. The path of Lamed or "the Faithful Intelligence" is linked with the zodiac sign Libra and represents the need for justice in the world. The beauty of Tiphareth can only exist because of the exercising of the justice of the path of Lamed. Sometimes this justice must be stern, and this is hinted at by the fact that Lamed translates as "ox goad." An ox goad is a whiplike implement used to drive oxen in the field.

If you turn to the Tree of Life diagram in Chapter 1, you will see how Geburah appears when written in Hebrew. The central letter Vau is associated with the element of Air and so links to ideas of thought and mental structure. Its presence at the heart of the spelling of Geburah is important. It reminds us that although Geburah is responsible for themes of severity and destruction in our lives, these forces are still an essential part of the underlying Divine structure of the universe. If you look closely at the shapes of the individual letters, you can see that each letter is in some way formed from the basic Vau letter shape. This emphasizes the importance of an objective rational viewpoint to a proper understanding of the sometimes harsh energies of Geburah.

When I consider the spelling of Geburah, I find a message regarding the importance of remaining faithful to our trust in the Divine structure, even when it is difficult to see the reasons for certain difficulties in our lives. It also continues the theme of balance that we found in Tiphareth. However, the balance we need to see now is the balance between birth and death, peace and turmoil. The spelling seems to say that we must follow the path of the Divine (Gimel) all the way to the home of Divine understanding (Beth). This can be achieved only with a fully cleared and objective mind (Vau). When our minds are properly balanced, we can see the necessity of both the benevolence (Resh) and the martial nature (Heh) of the Divine.

The value of the Hebrew word Geburah is 216. This can be reduced to the number 9 (2 + 1 + 6 = 9). The number 9 is the value of the Hebrew letter Teth, meaning "snake" or "serpent." The letter Teth is associated with the Tarot card Force and so has strong associations with the Mars-related energies of Geburah. It is also worth noting that it is the path of Teth that leads out of the Sephira of Geburah into the next Sephira of Chesed, and so the value of this Sephira points, in a hidden way, at the next stage of our journey. You will be aware from the Bible that it is a serpent who first introduces humanity to the concept of good and evil. The association with a serpent is important because one of the aspects of our journey through Geburah is the development of an understanding of the importance of the potential for evil in the world. The ability to make real moral choices can exist only in a world where it is possible to make the wrong choice.

The value 9 is also the value of a Hebrew word meaning "to make powerful." This relates to Geburah in two ways. First, Geburah refers to the awesome power of the Divine when in its destructive mode. It is essential that we come to terms with this level of power if we are to understand why it is that all things ultimately die and decay. Second, when we have a full understanding of the need for the seemingly negative energy of Geburah, we ourselves are made more powerful as a result.

The Sephira of Geburah may at first seem the least attractive of all the Sephiroth. Geburah literally means "power" or "severity." Another of Geburah's titles is Pachad, which literally means "fear." Given these somewhat ominous titles, you won't be surprised to learn that Geburah is linked with death, decay, and the destruction of all life. It is partly because of these associations that it is important that we don't try to work with the energies of Geburah until we have achieved a level of balance by passing through Tiphareth first.

It's easy to misunderstand the role of Geburah. We should avoid seeing this Sephira as being a justification for anger or violent behavior. What Geburah really refers to is the inevitability of death and decay in the universe in general. Without the breaking apart of forms that is presided over by Geburah, it would be impossible for new life forms to develop. In Kabbalah the term "forms" doesn't just mean animal or plant life, but relates to all kinds of structures within the universe, from galaxies to sub-atomic particles. It is very fitting that Geburah follows from Tiphareth when we are climbing the Tree of Life. It is attractive to think that when we achieve a sense of spiritual understanding the world will suddenly appear to be a peaceful and harmonious place. The presence of Geburah reminds us that inner development is not about denying the reality of the world, but of finding a way to understand and explain it.

Geburah is associated with Mars, or as it is known in Hebrew, *Madim* (Mah-Deem). Mars is known as the angry planet that presides over all war and conflicts. The Kabbalistic understanding of Mars follows this general understanding of the red planet. However, it's important that we appreciate the positive aspects that are also associated with Mars. As the archetypically male planet, Mars is responsible for such qualities as determination, honor, bravery, and resilience. We need to recognize that sometimes to behave in a just or fair way it is necessary to engage in some kind of conflict. To avoid conflict and destruction at all costs is as negative as to be someone who constantly seeks to create conflict.

The key Divine name of Geburah is Elohim Gibor, which is pronounced "El-Oh-Heem Gi-Boor." The "Gi" is pronounced with a short sound as in "give." This name translates as "the Almighty God," or perhaps more appropriately, "Lord God of Battles." These two alternative translations nicely summarize the role of this Sephira. On the one hand, we have the sense of ultimate power that is wielded by the Divine. On the other hand, we are faced with a reminder that we must also face our own battles and conflicts in our life if we are to genuinely empower ourselves as whole individuals.

Areas of Empowerment

Geburah is responsible for death, destruction, mortality, and conflict in our lives and in the universe at large. You might be wondering how on earth experiencing the energies of this Sephira is going to enrich your life in any positive way.

The main lesson of Geburah is one of acceptance, and this has much more to do with how we think and feel than with what we do. The exercises in this chapter show you how to deal with your own anger in a more productive way, and how to cope with and hopefully reconcile or nullify your inner fears. In addition, you will be able to come to terms with the whole notion of mortality, both at the human and at the universal levels.

Practical Activities

The two exercises in this section will encourage a deeper understanding of the importance and necessity of the destruction of forms. Additionally, these practices will, to varying degrees, encourage you to let go of your inner fears and become more accepting of changes and challenges in your life. You can do these exercises as many times as you like, but don't move on to the next chapter until you feel comfortable with each exercise.

Beating the Bogeyman

All of us are afraid of something, and many of us are more afraid than we care to admit. Of course we also know deep down that many of our fears are completely unfounded. Many of our deepest fears stem from events in our childhood, which although scary at the time don't need to scare us now. However, these events can stay locked in our unconscious and cause us to be scared as adults without us really knowing why we feel that way. Although the Sephira of Geburah is associated with the fearful, it also gives us the Mars-based or martial energy to deal with and remove those fears.

For this process of facing and controlling your fears, you need some paper and a pen, a blindfold, somewhere dark where you can sit, and most important, the determination to conquer your fears.

Before you move into the meditation and ritual sections of this chapter, it's important that you have begun to deal with your fears on a practical level. You don't want to have to meet them up close for the first time in an altered state of consciousness! Also, by reconciling your fears on a practical level, you will find it easier to live your life in a more courageous manner that will be true to your inner self.

1. Fears come in all shapes and sizes, and we want to recognize them all so that they can no longer interfere and hold us back in the way we want to live our lives. The simplest fears might be called "doing" fears. That might be a fear of heights or a fear of swimming. We all have some practical activity or activities that make us afraid. Start by making a list of the practical activities that make you feel uncomfortable. Then reflect on why those particular things bother you.

2. The next step is a toughie! Pick one of these activities and then go and do it. If your first reaction is to think that there is no way that you will ever be able to go and have a swim or take a flight, enlist the help of a friend for moral support. If this doesn't work, it is fine to take it a tiny step at a time, just going to a swimming pool or an airport, for instance, and spending some time there.

3. After you have conquered or begun to conquer one of your "doing" fears, it's time to move to the next level. Let's call the next set of fears "memory" fears. These are anxieties that you have that relate to events in your past that were disturbing for whatever reason. Again make a list of the events and places that make you feel uneasy or scared.

4. As you might have guessed, what you now have to do is find a way of trying to face at least one of the fears on your new list. These are likely to seem more overpowering than "doing" fears. You may find it helpful to practice your meditative breathing before trying to face these fears to give yourself a sense of being grounded and secure.

The best way to face a "memory" fear is to visit the place in question. You can then spend some time just wandering around and realizing that your fear association is a very partial memory of what the place you are visiting is really about.

5. As we get deeper into our anxieties, we need to focus on what I call "feeling" fears. Very often we don't know why we have these anxieties, but we feel them much more deeply than any of our other fears. I'm thinking now of the conviction that we are deeply unattractive or stupid or inadequate. Again, write these down, but remind yourself as you are doing so that these are not truthful statements. It is crucial that you keep telling yourself that these are reflections of your perceptions and not reflections of reality.

6. After you have the list, read through it very slowly. This may be difficult because you need to concentrate very hard on every nuance of what you have written. The conscious recognition that this is how we feel can be quite upsetting and disturbing. However, it is only when we are this honest with ourselves that we can begin to clear these blockages to our self-fulfillment.

7. After you have read through the list, write a positive response to each point. Don't think of it as writing to yourself. Instead, imagine that the negative points have been written by a friend about herself and you are trying to convince her that she is wrong. You will find it much easier this way to find arguments that show how wrong and unfair these self-perceptions are. After you have written them down, read them out loud. Every time your mind puts up an argument as to why your negative perception still applies, write down another counterargument and read it out loud.

8. When we get beyond our "feeling" fears, there is nothing specific left to fight. Instead, we are faced with a vague set of uncertainties and anxieties that can perhaps be best referred to as "dark" fears. To establish your power and control over the dark, you must learn to be in this darkness and not be afraid. Put on your blindfold and just allow the negative feelings to well up inside you. Soon you will feel hugely uncomfortable; when you do, remove the blindfold and play some uplifting music or go for a walk.

9. When you can manage 20 minutes or so blindfolded, move on to really immersing yourself in your "dark" anxieties. Find a room

that you can keep completely dark, such as a closet. Sit in your darkened space and then put on your blindfold.

10. All you need to do now is to just sit. The longer you sit in total darkness, the more your unformed fears will begin to take hold. It may take several attempts, but try to reach a point where you can stay in your dark place and allow these fears to descend. You will find that if you stay in the darkness for long enough, the fears will begin to take on a shape and at this point you can visualize yourself destroying them. A useful visualization is to see them falling into pieces and then crumbling into dust. There is no doubt that this is a challenging activity, but the results really will change your life in a hugely positive way.

Lament not that men suffer war, fear, pain and death, for these are but the inevitable accompaniment to love, desire, pleasure and sex. Only laughter can be gotten away with for free.
—Peter J. Carroll, *Liber Null* (1987)

Nature in Conflict

In a society dominated by technology and manmade environments, it's tempting to see nature in a sentimental and romanticized manner. If we are to absorb the inner lessons that Geburah has to teach us, however, we must be willing to see nature as it really is, "red in tooth and claw" as the poet would say.

This activity requires a number of videos and books, so you need to spend some time at your local video store or library. You also need to arrange some free time over a few weekends to complete the visits to the various places included in this exercise.

It's not healthy to spend our lives being afraid, but it's equally unhealthy to try to avoid the reality of life, and that reality inevitably involves conflict in various forms. Although we are constantly surrounded by conflict, we tend to grow up with the notion that conflict is always a negative experience. What you will begin to see in this set of activities is not only the necessity of conflict, but also that sometimes it can actually prove to be creative in its own right.

1. Although nature may be full of vigorous and violent activity, you don't have to be! Buy or rent some wildlife documentaries, preferably ones detailing the lives of carnivores. When you watch the predators stalking, catching, and eating their prey, try to appreciate it as part of the underlying structure of the universe.

2. If you really want to experience nature, though, at some point you need to come face-to-face with it. Take a trip to your local zoo or wildlife park. Make a point of watching feeding time, especially if you can find an animal that has to be provided live food. If you spend some time in the restaurant first watching people eat, you will have a more informative and thought-provoking experience.

3. It's not just animals that use conflict and violence to keep themselves alive. Many people eat meat. Spend a day on a fishing trip, and even if you don't catch a single thing, you will be able to get a feel for the complex drives involved when we hunt for prey.

4. After all that fishing, you have probably built up an appetite. As you eat, focus on the fact that although you have not hunted for this food, there is still a connection between your eating and the animals you were watching in Steps 1 and 2. After you swallow each mouthful, visualize the conflict that is going on at a cellular level as your enzymes "do battle" with the food to break it up into nutrients that your body can absorb.

5. Of course, conflict isn't just about food. There are any number of events where you can see human beings engaging in quite serious conflict. The best venue is a football game because this involves the suppressed violence of warfare but has the added complication of being entertainment and not intentionally damaging to anyone. If you support a particular team, concentrate on the interaction between the players and supporters and the action rather than on who's winning. Although it is best to go to a live event, you could also complete this step by watching a game on TV.

6. Time for some culture now! Visit your local art gallery or go to the theater or the ballet. Instead of enjoying the art as an expression of feelings, watch out for signs of conflict within the art. When you start looking, you will be surprised at just how much symbolic violence and conflict exists even in something as seemingly unthreatening as a dance performance.

7. When we think of violence, we tend to think of people and animals. However, we can find all the clashing of forces that we need within the physical world itself. Go to your local library and take out some books on natural disasters. When you have read about a few earthquakes and tidal waves, you may begin to wonder whether people aren't rather placid in comparison.

8. Even the weather needs a certain amount of friction to get along. Take out some books that explain the way in which weather cycles actually work. You will find that underlying all the shifts of temperature and rainfall is what amounts to a conflict between competing levels of pressure. You can also move on and explore more extreme weather such as hurricanes and tsunami.

9. To really appreciate the omnipresence of conflict within the world, you can look at life at the very microscopic level. Even when we get down to the level of bacteria or protoplasm, what we find are life cycles built around and dependent on conflict. You should be able to find some useful books detailing the world at the level of the bacteria or virus, and they make very revealing reading.

10. It is sometimes comforting to think that if only we achieve a great enough distance from the world we could see a pattern of peaceful harmony. If we are to fully understand the energies of Geburah, we must realize that although there is a Divine order in the universe, it is far from always peaceful. Having read all about the micro-lives of bacteria, you should now see the conflict that goes on at a much greater scale of existence, by reading about the Big Bang theory and the formation of galaxies.

Meditations

The two meditations in this section help to embed the positive energies associated with Geburah within your consciousness. You'll notice we are not building an astral kingdom in Geburah as we did with the Sephiroth in the previous chapters, and indeed, we do not build an astral temple in any of the higher Sephiroth. This is because the energies of the higher Sephiroth are extremely powerful, and so when performing rituals associated with the higher Sephiroth, we first enter our astral kingdom in Tiphareth and perform our ritual in that astral space. Because Tiphareth is a point of balance on the Tree of Life, our ritual will be properly grounded and balanced when it takes effect in our daily life.

We are now dealing with energies that are beyond the merely elemental, and so it is important that we feel properly protected when we are working with them on a deep level. This is particularly the case when we are working with the Sephira of Geburah because it is associated with all forms of severity and destruction. You may find it helpful to perform the Rite of Protection from Chapter 2 before each of these meditations.

Mars Meditation

This meditation awakens your inner connections with the energy associated with Mars. Before you begin, light five red candles and burn some pine-scented incense. Place this incense in the south along with the candles, which should be arranged in the shape of a pentagram. (See the five-sided symbol shown in Appendix B.)

1. Mars is a planet of activity and conflict. To encourage these energies within your psyche, you are going to spend this meditation in constant motion. It is often assumed that meditation must always be performed in a static position, but if we are trying to connect with our own martial energies, it makes sense to put ourselves in a state that is sympathetic to Mars. Begin by jogging in place until you feel your heart rate increase.

2. After you have increased your heart rate, try to establish your normal meditation breathing rhythm. This will understandably be difficult, and the internal tension that this will cause is ideal for accessing the explosive energy of Mars. For the rest of this meditation, walk back and forth in as soldierly a manner as you can manage.

3. As you march, feel the heat of your exertion make your skin prickle. Allow this heat to grow and surround you until you feel almost a boiling heat deep within you. Around you the landscape is a bleak reddish brown desert interspersed with outcrops of twisted iron.

4. You notice that you feel not only hot, but also heavier than usual. Looking down you see you are wearing heavy iron armor and carrying a large two-handed sword. Although this armor is heavy, the controlled rage and anger within you gives you the momentum to keep moving.

5. Across the deserted landscape, you see a large cat, such as a tiger or leopard, running toward you. Instinctively you know that it is going to attack, and so you swing your sword at it as soon as it leaps at you with its teeth bared. The animal falls dead, and from its bleeding body a dove flies upward.

6. As soon as the dove has flown out of view, a dust storm begins to gather. Your whole body is being buffeted by a cloud of red dust. The force of this dust cloud grows and grows until it literally tears the armor from your body. The sandstorm then knocks you off your feet, and the vision fades.

7. You are now wandering in a large forest of oak and pine trees. It is just before dawn, and as you walk around you can see the red sun beginning to rise in the east and the light giving the trees a somewhat eerie red glow.

8. As you walk through the trees, you hear a low bleating. You enter a clearing and see a young lamb. Approaching the lamb are two large crimson and green snakes. You approach the snakes, and grasping each one behind its head, you hurl them away from the lamb.

9. The lamb transforms before your eyes into a tall warrior figure, almost Arthurian in appearance. He takes his sword from its scabbard and hands it to you, nods formally in acknowledgment, and then walks away. You may sit among the trees for as long as you wish before returning to your normal waking state.

Meditation to Banish Fears

For this meditation, you need some paper and a pen with red ink. Light some pepper-scented incense if you can find it, or burn some strong tobacco in a bowl.

1. With your red pen write, "May Kamael the archangel of Geburah support me, under the strong guardianship of Elohim Gibor, in facing and defeating my fears." Underneath this draw a five-pointed star or pentagram (shown in Appendix B).

2. Be seated in a high-backed chair for the duration of this ritual. If possible, the chair should have metal details, failing that it should have at least one item made of iron that you can hold for the duration of

the meditation. To help set the mood, you might like to play some stirring music—the "Mars Suite" from Holst's *The Planets Suite* is particularly appropriate.

3. After establishing your normal meditation breathing, visualize a large red five-pointed star or pentagram. This pentagram is glowing as if made of living fire, and all around is nothing but blackness.

4. As you watch, the pentagram grows in size until you can no longer see it in its entirety. Eventually all you can see is the central space at the heart of the pentagram; although this is black, it has a slight hint of redness. You feel yourself being pulled into the heart of the pentagram as if into a black hole.

5. You are now standing in a dark room made of gray flint. In front of you is a tall mirror in an iron frame. You see yourself in the mirror. However, a crimson-colored whip in the shape of the Hebrew letter Lamed appears in the mirror image. It cracks itself, repeatedly striking your mirror image.

6. After five such blows, your mirror image explodes leaving just blackness in front of you in the mirror. As you look closer into the mirror, you can see the pieces of your broken body lying on the stone floor. Above the pieces of your body hover shadowy figures; they are thin and ghostly, but with long clawed fingers and malevolent glowing eyes.

7. These are your fears that have been set free by the harsh energy of the path of Lamed. You can destroy them under the guidance of the archangel Kamael. As you look at each ghostly figure, give it a name. Don't worry, a name will come to you—either of a fear or possibly some strange gibberish name that just somehow fits.

8. Hear your Higher Self in your head saying, "I banish you (name of fear) in the name of Elohim Gibor." As this is said, you see a sharp iron spear penetrating the body of that particular fear and it fades completely from view. Repeat this until all the figures have disappeared.

9. After the last fear has been banished, you begin to hear the roaring of water. A huge wave appears in the mirror washing over your broken body. When this water recedes, your body can be seen whole again and glowing with a warm pinkish sheen. Inwardly give thanks to the Divine before returning to your normal waking state.

Empowerment Technique for Geburah: Willpower

In Chapter 6, you focused on listening to your Higher Self. As you move into the higher Sephira of Geburah, it's important that you are also able to consciously take control not only of your actions but also of your thoughts. It's easy to see the negative side of Geburah, but its very severity is also one of its great strengths and benefits. We cannot begin to truly create unless we are also able to accept the need to get rid of those things that are no longer useful to us. When we learn to remove the surplus features from our life, we can concentrate on those aspects of our character and our lifestyle that genuinely help us to develop as individuals.

It might seem strange to see a section on willpower in a book devoted to a spiritual approach to self-development. We tend to think of strong-willed people as rather hard and unapproachable, but this need not be the case. A strong will is only negative when it is used in an unbalanced manner. The work that you've done in previous chapters has been all about making sure you have a proper level of internal balance. For this technique, you need one large red candle.

You'll recall from earlier chapters that the four powers of the Sphinx were described as "to know, to dare, to will, and to be silent." The following empowerment technique stimulates your ability to "will" in the mystical and magical sense of the word. When we think of our will in terms of Hermetic Kabbalah, we are not talking about the desires of our ego, but the strength of character needed to maintain a contact with our Higher Self. It is this contact that allows us to be in touch with our true will. The following steps gradually introduce you to a conscious control of your will. After you have achieved a level of conscious control, it will be easier for your true will to begin to act more powerfully in your life.

1. Exercising our will can be very arduous and challenging, so let's start with something relatively simple. Buy yourself a video or DVD of your favorite film. Fix yourself some nice snacks to go with it. Then take your treats into your TV room, put the film on, and promptly leave the room. Spend the duration of the film in a completely different room.

2. Having demonstrated to yourself that you have a basic level of will-power, it's time to move things on a little. Select something that you

really enjoy in your life. It might be a certain food, a television program, or even a particular hobby. Whatever you choose, you now have to exclude it from your life completely for at least one week.

3. One important aspect of developing a strong internal will relates to doing things that we would not normally do. In some ways this is harder than preventing ourselves from doing those things that we find enjoyable. Select a food that you dislike and eat at least a portion of it every day for a week. In doing so, you will begin to face up to whatever unconscious fear or unease causes your negative reaction. Eating a food that you don't like strengthens your internal will in terms of your unconscious and physical fears and anxieties.

4. Now decide on a particular viewpoint that you vehemently disagree with and make a point of arguing *for* this viewpoint when in conversation with your friends and colleagues.

5. Geburah is often referred to as the "sphere of severity." To fully develop our willpower, it is necessary to be strict with ourselves. This includes having the ability to exert a strict control over our body. Decide on some small and meaningless action, such as lightly scratching your left ear. Perform this small action once every hour for at least three days (and ideally for a week).

6. The next step can be followed in conjunction with Step 5 if you are feeling fairly ambitious. This exercise takes the controlling energy of Geburah and applies it to our language. This is very important because it will begin to impact on the way you actually think. Choose a word that you would normally use in everyday conversation, and make a commitment that you are *not* going to use that word at all for at least a week. If you do use it, you must impose some form of small penalty on yourself.

7. So far we have been practicing using our willpower in a fairly abstract way. However, the strengthening of your will has some very immediate and practical benefits. The next time you find yourself in a conflict with someone with whom you often disagree and tend to back down from, make a point of not giving up your position. When you feel like giving up, remind yourself of the progress that you have already made.

8. Develop your ability to cancel out certain words and practice canceling more complex ideas. Select a particular situation or memory

that you tend to spend a lot of time thinking about. When it next comes into your mind, visualize the scene that you are remembering dissipating and collapsing in your mind's eye. If the thought comes back, banish it with even more mental vigor.

9. By now you should be beginning to feel a sense of contact with your inner will. This new step will get you into the habit of allowing your inner will to be constantly present in your life. Create a mental image of a large crimson pentagram. Keep this image in your consciousness throughout the day as you go about your daily tasks. This will probably take a few attempts before you succeed, but the results are well worth it.

10. The final exercise is to light the large red candle and place it on a table about two feet away from you. Stare fixedly at the candle flame. Now will the flame to move. Don't wish the flame to move, or want it to, but be certain that it *will* move because of the exercise of your will. What counts here is not whether the flame actually moves, but that you see the flame moving. This is because the crucial factor in the work with the Tree of Life is its effect on your own perceptions. If you can make the flame actually move, so much the better.

We learn from every experience, particularly the unpleasant ones, and once we accept that and realize that every experience is there for a reason, life becomes so much easier.
—David Icke, *The Truth Vibrations* (1991)

Kabbalistic Rituals

The two rituals that follow use the two key energies of Geburah. On the one hand, we can recognize the way in which some aspects of Geburah can manifest in a negative way and seek to reduce this negative impact. On the other hand, this same powerful Marslike energy can also be used to a very positive effect in its own right in terms of strengthening our inner resolve.

Conflict-Resolution Ritual

For this ritual, you need some pine-scented incense, three red candles, three blue candles, and a metal (preferably iron) bowl of water.

We have explored the nature of conflict in earlier sections of this chapter and have seen that in many cases what appears to be negative conflict can actually be seen as a positive process of development. However, many conflicts are entirely nonproductive. The energy of Geburah can be used to control these genuinely negative forms of conflict. In particular, the following ritual uses the complementary energies of the two paths that lead into Geburah. When you have completed the ritual a few times, you should find that when faced with a conflict situation, you are better able to see the different sides of the argument. It will also help you to act with much greater confidence when faced with conflict situations.

1. Prepare your ritual space by lighting the pine incense and placing it in the south. Place the red candles in the east and the blue candles in the west. Place the bowl of water in the north.

2. Enter your temple in Tiphareth by performing the Building an Astral Kingdom in Tiphareth meditation described in Chapter 6. Move to the center of your ritual space and declare, "In the name of the most high Divine force, I call upon the energy of Geburah to be present in this balanced hall of Tiphareth."

3. Remain in the center of your ritual space. Raise your arms straight above your head and then extend them while saying in a loud voice, "I call upon the Divine force of Elohim Gibor (El-Oh-Heem Gi-Boor) to be present in this working." As you say these words, visualize a large red flaming pentagram forming around your whole body.

4. In front of you, running from the east to the center, you now visualize a vivid blue-green ray of light. As loudly as possible, say, "Under the guidance of Kamael (Ka-May-Al), I will enter the path of Lamed." Begin walking toward the east.

5. As you walk, you are aware of the sounds of a large number of whips cracking and low groans of pain that seem to come from each side as you walk. Declare, "The path of Lamed is severe, but I shall remain faithful and just." Take the last steps toward the east as very definite strides and be aware of the disquieting sounds fading.

6. Retrace your steps to the center of your ritual space. While facing west, visualize a vivid olive green ray of light coming from the west. Say in a very quiet and dignified tone, "Under the guidance of Kamael, I will enter the path of Mem." Begin walking toward the west.

7. When you are halfway between the center of your ritual space and the west, visualize a violent storm at sea blocking your way. On your right side stands a small flask of oil. You pick this up and pour it over the stormy waters. The storm ceases and you can continue to walk until you are standing in the west.

8. In the west you say, "The path of Mem brings me to a place of stability and calm." Now turn round and retrace your steps back to the center of your ritual space. Once there, declare, "In the name of Elohim Gibor and under the guidance of the great archangel Kamael, I shall be just in all and commit myself to bringing stability where there is negative conflict."

9. Stretch your arms out in the form of a cross. Lift your head upward and see two rays of light emanating from the Divine covering your body. One ray is emerald green, and the other is a deep blue. As you stand in this position, you should feel a great sense of calm descend on you.

10. You may stay in this position for as long as is comfortable. When you are ready to end the ritual, give thanks to the Divine and to the particular force of Elohim Gibor. Ensure that you feel balanced within your temple in Tiphareth before returning to your normal wakeful state.

Ritual of Inner Fire

For this ritual, you need five red candles, pepper-scented incense or some strong tobacco, a bloodstone or ruby, a bell or tambourine, some paper, and a pen with red ink.

In this ritual you activate all the positive aspects of the Sephira Geburah within your psyche. The more productive qualities of Geburah are also associated with the planet Mars, or *Madim* as it is known in Hebrew. This is the planet traditionally associated with Geburah, and this ritual calls on the energies of Mars to reinforce those energies within your life.

The energies that you will be activating have the potential to be misused, so it's a good idea to perform the Rite of Protection (see Chapter 2) before starting this ritual.

1. Before you begin, lay out your ritual space as follows: The candles belong in the south, and the incense or tobacco should be lit and placed in the east along with the paper and pen. Your bloodstone or ruby belongs in the north, and the bell or tambourine should be positioned in the west.

2. When you have set up your ritual space, enter your temple in Tiphareth to help ensure that the energies are experienced in a fully balanced manner. Then stand in the east and write on your piece of paper, "In the name of Elohim Gibor, I seek to activate the energies of Madim (Ma-Deem) within my psyche." Beneath this draw the symbol of the planet Mars (see Appendix B) and place the paper next to the incense.

3. Walk to the center of your ritual space and declare, "It is my will that I absorb the positive energies of Geburah under the guidance of Kamael and through the authority of Elohim Gibor." As you say this, visualize a crimson pentagram glowing on your forehead.

4. Walk with a very martial, almost marching, step to the west from the center of your ritual space. Pick up the bell or tambourine and strike it five times. Then say as loudly as possible, "In the name of Elohim Gibor, I call upon Zamael (Za-May-Al), the archangel of the palace of Madim, to be with me in this working." Strike the bell or tambourine five more times.

5. Now return in a straight line to the east. Breathe in the incense or tobacco smoke, stand up very straight, and declare, "Let Zamael assist me in the purging of all weakness of thought in my life, for weak thoughts lead only to inaction."

6. Walk around to the south and warm your hands over the candles. Again stand very straight and declare, "Let Zamael assist me in ensuring that my spirit is filled with drive and determination at all times, that I may complete the Great Work."

7. Move around to the west. Strike the bell or tambourine five times and while standing at attention declare, "Let Zamael assist me in acting with honor in all my relationships, for from honorable actions flows trust."

8. Walk around to the north and hold the ruby or bloodstone in your right hand as you declare, "Let Zamael assist me in showing courage in all my endeavors, for without courage all my efforts will be in vain."

9. Walk back to the east and pick up the paper on which you wrote the ritual's intent. Wrap the stone in this paper and move back to the center of your ritual space. Visualize a bright crimson glow in your solar plexus area. This glow becomes a ray of light that emanates upward away from you, making contact with the Divine force out of your sight.

10. Feel yourself being filled with a sense of purpose and resolve. When you are ready, give thanks both to Zamael and Elohim Gibor for their guidance and assistance. Make sure that you feel fully balanced in your temple of Tiphareth before returning to your normal waking state.

Signs and Symbols of Geburah

This section lists symbols, colors, and other associations with Geburah. These are interesting in their own right and can be meditated on to arrive at your own deep understanding of their meaning. Additionally, while you are working with the energies of Geburah or when you want to attract positive energies relating to a matter governed by Geburah, you may want to wear or carry with you something that relates to Geburah. If you're hoping to succeed in a competitive sport or win a legal battle, for instance, you could keep a bloodstone with you or burn some pine incense.

Appendix A shows the pathway correspondences at a glance, and Appendix B lists more symbols, including easy-to-copy planetary and elemental symbols.

- **Symbols:** Five-sided figures, Mars symbol, sword, whip, or scourge
- **Colors:** Red, crimson, green
- **Numbers and letters:** 5, 9, 25, 65, 70, 95, 325, Mem (M), Lamed (L), Teth (T)
- **Crystals and stones:** Ruby, bloodstone
- **Plants and incense:** Oak, pine, tobacco, pepper
- **Archangel:** Kamael
- **Direction:** South
- **Element:** Fire, whose archangel is Michael and whose spirits are the salamanders
- **Planet:** Mars (Madim), whose archangel is Zamael

Chapter 8

Chesed: The Kingdom of the Father

You will be pleased to learn that the next Sephira is less challenging despite being higher up on the Tree of Life. In Chesed we are dealing with a more spiritually attuned energy, but one that is forgiving and benevolent in nature, rather than stern and severe.

It may seem strange that you are progressing from a very difficult phase to an altogether gentler experience. However, to experience the mercy of Chesed before fully understanding the necessity of the severity of Geburah could have a negative impact on your overall personal empowerment. With an appreciation of the need for decay and conflict in the world, we can enjoy the protective energy of Chesed in its proper context.

We pronounce Chesed "Che-Said," with the initial "Che" sound pronounced with a guttural "ch" as in the ending of the Scottish word *loch*. Chesed is spelled Cheth, Samech, Daleth. We can reach Chesed by three paths. From Netzach we follow the path of Kaph, from Tiphareth the path of Yod, and from Geburah the path of Teth. The path of Kaph is linked with Tarot's Wheel of Fortune card, and this links with the notion of Chesed as a benevolent force in our lives. The path of Yod is also known by the title "the Intelligence of Will." As a link between Tiphareth and Chesed, this title emphasizes that we are now able to rely more on our inner will. The path of Yod is also associated with the zodiac sign Virgo, and this suggests that we need to be spiritually innocent and emphasizes the importance of appreciating the beauty of the Divine. The path of Teth also goes by the name "the Intelligence of Spiritual Activity." It is a fiery path and is associated with the Tarot card Strength. As a link between Geburah and Chesed, this path emphasizes the need to carry with us the strength and restraint that we have learned from Geburah into the more merciful arena of Chesed.

If you look at the Tree of Life diagram in Chapter 1 you will see what the Hebrew spelling of Chesed looks like. The central letter Samech in the spelling of Chesed reminds us of the middle pillar of the Tree of Life as the path of Samech leads into Tiphareth. This connection to the middle pillar reminds us that as we climb further up the Tree, the Sephiroth represent an increasing level of balance, even when they are positioned away from the middle pillar. The shapes of the Hebrew letters in the spelling of Chesed are suggestive of entering an ancient temple. The initial letter Cheth symbolizes the pillared entrance. We then have the round shape of Samech, which suggests the hallway or tunnel leading to the doorway to the inner sanctum, which is represented by the final Daleth. Appropriately enough, the name Daleth translates as "door."

When I consider the spelling of Chesed, I find a message related to Chesed's meaning as "mercy." We are reminded that the Divine is always there to protect us (Cheth), and that if we rely on the support of the Divine (Samech), we will be able to open the doorway (Daleth) to a new and richer way of living. We can also look at the spelling in terms of the associated Tarot cards. The Chariot card (Cheth) represents our ongoing quest for truth, and the Temperance card (Samech) points to the need to maintain a sense of balance in our search. The final card is the Empress (Daleth), and this reminds us that although our search may be spiritual, its results will also manifest in a more creative physical life.

The value of the Hebrew word Chesed is 72. This can be reduced to the number 9 (7 + 2 = 9). You may recall that the reduced value of Geburah is also 9. At one level this connection reminds us that within the heart of Chesed lies the necessary severity that we learned in Geburah. At another level, we can see that because Geburah and Chesed are balancing Sephiroth on opposite sides of the Tree of Life, this shared value emphasizes the fact that they work in a harmonious partnership.

The number 9 also has a very special place in the esoteric tradition. Because it is associated with the letter Teth, meaning "serpent," we can link it to the powerful energy that resides within all of us and which can allow us to make a connection with the Divine. This idea is found in many forms of mysticism, perhaps most obviously in kundalini yoga, where the release of this serpent energy is a key aspect of finding one's spirituality. The path of Teth is also the route by which we reach Chesed if we cross horizontally across the Tree of Life from Geburah. As mentioned in Chapter 7, the value 9 is also the value of a Hebrew word meaning "to make powerful." Although it's easy to see the power of Geburah, the qualities of mercy and justice associated with Chesed are just as powerful in their own right.

Chesed is often associated with good fortune, and the number 72 is also relevant in this context. In Kabbalistic tradition, there are 72 names of God known as the Shemhamphoresch, which can be located by a special way of reading certain sections of the Jewish Bible. These 72 names allow the Kabbalist to contact 72 angels that can bring wonderful revelations and great fortune.

The Sephira of Chesed literally translates as mercy or kindness, and it is a representation of the kindness and mercy of the Divine as it manifests in the universe. The color associated with Chesed is deep blue, a color regarded as calming and soothing. Although Chesed is a soothing and gentle force, we should never forget that it is also associated with justice and responsibility. This means that we cannot expect the energies of Chesed to be soothing and merciful unless we behave in a way that deserves compassion and mercy.

Chesed is the last Sephira before we reach the realm of the supernals. The supernals are the three highest Sephiroth. In the One Tree model (see Chapter 1), they are regarded as being so close to the Divine as to be beyond our understanding. As a result, Chesed is often associated with deities that we can understand, and so we find that many of the qualities that we associate with God in the major religions of the world are reflected in the Sephira of Chesed.

Chesed is associated with the planet Jupiter, or as it is known in Hebrew *Tzedeq* (Tzed-Eck, the initial *Z* should be pronounced like "Tz" in "tzar"). One of the names for the planet Jupiter is Jove, which is a corruption of the God name Jehovah. In Roman mythology, Jupiter was the supreme God. Since ancient times, Jupiter has been seen as a planet of general good fortune, particularly good luck that is connected to hard work. As Jupiter is seen as the "king" of the planets, it is also linked with notions of justice. This is not justice in the sense of retribution (this is the role of Geburah), but justice in the sense of fair play and equality between people. The expression "jovial," meaning to be cheerful, comes from the fact that Jupiter is also regarded as a planet with a very happy and benevolent energy. We can see the Father association again in the fact the name Jupiter derives from the Latin *Zeus Pater*, meaning "God the Father."

The key Divine name of Chesed is El. This name translates as "the mighty one" or "the Divine one." It is also possible to translate the name El as meaning simply "God." The value of the word El (A = 1, L = 30) reduces to 4 (1 + 3 + 0 = 4), which puts us in mind of the four-lettered name of God or tetragrammaton YHVH. The letters Aleph and Lamed point both to the unity of the Divine (Aleph) and its capacity to act as a driving force in our lives (Lamed). It's also worth noting that the number 4 is the value of the Hebrew word Daleth, meaning "doorway." Chesed is indeed the doorway to the supernal Sephiroth.

Areas of Empowerment

The responsibilities of Chesed could be summarized as compassion or mercy, acceptance of responsibility, and the workings of fortune or luck. In addition, Chesed inevitably brings up issues to do with our relationships with our parents. We are especially likely to work through any emotional baggage that we have in relation to our fathers in Chesed. This is because Chesed represents our notion of God as a paternalistic dispenser of justice.

By the time you have worked through this chapter, you should have made significant advances at both a practical and a spiritual level. In practical terms, the positive energy relating to good fortune can be enormously helpful when it comes to our careers. At a spiritual level, you will find that your confidence in the ultimately benevolent nature of the Divine will increase. This in turn will lead to a greater confidence in yourself and your own ability to complete the Great Work. As always, much of the work in Chesed will be more successful the more you trust in the Divine and your own Higher Self. However, because we are dealing with the forces of fortune in this chapter, the trust is especially important. Your success traveling through the lower elemental Sephiroth will have prepared you for the level of trust required when working with certain aspects of Chesed.

Similarly the experience of Geburah will have given you the inner courage and determination to succeed.

> By three things is the world sustained: by truth, by judgment, and by peace.
> —From the Jewish Talmud dating from the fifth century C.E.

Practical Activities

The two exercises in this section will increase your awareness of your responsibility to take control of your life, and also to begin to explore the way in which the power of the Divine and your own Higher Self can increase your potential for good fortune. As we move toward the supernal Sephiroth, even the practical exercises require more depth of thought. Some of the exercises that you explore in the next four chapters may have fewer steps, but each step will require more from you. This is because you will be reflecting on the what and the why of what is happening. The more you are able to think clearly and deeply about what you are doing, the more you will find that the exercises really activate aspects of your personality and cause positive changes in your life.

Test Your Luck

We live in a world where almost everything is carefully designed and planned. Even our food choices have been researched and market-tested to ensure that we know exactly which cereal is right for our particular lifestyle. In such a system there is little room for the rules of chance. Part of the benevolent nature of Chesed is expressed through its responsibility for good fortune and luck—and this next activity puts you in touch with that energy.

You need to spend some time at a fairground, amusement park, arcade, or other setting that offers games. (Most areas will have at least one within driving distance.) You also need a pair of dice and a friend with whom you can play a game.

The path of Kaph leads into the Sephira of Chesed, and this path is associated with the Tarot card, the Wheel of Fortune. The spreading of fortune is the responsibility of both the planet Jupiter and Chesed. It may not seem that luck has any place in a spiritually based approach to empowerment. However, allowing good fortune into your life is all about placing your trust in the Divine. Additionally, if we are to be lucky in our lives, we have to be prepared to take an occasional risk, because without risks there is no opportunity for good luck to actually happen. The next series of activities is intended to help you open yourself up to the possibility of positive risk-taking so that you may also allow some fortune into your life.

1. The most obvious way to start allowing some luck into your life and learning to take a risk is to place a small bet. However, although this is possible in my own country (England), there are only certain places in the United States where gambling is legal. So, instead, there is a game you can play with a friend for which you only need a pair of dice. The aim of the game is to throw a six and the first person to roll 12 sixes is the winner and can receive some small token prize.

2. When you first play the game, really concentrate on how much you want to roll a six. Chances are that you will lose the game, because the more we concentrate on wanting something, the less likely it is to happen. The second time you play the game, roll the dice with complete abandon, and you will probably be surprised at how much better you do. At the very least, you will enjoy yourself more— which is also a key aspect of Chesed's jovial nature.

3. Now you're ready to take a trip to the fairground or other setting. All old-style fairs have some form of dubious game where you can win a prize by throwing hoops over deceptively large obstacles or try to shoot down cans that are remarkably stable! Pick one of these games and instead of carefully aiming, just close your eyes and think positively as you throw the hoop or pull the trigger.

4. While at the fairground, you will see someone whom you think you might be able to be friends with, or if you are single, someone you might like to take on a date. It's now time to really take a risk. Rather than doing the usual thing of merely thinking about talking to this person, go up and start a conversation—and suggest that it might be fun to go on some of the rides together. The point of this is not necessarily to be successful, but to realize that you are able to face that kind of emotional risk.

5. Many people take part in some kind of sport such as baseball, football, or something less active such as billiards. Whatever your sport, this next step will help you remember why you first enjoyed it so much. Instead of playing cautiously or even sensibly, at least four times in every game try to take the riskiest option, where there is the slight possibility of a goal or of making a shot. The first time you take this option and actually have the luck to make the point, you will get far more satisfaction than from following the rigidly safe approach to the game.

6. There is no reason why you should only let luck into your personal life and your weekends. We all have work-related ideas. Most often we decide not to say anything about our idea in case our boss thinks it's foolish, or even worse, that it's tried and flops. In the next month, make at least one significant suggestion at the office. You never know—you might even be promoted!

7. We tend to think of luck least in terms of our relationships. Yet, relationships are also the area of our life where we are most exposed to risks. The simple act of exposing your emotional nature is hugely risky, but also hugely beneficial. There are still many things that we don't say to our loved ones because we are not sure how they will react. In the next month, say at least one thing to someone who is very close to you that you would normally not tell that person. For instance, you might say how you often think of him even when he's at work, or mention some habit that seems trivial but that you would really miss if she were ever to stop doing it.

Self-Affirmation

Chesed is also known as "mercy." We tend to think in terms of other people when we think of being merciful or compassionate. However, there is no reason why we should not also be merciful and compassionate to ourselves. In fact, until we are able to be properly empathetic and benevolent with ourselves, we are unlikely to be able to be genuinely sympathetic to those around us.

For this exercise, you need a small mirror and a piece of paper and pen.

The process of self-affirmation is a simple but effective tool for self-empowerment. The idea of self-affirmation reinforces the fact that you are a person of value who is allowed to have weaknesses and foibles. After all, if we were all perfect there would be no need for any of us to learn the lessons of compassion in Chesed.

1. Write down seven sentences about yourself that reflect positive aspects of your character. These should all be written as definite statements of value, such as "I am always friendly when meeting new people."

2. Next list seven characteristics that you would like to acquire. These should be written as definite statements of what you will achieve; for example, "I will feel more confident about my appearance."

3. Finally, write down seven aspects of your personality that you recognize as less than ideal. Write these statements in a way that accepts the inevitability of imperfection; for instance, "Sometimes I can seem cold, but I am honest with my friends about this trait." (If having reached this point in the book you still have traits that you regard as deeply wrong, such as consistently lying, it's a good idea to work through the lower Sephiroth again. Self-development is not a race, and there is no fault in recognizing that you may need to spend more time working with a particular Sephira.)

4. Now that you have your lists, read them out loud while looking at yourself in the mirror in as understanding and empathetic manner as you can muster. Read the imperfections in the morning, the wholly positives in the evening, and the aspects that you intend to develop last thing at night. If you do this for a month, you will begin to find that you feel more comfortable with yourself and that you are starting to develop the positive traits that you are seeking to acquire.

Meditations

The two meditations in this section help to embed the positive energies associated with Chesed within your consciousness. The meditations build on the practical activities but function at a deeper level. Their impact is more subtle; if you perform one meditation per week, however, you will gradually notice a very definite shift in the way that you approach your life.

Jupiter Meditation

This meditation awakens your inner connections with the energy associated with the planet Jupiter. Before you begin, light four dark yellow candles and burn some saffron-scented incense. (See Appendix C for some online suppliers.) Place the incense in the north and the candles in the east in a square formation.

1. When working with the energies of Jupiter, we are dealing with a force that is both magisterial in nature and benevolently good-humored. It will help you find the right mood if you play some music that is traditionally classical but with a rousing and upbeat tone. Sit in a high-backed chair, ideally on a gold- or silver-colored cushion, and place your hands one on each thigh.

2. It is very important for this meditation that you maintain a strict breathing rhythm where each element of the breathing process lasts for four beats. This is because of the association of the number 4 with the Sephira of Chesed. After you have established your breathing rhythm, allow yourself to become aware of sitting in a very upright and dignified manner.

3. As you look down at yourself, you see that you are wearing very heavy and expensive robes trimmed with white fur and alternating sapphire and emerald stones. On your wrists are white bracelets of tin engraved with the numbers 34 and 16. The metal and the numbers are all linked with the planet Jupiter. While you feel your sense of majesty growing, you are also aware of a great sense of responsibility toward your kingdom and its people.

4. By your side is a tin cup containing olive oil. Dip your index and middle fingers of your right hand into the cup of oil and anoint your forehead by drawing the outline of a square within a circle. Stand up and walk down the steps leading from what has now become a large throne, the feet of which have been carved into a likeness of eagles' heads.

5. You are now walking through the gray stone corridors of your castle. The walls are hung with heavy tapestries showing you spending time walking in fields, spending time with the people, and presiding over disputes between citizens. As you leave the castle, you face an avenue of poplar and apple trees.

6. Walking down this avenue, you approach a large golden eagle tethered to a perch. You release it from the perch, and it promptly flies away. Within a few minutes, it flies back to you and drops into your hand a small square of tin on which is inscribed the symbol of the planet Jupiter (like an exaggerated number 2 with a vertical line running through the bottom horizontal line; shown in Appendix B). You thank the eagle and continue walking down the avenue of trees.

7. You arrive at a heavy wooden gate with a complicated-looking lock. Beyond the gate is a large lake with a rowboat on the bank. You drop the square of tin into a small slot in the lock mechanism, and the gate slowly opens.

8. Passing through the gate, you approach the rowboat and push it into the water. You begin to row into the center of the lake, following the eagle guiding you, flying slowly and slightly ahead of you.

9. In the center of the lake, you sit and wait. As the sun sinks over the horizon, a dolphin appears at the side of your boat. (A dolphin in a lake may seem strange, but remember, meditations take us into a symbolic rather than a realistic world!) In its mouth, it holds a plain crown, which is little more than a circlet of gold. You take the crown and place it on your head. You have an immediate sense of the responsibility and duty that comes with kingship as well as the capacity that you now have to do enormous amounts of good in your kingdom. You may remain in this state as long as you wish before thanking the spirits of Jupiter and leaving the meditation.

Hatred does not cease by hatred at any time; hatred ceases by love. This is an old rule.

—Attributed to Siddhartha Gautama, the Buddha (approximately 500 B.C.E.)

Meditation to Restore Innocence

For this meditation, you need some cedar incense burning in the north, a blue bowl of water placed in the west, and four blue candles burning in the east.

1. Because this meditation is going to take you back into a childhood state of consciousness, you need to be properly prepared. If you have significant issues relating to your parents, you might want to perform the Rite of Protection (see Chapter 2) before beginning this meditation. When you are ready, sit on the floor in any comfortable position.

2. After you have established a breathing rhythm, imagine that you are a child back in your bedroom playing with your toys. Spend as much time as you need to in this part of the meditation to really connect with your childhood self.

3. The door of your closet opens, and you see a pure white unicorn walking through the doorway. It paws at the ground while looking at you. Filled with excitement and wonder, you follow the unicorn as it walks back into the closet and find yourself in a meadow with a winding pathway that is strewn with shamrocks.

4. As you walk along, you can hear the sound of cuckoos in the distance. It is early morning, and there is still a fine layer of pearlescent dew on the grass. The landscape is gently rolling rather than flat or hilly. Around a bend, you see a shepherd walking toward you followed by a flock of sheep.

5. The shepherd is very old and bearded. He holds a traditional shepherd's crook in his right hand and wears a cloak of gray wool trimmed with blue. The shepherd asks you if you are lost. You nod politely and explain that you are looking for yourself, but don't seem to be able to remember where you are.

6. Beckoning with his crook, the shepherd indicates that you should follow him. When you draw level with the shepherd, he takes you by the hand and leads you to a group of apple trees, in the middle of the trees sits a tiny lamb wearing a blue collar.

7. The lamb stands up as soon as it sees you. The shepherd picks up the lamb and hands it to you. As you hold the lamb in your arms, however, it slowly metamorphoses into a small child who you quickly recognize as yourself. At the same time, you realize that you are no longer a child but are fully grown and wearing the same clothes as the shepherd.

8. Smiling at the small child, the younger version of yourself, you tell the child that he or she was lost but now has been found forever. The shepherd hands you his crook and slowly walks away. Cradling the child in your arms, you begin to walk back along the shamrock path.

9. As you carry the child, you realize that you are now your own shepherd. When this sense of being the shepherd of your own childhood is felt on a very deep level, you may return to your bedroom and place the child gently in bed, before returning to your normal waking state.

Empowerment Technique for Chesed: The Universe Contained Within the Self

In Chesed we get in touch with a sense of the Divine as an ever-present protective force in our life. As always, however, there are two ways to approach any Sephira. We can look at the Sephira as a source of power from which emanates certain energies. However, we can also look at the energies associated with that Sephira and seek to absorb them within our own sphere of influence. So when we work with Chesed, as well as recognizing the awesome and merciful power of the Divine we can seek to realize within ourselves some of that all-encompassing responsibility and understanding.

One of the great maxims of Hermetic Kabbalah is the statement "As above, so below." This suggests that although we are all part of the Divine, each of us contains a spark of the Divine within ourselves. It also suggests the universe is in some ways a reflection of our own selves. So we also need to try and see ourselves as containing the same infinite potential within ourselves that we associate with the universe. Achieving this realization leads to a recognition of our own power to cause change, and also of our deep responsibility to ourselves and to the world around us. Thanks to our journey through Geburah, we can be sure that we will not allow this insight to cause any arrogance or inflation of our ego.

For this technique, you need some readily available books and a large blue candle.

This empowerment technique encompasses two of the legendary powers of the Sphinx, namely "to know" and "to dare." It takes a leap of will to dare to regard ourselves as containing a mirror image of the

whole universe within ourselves. This awareness is also one of the great
secrets of the Western Mystery Tradition, and so developing an internal
acceptance of this knowledge is a major fulfillment of the requirement
"to know." In terms of personal empowerment, internalizing the reality
of the mirror relationship between ourselves and the universe helps us
believe we can make profound changes in our lives. At another level, this
technique is intended to help us take responsibility for improving the lot
of those around us and the world in general.

1. Before beginning any physical activities, you should develop an
    appreciation of the amazing complexity that exists within your own
    body. This is important because Kabbalah does not seek to elevate
    the spiritual at the expense of the physical, but sees the Physical
    world as an expression of the beauty of the Divine. Obtain some
    books on human biology and evolution. When you learn about the
    intricate nature of the processes that occur even within a single cell,
    you will start to fully appreciate just how amazing your physical
    existence is.

2. You are now ready for the first meditation. Having established
    your normal breathing rhythm, imagine a point in your mind's eye.
    Try to visualize that point just existing in space. When you can see
    the point clearly in your mind's eye, begin to consider what exactly
    a point means.

3. Remind yourself that a point has a position but no dimension. In
    other words, it can be located but has no size at all. Allow the
    physical impossibility of this to sink into your mind. Reflect on the
    fact that everything in the universe is built around the notion of a
    point because the most basic shape in the universe, a sphere, can
    only be built around a point.

4. As you realize that logically the universe should not exist because it
    is based on an idea that only works in an abstract way (even an
    atom has dimensions as well as a location), remind yourself that
    you definitely experience the universe as existing. This should lead
    you to an understanding that the existence of the universe proves
    the presence of the will of the Divine in calling it into being.

5. This next meditation is even more likely to make your head feel
    rather dizzy! Establish your normal breathing rhythm and then
    begin to focus all of your awareness on your feet. Ask yourself

whether you would still be the same person if you had no feet. Realizing that your feet are not essential to your sense of self, withdraw your awareness away from your feet so that they seem no longer to be a part of you.

6. Continue this process with the rest of your body. Keep removing your consciousness from each limb in turn until your whole awareness is centered not in your physical brain but in your mind—that part of you that has no physical needs at all. After achieving this, reverse the process, reminding yourself of the way in which each part of your body enriches and enlivens your existence.

7. As a result of these meditations, you should be developing an innate understanding of not only the benefits but also of the ultimately flimsy nature of the physical universe and of your own physical existence. You are now going to inwardly absorb the physical universe within yourself. Begin by lighting the large blue candle and then establishing a normal meditative breathing rhythm. See yourself growing larger and larger until you are no longer aware of your body because it has become so vast.

8. Your mind still carries an awareness of where your extremities should be. In the space where your feet would be, you see the planet Earth spinning gently. At the level of your solar plexus, you are aware of the other planets orbiting gracefully. The spaces where your arms and legs would be are filled with stars.

9. At your heart center lies the sun, the largest of the celestial bodies that you have now absorbed into yourself. Its warm orange glow adds a bright tint to all the planets and stars. Finally, at the crown of your forehead you visualize a spiral-armed galaxy (like the Milky Way) filled with a milky-white light and a pulsing resonance of life that you can feel rushing through your expanded self.

10. Remain in this awareness for a while, focusing on a sense of oneness with the universe. It is not at all clear or even important whether you are the universe or the universe is you. All that you can sense is a unity with the Divine. When you are ready, return to your normal waking state. It is very useful to repeat all these activities on a regular basis throughout your life.

Kabbalistic Rituals

The two rituals that follow incorporate the two main responsibilities of both Chesed and Jupiter. In the first ritual, we work with the sense of Chesed as "mercy," and the second ritual is concerned with accessing the benevolent and Jovian energies of this Sephirah. In this way, our ritual work will help us to benefit our own lives and those of our friends and family.

Ritual of the Merciful Father

For this ritual, you need some sage and cedar incense, four blue candles, a blue bowl, some olive oil, and an amethyst.

The more that we spiritually advance, the greater our responsibility to others becomes. At one level the process of self-empowerment is about improving our own quality of life both practically and spiritually. At the same time, it is only really possible to fully develop as a spiritual being when the way in which we interact with others is also transformed. This ritual calls into us the unquestioning compassion and mercy that we associate with Chesed. After you have completed it a few times, you will be more inclined to assist those around you who are in need of help or just a little sympathy in their lives.

1. Prepare your ritual space by lighting the cedar and sage incense in the east and lighting the four blue candles in the shape of a cross in the south. In the west place the blue bowl filled with olive oil, and in the north position the amethyst.

2. Enter your temple in Tiphareth by performing the Building an Astral Kingdom in Tiphareth meditation described in Chapter 6. Move to the east and declare, "I call upon the almighty El to send the archangel Tzadqiel (Zad-Key-Al) in order that I may be instilled with the power of righteousness." Pick up the incense and wave it toward the east four times.

3. Move to the south and repeat this declaration. Then pick up one of the candles and make the sign of an equal-armed cross in the air in front of you. Visualize this cross as glowing blue.

4. Move to the west and repeat the declaration from Step 1. Dip your index and middle fingers in the olive oil and anoint yourself on the forehead in the shape of a square within a circle.

5. Approach the north and pick up the amethyst as you utter the declaration for a fourth time. After you have made the declaration, draw an equal-armed cross in the air in front of you with the amethyst. See this cross as a glowing blue in color.

6. Return to the east and then turn so that you are facing west. Say, "Tzadqiel lead me into the path of Yod." The floor beneath your feet and extending to the west becomes a grayish green color. As you walk along this path, a number of lightning flashes strike you. Rather than being painful, you feel their heat settle within you and a sense of increased dignity fills your whole being.

7. Turn again so that you are facing the north and say, "Tzadqiel lead me into the path of Kaph." The floor beneath your feet and extending toward the north becomes a rich purple color. When you are halfway toward the amethyst in the north, you are approached by a group of ragged people. You place your hands in your pockets and find that they are filled with food and coins. You distribute these to the people and then move on to the north.

8. Turn so that you are facing south and say, "Tzadqiel lead me into the path of Teth, that I may absorb the merciful greatness of Chesed." The floor now becomes a plain gray color extending toward the south. When you are halfway from the candles in the south, a large green and yellow serpent appears, its fangs bared and ready to strike. In your hands you find that you are holding the bowl of olive oil. Having dipped your index and middle fingers in the oil, you draw a cross over the head of the serpent, which promptly disappears.

9. Return to the center of your ritual space. Facing east you kneel on one knee and declare, "Having traversed the three intelligences that lead into the great intelligence of Gedulah (Ged-You-Lah), I pledge myself to working in the name of mercy and compassion, and I call upon Tzadqiel to convey the truth of this pledge to the almighty El."

10. As you make this declaration, you become bathed in a pyramid of blue light. On each of your shoulders, you can also see an equal-armed cross of saffron yellow. You may stay in this position absorbing the energy of Chesed as long as you wish. Ensure that you feel balanced within your temple in Tiphareth before returning to your normal wakeful state.

Ritual to Bring Good Fortune

For this ritual, you need some basil-scented incense (or some basil leaves), a cutting from a hazel shrub or tree (or a cutting from an oak tree), four yellow candles, a sprig of sage, a cutting from a violet plant, and, if possible, a square of tin.

In this ritual you internalize the benevolent energies of Chesed and call upon the power of Tzedeq to increase the good fortune in your life. Don't assume that this ritual is going to make you win the lottery or suddenly come into a lot of money. When we speak of activating good fortune in our lives, we are referring to a generally benevolent influence that will be felt in all aspects of your life rather than in a purely material or monetary sense.

1. Before you begin, lay out your ritual space. Place the basil incense and hazel in the east, the four yellow candles in the south in the shape of a square, the sage in the west, and the cutting from a violet plant in the north (ideally on the tin square).

2. Enter your temple in Tiphareth to help ensure that the energies are experienced in a fully balanced manner. Stand in the west facing east and declare, "I call upon the almighty power of El to bring Sachiel (Sa-Key-Al) the archangel of Tzedeq (Zed-Eck) to guide me through the Hall of Fortune."

3. Walk to the south. In front of the candles, you see a large eagle. Salute the eagle and declare, "In the name of Sachiel, I call upon the spirits of Tzedeq to bring me good fortune."

4. Pass straight across to the north. Pick up the cutting of violet and state, "In the name of Sachiel, I call upon the spirits of Tzedeq to bring me good fortune." Inhale the scent of the violet before replacing it on the square of tin.

5. Walk from the north directly to the center of your ritual space. As you stand in the center, visualize a large, gray, metal, equal-armed cross before you, which you now pick up in your right hand.

6. Holding the cross in your right hand, walk from the center of your ritual space to the east. Standing in the east declare, "Having traced the sigil [a symbol with inner power] of Tzedeq through my wanderings in the Hall of Fortune, I call upon Sachiel to urge the spirits of Tzedeq to bring me good fortune in my life."

7. Return to the center of your ritual space. Stretch out both arms in the form of a cross and declare, "I call upon almighty El to send the archangel of righteousness Tzadqiel to open the way to the benevolence of Gedulah." Visualize a dark blue pathway extending from the west to the east.

8. Walk to the east again, and as you are walking say in a loud and dignified voice, "Let the Chashmalim (Shash-Ma-Leem) be present, let the shining ones light my way to the path of good fortune." As you make this declaration, the sky fills with clouds edged in gold and copper.

9. As you arrive in the east, turn around and face west. As you do so, the clouds release showers of bright sparks that circle down toward you, forming a pyramid of light over your whole body. At the same time, a path of deep blue light also forms running from north to south, creating a cross of deep blue light in your ritual space.

10. As the sparks whirl around, you feel a growing sense of happiness and genuine joviality. You may enjoy this sensation for as long as you wish. When you are ready to leave, thank the Divine El and the spirits of Chesed and Tzedeq before returning to your normal waking state.

Signs and Symbols of Chesed

This section lists symbols, colors, and other associations with Chesed. These are interesting in their own right and can be meditated on to arrive at your own deep understanding of their meaning. Additionally, while you are working with the energies of Chesed or when you want to attract positive energies relating to a matter governed by Chesed, you may want to wear or carry with you something that relates to Chesed. If you are trying to forgive someone you feel has wronged you, for example, you could wear a piece of amethyst on a necklace.

Appendix A shows the pathway correspondences at a glance, and Appendix B lists more symbols, including easy-to-copy planetary and elemental symbols.

- **Symbols:** Four-sided figures, square within a circle, Jupiter symbol, crook, scepter, and orb
- **Colors:** Blue, dark yellow
- **Numbers and letters:** 4, 9, 16, 34, 72, 136, 194, Teth (T), Yod (Y), Kaph (K)
- **Crystals and stones:** Sapphire, amethyst
- **Plants and incense:** Basil, cedar, hazel, saffron, oak, apple
- **Archangel:** Tzadqiel
- **Direction:** West
- **Element:** Water, whose archangel is Gabriel and whose spirits are the undines
- **Planet:** Jupiter (Tzedeq), whose archangel is Sachiel

Chapter 9

Binah: The Kingdom of the Mother

Congratulations! You have now reached the highest stage of the Tree of Life. The three highest Sephiroth, the so-called supernal Sephiroth, represent forms of energy that are as close to the Divine as is possible for us to understand. In the One World model of the Tree of Life, the supernals represent aspects of what we might call the "body of God." In particular Binah represents the ability of the Divine to create forms out of what would otherwise be formless energy. If we had been using the One World model, our exercises would have to have stopped at Tiphareth, because it would not be possible for us to handle the amount of energy represented by Sephiroth operating at the Archangelic or Divine level.

As you'll recall from Chapter 1, we are using the Four Worlds model of the Tree of Life. In this model, even though we are now entering the realm of the supernal Sephiroth, we are experiencing them only as physical manifestations of Divine energy. In other words, the fact that we will be absorbing the energy of Binah in this chapter does not mean that we will attain a state of Divine enlightenment. However, even at a "diluted" level, the understanding and insight that you'll gain from working with Binah will still be profound and empowering.

We pronounce Binah "Bee-Nah" with the emphasis on the second syllable. Binah is spelled Beth Yod Nun Heh and the title Binah translates as "understanding." We can reach Binah by two paths. From Tiphareth we follow the path of Zayin, and from Geburah we follow the path of Cheth. The path of Zayin is also known as "the Disposing One," and this relates to Zayin's association with the ability to discriminate between different courses of action. This aspect of the path of Zayin is also represented by its literal meaning, "sword." The Tarot card linked with the path of Zayin is the Lovers. Because this card is all about choices in life, it neatly fits with the idea that Zayin refers to the ability to "dispose" of wrong choices.

The path of Cheth is also known as "the Intelligence of the House of Influence." It is linked with the Tarot card the Chariot. The idea of influence can be linked to the Sephira of Geburah, which the path of Cheth links with Binah. As we enter Binah, which is also known as "the Great Mother," we are in a sense returning to the universal womb, the place where all forms of life are created. The path of influence reminds us that this creation of forms is in some ways a constraining force. For example, if we are to create a female organism, we must constrain those genetic instructions that would lead to the creation of a male organism. On the more benevolent and maternal side, we can see the path of Cheth as representing the protective energy of a mother. The letter Cheth literally means "fence" and depicts a protective wall, which itself could represent the womb.

If you look at the Hebrew spelling of Binah in the Tree of Life diagram in Chapter 1, you can see that the shapes of the letters also represent the idea of Binah as the Universal Mother in the sense of being a protective womblike force. At the end of each word, we have letters whose shapes act to enclose the smaller letters in the center. This idea becomes more convincing when we look at the associations of the central letters. The initial Yod is often regarded as being symbolic of the initial spark of creation, and the letter Nun literally means "fish" and so can be associated with the embryonic state.

When I consider the spelling of Binah, I find a message directly related to the literal translation of Binah as "understanding." The spelling of the Sephira tells us that Binah is the home (Beth) of the creative force (Yod) that will lead us to profound emotional change (Nun) through which we can see the Divine creation (Heh) more clearly.

If we look at the total value of the title Binah, we find the letters Samech (60) and Zayin (7). The letter Samech literally means "support," and the letter Zayin means "sword." We can interpret this as meaning that Binah supports the ability of the individual to make strong and active decisions. This may seem strange in the context of a Sephira that is also representative of maternal energies. But remember, we can only define what something is in terms of what it is not, and also that a key maternal role lies in the formation of identity. When we consider the letter Zayin from this perspective, it makes much more obvious sense.

The total value of 67 can be reduced to the number 13 (6 + 7 = 13). The number 13 is also the reduced value of the Sephira Netzach. This number is associated with major changes and is well suited to Binah, because it is Binah that is responsible for taking the raw energy from Chokmah and turning that energy into a definite shape or form. This again calls to mind the idea of Binah as the Great Mother. From our point of view of climbing the Tree of Life, the great change is in the shift from a trust in the Divine that we learn in Chesed to a deep understanding of the way in which the Divine works.

A relationship exists between Binah and Netzach as well. Netzach refers to human creativity, whereas we can see Binah as representing the creativity of the Divine. It is in the womb of Binah that all the potential life forms in the universe are given a shape and a possibility of existence. This is where the further reduction of 13 to 4 (1 + 3 = 4) becomes significant. Recall from Chapter 5 that the number 4 is a symbol of the material world. Although Binah only provides the form or blueprint for life, this process of giving form is absolutely essential if anything is ever going to manifest. You could compare this to the fact that before a car can be built, it has to be planned and designed on paper.

The Sephira of Binah is also known as "the Sanctifying Intelligence," and this emphasizes its protective and nurturing influence in the universe. As well as being referred to as "the Great or Supernal Mother," Binah can be translated as "understanding." The term *understanding* is significant because it implies more than simple factual knowledge, and it is this intuitive level of insight that also links into the nature of Binah.

Binah is associated with the planet Saturn, or as it is known in Hebrew, *Shabbatai* (Shab-A-Tie). Traditionally Saturn has been associated with Old Father Time and is regarded as the planet of old age. Saturn's connection with Binah is based on the fact that it is also the planet most associated with the wisdom of experience, and in this sense we can see a definite association with the qualities that one would expect to find in the Supernal Mother. Saturn was also regarded by the ancient Greeks and Romans as the God responsible for agriculture, and in this sense we see another link to Binah because of the associations of farming with natural growth and the need to nurture the crops with appropriate care and attention.

The key Divine name of Binah is YHVH Elohim. This name translates as "the Lord God." Because Elohim is a plural, however, we should perhaps translate this title as "the Lord Gods." The Divine name of Binah contains a feminine noun and this indicates the need to view the Divine as containing, but also transcending or rising above, both genders. This is particularly important when thinking about a Sephira known as the Great Mother, because we need to think of its qualities as relevant to all of us, regardless of our gender.

Areas of Empowerment

The responsibilities of Binah are largely those that we would expect of an archetypal mother figure. Binah oversees family relationships, deep understanding, and the development of good relationships with our children. When we work with Binah, we can open ourselves to the maternal energies of this Sephira, but we should also try to emulate those protective forces in our own relationships with others. The best mothers know when to be strict as well as when to be affectionate. The influence of Saturn comes into its own with this aspect of the Supernal Mother. By the time you have worked through this chapter, you will be more understanding in your relationships with others. You will also be much better at establishing clear limits of what you will accept, not only from your children but in other areas of your life, such as in the workplace or from your partner.

Practical Activities

The two exercises in this section will begin to solidify the energies of Binah within your consciousness. Even as we reach the highest Sephiroth of the Tree of Life, the impact of their energies is felt at every level of our existence. This is because we experience ourselves and the world around us in a holistic way, and so a practical action will resonate within us on a whole range of levels, including the spiritual.

The Urban Family Tree

As we would expect from the Great Mother, family is a very important aspect of Binah's responsibilities. A hundred years ago, our family ties would be easy to draw. People tended to move around less and stayed in very close contact with large extended families. In today's society, more and more of us live alone, move away from home for our careers, and spend more time with friends than we do with our relations. This can often lead to feelings of isolation and even confusion about who we really are, because families often provide a psychological anchor around which we can safely construct a clear sense of our individual identity.

For this exercise, you need some paper, including large sheets of drawing paper, pens (any color of ink), and some greeting cards.

The title of this particular activity was suggested by a scene from the movie *Bridget Jones's Diary*, in which the main character is reminded by her friends that they are more than just acquaintances—they are her "urban family." The idea of an urban family is one positive way to respond to the loss of the extended family. This exercise should make you aware that the important thing about family is the level of emotional connectedness and not the biological relationship.

1. Family is both a social and a very personal matter. Society holds certain broad ideas about the role of a father or uncle in the family, for example, but ultimately we all add our own particular twist on these definitions. Make a list of different relationship roles and what earmarks each specific role for you. For example, the key aspect of a father for you may be a person who will always be there to protect you. Your idea of what each relationship role should involve may be unusual, but that doesn't matter; what counts here are your feelings about what you expect in different types of relationships.

2. On a large sheet of paper, begin drawing your first family tree. This first diagram should include actual relatives, both by blood and marriage. If you are not sure how to lay out your family tree, there are lots of books available on genealogy to help you.

3. Don't worry about trying to research members of your family whom you don't know. This activity is about establishing a "real" family rather than constructing a diagram of family history. Include relatives whom you know but don't see very often; they are still a part of your known family.

4. Looking at your list of family roles, assign a role to each person on the tree. If someone is important in your life but doesn't really fit any of your roles, try to think of a single label word that best sums up that person's importance to you. For those relatives who do not play any meaningful part in your life, just mark as "no significant role."

5. On a new sheet of paper, construct a second family tree. However, instead of relatives, this family tree should include your friends and colleagues.

6. Allocate various family roles to your friends and colleagues. If someone plays no major part in your life, just note this. What may surprise you is that it is quite likely that you will find more "family"-type roles for your friends and colleagues than you did for your relatives.

7. With two family trees, you may have built up quite a large and extended family. You can now combine the significant individuals from each tree to make one large family tree that should cover all the particular relationships that you are looking for in your life. If there are still gaps, write a brief description of what the missing relationship would provide for you.

8. A family should be mutually supportive. Think about the different roles that you take on in relation to all the people in your "family." If you can't think of anything you do to help anyone who appears in your completed family tree, think about how you can change the situation so that you are supporting that person as much as he or she is supporting you.

9. It's important to let our family members know how much they mean to us, so send a greeting card to each family member and friend on your final family tree. Make sure that each card is personal to the person who is going to receive it so that he or she really understands your appreciation.

10. Family trees can be great fun as well as thought-provoking. Add to your tree as you meet new people. Make sure you don't forget people who have been important in your past, too.

Intuition Training

People often talk of the existence of "women's intuition," but it's not just women who can develop their intuition to its full potential. We all have the potential to be intuitive. It is certainly true that women tend to be more intuitive than men. This is because society still values the caring, listening qualities that encourage intuitive ability far more in women than it does in men. As the Universal Mother, Binah is especially associated with intuitive ability. In practical terms, it is much easier to develop an intuitive awareness when you have already explored the energies that lie on the Tree of Life below Binah.

There are no particular needs for this activity, although it does involve spending time with friends, colleagues, and even some people whom you don't know at all right now.

One of the key aims of self-empowerment is to be in touch with not only ourselves, but also those around us. The more we understand and empathize with other people, the better we will understand ourselves. The aim of the following activity is to encourage your innate listening skills. When I say listening, I don't just mean with your ears, but listening with your higher consciousness. This can only be developed by regular practice, but the increase in understanding will make the effort worthwhile.

1. We all use intuition in our lives often without realizing that we're doing it. Whenever you run into someone, before you begin to speak, you have a moment when you sense how the other person is feeling. The first thing you are going to do is make a point of noting that feeling and then seeing as the conversation develops whether your feelings were right.

2. When you start achieving some success with this mood-sensing activity, pick a few close friends and write down three significant things about each friend. These should not be things that you know or things that you could just deduce—for instance, if you have a fit friend, it doesn't really count if you write down that he exercises a lot! These should be things that you feel without thinking about them. When you have your list, check it out with your friends and see how accurate you were.

3. It's not just people who have feelings and atmospheres around them. Places are very evocative and seem to retain something of a trace of major events that have taken place there. Take a walk around some older parts of your town. Notice the feelings that you experience in different places. Go to your local library and look up any places that created significant feelings. You may well find that the records of the place in question detail an event that makes perfect sense of the feelings that you experienced.

4. So far we have been dealing with the familiar. Your next challenge is to get out there and start talking to some people you don't know. The venue doesn't matter; the important thing is that you make a mental note of your feelings when you first see the person. As you talk with the person, consider whether your initial feelings are reflected by the person's actual character. The more you practice this, the more accurate you will become.

5. Of course, we all give each other all sorts of unconscious visual cues through our body language, and some of what we might call intuition is really about improving our instinctive reading of body language. A good test of pure intuition is to speak to someone on the phone or over the Internet. Then allow your intuitive feelings about that person's appearance and mannerisms to come to the surface. You can then arrange to meet the other person and see just how close your intuition was. Of course, be very careful about meeting strangers in person with whom you've corresponded over the Internet. One good approach is to have an e-mail correspondence with a colleague who works in another city or state and then arrange to meet. Another possibility is to phone in a repair request and later meet the person when he or she comes to make the repair.

6. Up to now we have looked at things that we might consider static aspects of personality and atmosphere. With practice, however, you can use your intuition for some insight into what the day ahead might have in store. We all have days when we wake up feeling that the day will go great, or indeed that it really isn't worth getting out of bed. From now on, start paying conscious attention to those feelings. The more you do, the more your feelings will become increasingly accurate. Don't just focus on how you feel throughout the day. You'll find that as you pay attention to these feelings, you

actually impact what happens; for example, you feel that it will be a good day, and then you bump into an old friend from college.

7. The best thing about being a good friend is being there when someone really needs us. Often we find out only after the fact that someone has had a rotten time. This can be frustrating because we want to be there supporting that person right away. If you allow it to, your intuition can tell you how those you are close to are feeling. Pick a close friend and make a point each day of sensing rather than thinking about how he or she feels. If you sense your friend needs a hug or a chat, act on that feeling. You'll be surprised by how often you turn out to be right.

8. As your intuition grows stronger, you can also have some fun at work. We all know that for every meeting there will always be at least one person who is late, one person who will make a suggestion that he or she really regrets, and someone who won't say anything during the whole meeting. Try to sense which colleague will fill each role— if you do it often enough, you may be quite surprised at just how accurate you can become.

(One) must strive to attain to the TRUTH behind the symbol—one can use these images as a tool, a device, to attain to the truth.
—Frater A.H.E.H'O, *Angelic Images* (1996)

Meditations

The two meditations in this section help to embed the positive energies associated with Binah within your consciousness. When working with Binah, it's important to recognize the full nature of this Sephira. It's all too easy to focus only on what we might call the "soft" aspects of Binah that we associate with its role as the Supernal Mother. Although these elements of Binah's "personality" are important, they have to be understood in the context of the associations with the planet Saturn. The first meditation in this section focuses on the energy of Saturn. The Saturn Meditation prepares you for the next meditation in this section and is a good meditation to do before the rituals later in this chapter. Doing so ensures that you are maintaining an appropriate balance of the complex energies that you are absorbing when you work through the Sephira of Binah.

Saturn Meditation

This meditation awakens your inner connections with the energy associated with the planet Saturn. Before you begin, light nine gray candles, ideally set in dark gray candleholders, and place them in the north in a circular pattern. Also place some sprigs of ivy around the room. If possible, drape your chair with a dark gray cloth before sitting down.

1. Saturn is the regulator of time and is often portrayed as a venerable old man. You are seeking to emulate this sense of wisdom and experience when meditating. As silly as you may feel at first, perform this meditation leaning slightly forward with one hand resting on your chin. Tilt your head slightly as if listening. By taking up a physical position that mirrors the personality of Saturn, you will find it much easier to absorb its energies.

2. After establishing your breathing rhythm, see yourself sitting in a chair made of solid lead. You are wearing a heavy gray cloak with the hood pulled forward. In your free hand, you hold a large staff that is covered with strange inscriptions. Beneath the cowl of your robe, you are wearing a skullcap made of solid lead.

3. Around your feet are coils of ivy tendrils; as you look closely, you see that they are growing very slowly but perceptibly. Although it is quite dark, you can see that your chair is at one end of a stone hallway. You now stand slowly and take a step forward. You carry on walking forward, and as you do you notice that the ivy is growing up around your legs. You move slowly with the heaviness of age.

4. Walking along the stone hallway, you come to a large lead plinth. On this plinth are a number of scrolls. You open them—they are covered in mystical symbols and writing in some strange language that you somehow recognize and can understand. You place the scrolls in the pocket of your robe and walk on along the hallway until you come to a heavy, lead-colored door.

5. Opening the door, you step out into the daylight. You look behind you and see that you have just left a large, stone mansion. You are now outside in the grounds of this building. You can see people of all ages milling around; they are all dressed in peasant clothes. As you walk past, each person falls down slowly and sinks into the ground. However, there is no sense of loss or pain here, only peace. As they fall into the ground, stalks of wheat and barley spring up around them.

6. The staff in your hand has now turned into a scythe, and you have to scythe your way through the crops. You cut a winding path that leads toward a small gray stone building. On the door of the building is a doorknocker shaped like a crow's head.

7. You knock slowly three times on the door. You notice that the building has no windows and that even the door is gray—made of some metallic material. The door slowly opens after the third knock, and you walk in.

8. Inside, the building is bare except for thick cobwebs and inquisitive spiders that seem to peer at you as you enter. A number of lead-framed mirrors hang on the walls.

9. You look in each of the mirrors in turn. As you look at each one, you are shown an image of yourself at a different moment in time. Each image provokes a set of memories associated with that particular time in your life. You feel no regrets but only an awareness of the growing insight and experience that each memory has provided. You may stay as long in this building as you wish before leaving the meditation and returning to your normal waking state.

Rebirth Meditation

For this meditation, you will need some gray paper and a pen with black ink. You also need some myrrh-scented incense, which you should ideally burn in a receptacle made of lead. Light the incense and place it in the west.

1. Write the following, "May Tzaphqiel, the archangel of Binah, who beholds the true face of the Divine bring down the blessings of YHVH Elohim that I may be reborn in the heart of the Great Mother." Beneath this draw a large triangle inside a circle, as shown in Appendix B. Place the paper next to the incense in the west.

2. Perform this meditation lying in bed. Rather than lying with a straight back, though, curl yourself up into a comfortable fetal position. It may help the meditation to play some soothing classical music; anything featuring the flute would be especially appropriate.

3. After establishing your normal meditation breathing rhythm, you become aware of a silvery oval above you. This oval gradually forms into an egg around your body. Although you are completely enclosed in this silver egg, you feel entirely relaxed.

4. You see a light shining through the silvery membrane of the egg. This single light becomes three distinct points of light. Behind each point of light you are gradually able to make out the figure of a woman dressed in Grecian-style robes.

5. The lights cause the surface of the egg to become translucent, enabling you to see through the egg membrane more clearly, although everything still has a silvery tinge to it. The three women smile reassuringly at you and hold their hands out over the top of the egg.

6. As they do this, the egg fills with a soft pink glow. In the base of the egg, the light seems to coalesce, and you watch as pearls begin to form out of the gathering light. The pearls increase in number until you are lying in an egg full of soft, shiny pearls.

7. The three women now link hands around the egg. As their hands touch, the egg is bathed from the outside in a bright yellow light. Suddenly a shaft of light strikes the outer shell and the egg begins to crack and open. You stand up and stretch your arms up, looking up at the sun overhead as you do so.

8. The three women lead you to a simple-looking wooden chair and help you sit down. The chair itself is standing inside a silver triangle marked out on the floor, and the three women form a triangle around you.

9. Sitting in the chair, you see the vast ringed planet of Saturn above your head. You are filled with a sense of calm as the woman in front of you marks a triangle on your forehead with myrrh from a gray metallic jar. You may stay seated in this chair for as long as you wish before returning to your normal waking state.

Empowerment Technique for Binah: Spiritual Healing

In Binah we open ourselves up to the protective influences of the Supernal Mother. In the meditations, you were the receiver of these energies. When you work with the empowerment technique of Binah, however, you use those protective energies that you have developed to assist others. This is very much a part of the role of Binah. One of the key energies associated with the Sephira of understanding is that of concern and compassion for others.

Before we begin, let me emphasize that spiritual healing is *not* a substitute for medical treatment. If you are ill, always consult your doctor and follow the medical advice that you are given. Spiritual healing should be seen as a complement to and not a substitute for medical treatment. This is not to claim that spiritual healing cannot work, but especially at this level, the healing that we will perform is more likely to ease our pain rather than actually cure the cause of our symptoms. If you practice healing techniques, you should find that over time you will be able to rid yourself of minor ailments such as headaches or colds, but this will take time and most important, requires an absolute conviction that the technique you are using will work. After you have achieved a reasonable measure of success with yourself, you can consider trying these techniques to help friends and family when they are feeling under the weather. *Always* ask permission before trying to help; individuals must decide for themselves whether and when to let the spiritual, in whatever form that may take, into their lives. No matter how much success you achieve, always remember that the healing is coming from the Divine and not from any power that resides solely within you.

The aim of these techniques is to help you in realizing the desire to be of assistance to others. On a more personal level, they will make you realize beyond any doubt that the whole process of personal empowerment has had a positive effect on your ability to engage with your latent abilities.

You don't need any special tools or equipment for this first healing technique.

1. Learn to feel the internal energy flowing within you. Stand up straight with your feet comfortably apart and begin swinging your arms loosely from the shoulder. Don't be too vigorous, but allow your arms to move in a relaxed manner. As they swing forward, focus closely on the feeling of energy rushing toward your fingertips.

2. Keep swinging your arms and feel the heat growing in your hands. The more you swing your arms, the greater the feeling of heat in your hands. When you stop swinging your arms, hold your hands above the surface of your skin. You will feel heat emanating from the palms of your hands.

3. Now create that same flow of heat and energy without swinging your arms. Hold your leading hand (your right hand if you're

right-handed) over the back of your other arm. Try to recall the sensation that you had when you were swinging your arms and visualize the heat growing, especially in the palm of your hand. Do this in a relaxed way. If you try to force the results, you will just become physically tense and this will restrict your flow of energy.

4. After you have reached a point where you can generate a sensation of heat with relative ease, you are ready to move on to the next stage. When you next scratch yourself or have some other minor source of pain, place your leading hand over the affected area. (As I've mentioned, make sure that for anything more than minor pain you also see your doctor.) Focus on generating the heat and then visualize the heat moving from your hand to the area in question. As this happens, you should see a pink glow surrounding the area that you are seeking to heal.

5. Don't think about the pain itself. Just focus on a sense of positive health and watch the pink glow surrounding and supporting the part of you that is in pain. When you have practiced this for a while, you will begin to feel definite results.

The next healing technique is especially useful for self-healing or for helping people when you cannot be in physical contact with them. It builds on your growing expertise in meditation but applies it in a very directed way. Before you begin, light a pink candle and place it in a gray candleholder. It will also be helpful to burn some myrrh incense.

1. Establish a definite breathing rhythm, and then build up an awareness in your mind of a glowing pink and golden cloud of energy that you should perceive as being located at the crown of your head.

2. While keeping the cloud of energy in your mind, focus on the area that is in need of healing. After you have a strong image of the affected area in your mind, see the cloud of energy steadily moving in its direction. If you are seeking to heal yourself, visualize the cloud moving into your body. If you are seeking to heal someone else, keep the cloud on the surface of the person's body. You don't want to move the cloud inside that person's body because this would merge your energy with the other person's, which can be very disturbing for both of you unless you are experienced in this sort of technique.

3. When the energy cloud reaches the affected area, see it surround the site of the pain. The pain should be seen as a very deep red glow. As the cloud surrounds your pain, you see the color red gradually fade until it's the same shade of pink as the energy cloud. As the color fades, you become aware of the pain also dissipating. If you are healing someone else, visualize the sense of pain fading away as you hold a mental image of a red glow around the person fading to pink.

4. When the affected area is the color of the energy cloud, say "In the name of YHVH Elohim may you [I] be free from pain." Give thanks to the Divine before returning to your normal waking state. If you are doing a lot of healing for other people, it is advisable to perform the Rite of Protection (see Chapter 2) before you begin to ensure that you do not reduce your own energy levels.

Healing is my way of giving back, giving back to the Mother Universe, it doesn't really matter whether that's healing a friend, myself or the pets, it always feels like a way of thanking the Divine.

—From a modern-day member of a Western Mystery Tradition group based in England

Kabbalistic Rituals

The two rituals that follow incorporate the two main responsibilities of both Saturn and Binah. In the first ritual, you work with the sense of Binah as a source of understanding. In the second ritual, you access the energies of Saturn as they relate to memories and the past and then channel them through the maternal aspect of Binah.

Harmony Ritual

For this ritual, you need some myrrh incense, three gray candles, a silver bowl or cup, a gray silk square, a pearl (a cultured pearl if necessary), and a low table or stool.

You have now reached a stage in your personal development where to move forward it's important that your main goals are focused on helping others rather than yourself. In this ritual, you seek to increase the overall level of harmony in the world. You do this by trying to spread the power of understanding through your ritual. You might think that one person cannot make a great deal of difference. However, the more of us there are in the world working for understanding, the better all our lives will become. You can perform this ritual in two different ways. You can choose to focus on particular individuals who you know are going through a difficult time or you can just concentrate on the world in general becoming a more harmonious place.

1. Prepare your ritual space by lighting the myrrh incense and placing it in the east. Place the candles in a triangle shape in the south, the cup or bowl goes in the west, and the pearl should be wrapped in the silk and placed on the low table or stool in the north. If you are performing the ritual for a particular person, place his or her photograph or an item associated with the person next to the incense in the east. As with healing, if you are focusing on a specific person or group of people, ask for permission first. Respecting the space of others is one of the lessons that we learn as we develop an understanding of our own unique individuality.

2. Enter your temple in Tiphareth by performing the Building an Astral Kingdom in Tiphareth meditation described in Chapter 6. Move to the east and declare, "I call upon YHVH Elohim the Divine hosts to send the archangel Tzaphqiel (Zaf-Key-Al), the contemplation of God, to assist me in spreading the harmony that we learn from true understanding."

3. Walk clockwise around your ritual space while focusing on the notion of *understanding* in the spiritual sense of the word. When you arrive back in the east, extend your arms in the shape of a cross and intone the Divine name "YHVH Elohim." Then cross your arms over your chest.

4. Move to the center of your ritual space and declare, "In the name of YHVH Elohim, I will enter the path of Zayin." Before you and extending toward the south runs a deep yellow path.

5. As you walk toward the south, you can feel yourself being pulled to the left and right. This makes it difficult for you to walk forward, but again intone the Divine name "YHVH Elohim" and feel the strength of the forces pulling you get weaker and weaker.

6. As you arrive in the south, you see a magpie sitting on a perch made from a yew branch. You declare, "I have passed through the path of Zayin and brought calm and clarity where there was confusion." Face west and declare, "In the name of YHVH Elohim, I shall enter the path of Cheth, the influencing intelligence." You see a russet-colored path extending toward the west.

7. As you begin walking toward the west, a wall springs up on either side of the path. Rather than making you feel claustrophobic, you feel the wall as protective. You can hear clamoring noises from the outside of the wall, but you feel no fear. As you arrive in the west, you visualize a lotus flower lying on an altar of silver. You hold the flower in your right hand.

8. Declare, "I have passed through the path of Cheth and offer protection and security to those who feel none." Still visualizing yourself holding the lotus flower, walk around to the north. Stand in front of the table with the pearl and say, "I have completed the journey into Binah that I may bring harmony to [name of person or "the world"] in the name of YHVH Elohim."

9. Physically unwrap the cloth that covers the pearl. With your forefinger, but visualizing yourself using the lotus flower, draw a circle over the pearl and then draw a triangle inside the circle and declare, "May the Eralim (Air-A-Leem) assist me in blessing this symbol of [name of person or "the world"] with the harmonious energies of Binah. Let the thrones of the Divine, the blessed Eralim, carry the understanding of YHVH Elohim out of this temple and into the world."

10. Physically rewrap the pearl in the cloth and continue around to the east. Here give a brief prayer of thanks to the Divine as embodied in YHVH Elohim. Ensure that you feel balanced within your temple in Tiphareth before returning to your normal wakeful state.

Ritual of the Family

For this ritual, you need some myrrh incense, some fronds of ivy, three gray candles, a silver cup, and a piece of onyx.

In this ritual, you work with the energies of both Binah and Saturn to strengthen the bonds that tie your extended family together. As mentioned earlier, when we talk of family we are referring to all those people who constitute family members in terms of their importance in your life. If there are other members of your family who are interested in spiritual empowerment and working through this book with you, you could perform this ritual with them as a group to strengthen the bonds that it is enhancing in your life.

1. Before you begin, lay out your ritual space by placing the myrrh incense and ivy in the east. Place the three gray candles in the south in the shape of a triangle. (Ideally they should be placed on a circular stand.) The silver cup goes in the west of your ritual space, and the onyx should be placed in the north.

2. Enter your temple in Tiphareth to help ensure that the energies are experienced in a fully balanced manner. Then stand in the east and declare, "May the power of the almighty YHVH Elohim be present in this ritual and look down through the archangel Tzaphqiel with favor upon this working."

3. Walk clockwise around your ritual space until you arrive in the north. Stretch out your arms in the shape of a cross and declare, "I call upon the great angel who works with the power of Shabbatai (Shab-A-Tie), the great angel Kassiel (Kass-Ee-Al), to revive our family's memory of times past." You see Kassiel appear before you dressed in a long gray robe and carrying an hourglass.

4. Pass to the east and declare, "Kassiel send us memories of our family and our fond thoughts of them." Move to the south and declare, "Kassiel send us memories of our many activities and passions that we have shared with our family."

5. Move to the west and declare, "Kassiel send us memories of our emotional relationships with our family." Finally, walk back to the north and while facing the archangel declare, "Kassiel, in the name of YHVH Elohim make these memories manifest in the mind of our family."

6. Pass to the east and with arms outstretched in the form of a cross declare, "YHVH Elohim send your great angel Tzaphqiel to assist me in strengthening the bonds between my family and me." After

this declaration, cross your arms over your chest and remain still while feeling the energy of Binah enter your consciousness.

7. Pick up the incense and trace a circle with a triangle in its center while saying, "Let the Eralim descend and fill the minds and hearts of my family with certainty in the protection of the Divine and of the ties that bind us." As you say this, visualize a shaft of yellow light emanating from the ritual space into the east.

8. Repeat this declaration and visualization in the south, west, and north of your ritual space. In each quarter, trace a triangle within a circle with the symbolic element that is placed there. After completing the declaration in the north, return to the east.

9. Take the fronds of ivy in your hands and begin to bind them together, saying, "In the name of YHVH Elohim, as I bind this ivy symbolic of the power of Shabbatai and of Binah, may the ties between my family and me be strengthened and enhanced. In the name of the Great Mother, I call upon Tzaphqiel to assist me in bringing protection and peace to my family."

10. Place the knotted ivy next to the incense. Give thanks to the spirits of Binah and Shabbatai on behalf of yourself and your family. You can then return to your normal waking state after you have balanced yourself in your temple of Tiphareth.

Signs and Symbols of Binah

This section lists symbols, colors, and other associations with Binah. These are interesting in their own right and can be meditated on to arrive at your own deep understanding of their meaning. Additionally, while you are working with the energies of Binah or when you want to attract positive energies relating to a matter governed by Binah, you may want to wear or carry with you something that relates to Binah. If you want to ensure that you retain a healthy attitude about the process of aging, for example, you might want to keep a triangle of lead in your bedside drawer.

Appendix A shows the pathway correspondences at a glance, and Appendix B lists more symbols, including easy-to-copy planetary and elemental symbols.

- **Symbols:** Triangle within a circle, Saturn symbol, ovals and circles, cups and goblets, hourglasses, scythe
- **Colors:** Gray, gray flecked with pink, silver
- **Numbers and letters:** 3, 7, 8, 13, 15, 27, 45, 67, 713, Heh (H), Zayin (Z), Cheth (Ch)
- **Crystals and stones:** Onyx, pearl
- **Plants and incense:** Myrrh, assafoetida, ivy, yew
- **Archangel:** Tzaphqiel
- **Direction:** West
- **Element:** Fire, whose archangel is Michael and whose spirits are the salamanders
- **Planet:** Saturn (Shabbatai), whose archangel is Kassiel

Chapter 10

Chokmah: The Kingdom of Destiny

In earlier Sephiroth, you have balanced the four elements within your personality, then begun to try to access your Higher Self. In Chokmah you work toward developing a relationship with the Divine itself. This may sound quite a bit removed from the notion of self-empowerment, but that all depends on how we understand the nature of this relationship. The closer we feel to the Divine, the more we will be able to see meaning in every aspect of our lives.

One of the key beliefs in all forms of Kabbalah is that the physical universe is as much a part of the Divine as the spiritual dimension. Unlike many religions, Kabbalah does not see the Physical world or physical life as somehow a tainted experience from which we should try to escape. Instead Kabbalah teaches us that the Physical world is "the bride" of the Divine world. What we need to do is to understand it properly rather than just reject it. One of the key titles of Chokmah is "wisdom," and when we are exploring its energies, one of the things that we are trying to develop is the true wisdom that enables us to see our own lives and the world in general as being linked with the wider spiritual dimensions.

We pronounce Chokmah as "Chuk-ma" with the emphasis on the first syllable and the initial "ch" sounded like the "ch" in *loch*. Chokmah is spelled Cheth Kaph Mem Heh, and although its translation in English gives us "wisdom" it is also known by the title "the crown of creation." We can reach Chokmah by three paths. From Tiphareth we follow the path of Heh, from Chesed the path of Vau, and from Binah the path of Daleth. The path of Heh is associated with the Emperor card in Tarot and represents the inner strength that we need to carry us beyond the realm of the wholly physical. Its association with the zodiac sign of Aries also points to the need for curiosity to stimulate our continuing explorations.

The path of Vau is also referred to as "the Eternal One." This is a reminder that the energies we are now experiencing are coming almost directly from the Divine and so they have a significance and power that is not affected by the changes of time. The path of Vau is linked with the zodiac sign of Taurus; this is significant because the era of the very first civilizations occurred in the astrological period known as the age of Taurus. The path of Vau is often regarded as the path of the initiator into the mysteries. This is reflected in its link with Tarot's High Priest card, or the Hierophant, as this card is sometimes known. A hierophant in ancient times was the priest particularly in charge of initiation.

The path of Daleth is also called "the Illuminating Intelligence." Interestingly, this is also one of the titles in the *Sefer Yetzirah* of the Sephira Chokmah itself. This tells us very clearly that it is in the journey from the understanding of Binah that we gain the wisdom associated with Chokmah. The Tarot card the Empress is linked to this path. The Empress is associated with fertility and plenty. At a spiritual level, this tells us that when we pass along the path of Daleth we are about to receive a great deal of spiritual "nourishment." The path of Daleth is not linked with any zodiac sign, but is associated with the planet Venus; this again reinforces the notion of God as love and also the fact that the Divine combines both male and female qualities. In addition, the literal meaning of the letter Daleth is "door." We can see the path of Daleth as being quite literally a doorway into wisdom, and for this reason it shares the same title as the Sephira to which it belongs.

When we look at the shape of the Hebrew letters that spell out the word Chokmah (see the Tree of Life diagram in Chapter 1), we can see certain similarities to the spelling of Chesed, the Sephira that lies directly below it on the Tree of Life. Whereas Chesed is associated with paternalistic deities such as Zeus and Jupiter, Chokmah is sometimes referred to as the Father of the Supernal Sephiroth. Both Sephiroth begin with the same letter, which represents the two pillars at the entrance to the temple. However, whereas in Chesed this is followed by a tunnel-like image, in the Supernal Father we can see a shape that is much more open, suggesting that at this stage on the Tree we are much more open to the Divine light. If we then look at the final letter, Heh, we can see that it is made out of the shape of the letter Daleth with the letter Yod beneath it. The letter Daleth represents the doorway of the inner sanctum in the spelling of Chesed. Now that we are in Chokmah, this doorway has been opened and we can just make out beyond the door the flame or spark of creation represented by the letter Yod.

When I consider the spelling of Chokmah, I find a message that reminds us of the need to have faith in the Divine as we try to approach a full level of self-understanding. The protective force of the Divine (Cheth) will guide us (Kaph) and protect us (Mem) as long as we have the vision to see its presence (Heh). We can also look at the last two letters in Chokmah as reminders of the fact that the nature of the Divine transcends all human divisions of male and female. This is because Mem represents the protective maternal force and is associated with the element of Water, whereas Heh represents the outgoing vigorous masculine force and is associated with the element of Fire.

The value of the Hebrew word Chokmah is 73. This can be reduced to the number 10 (7 + 3 = 10). You'll recall from earlier chapters that the values of the Sephiroth Malkuth and Tiphareth both reduce to 10. In Malkuth we further reduce the value to 1, but this is due to the particular energies of the first Sephira on the Tree of Life. In their own way, each of these Sephiroth represented a form of completion. In Chokmah the completion relates more to the Divine than to us as people. After the Divine had produced Chokmah, the raw force that led to the creation of the universe had been released. Once released, this energy could not return to Kether but had such force that it caused the emanation of all the other Sephiroth. From the point of view of the Divine, the act of creation was complete as soon as Chokmah appeared. Everything that followed after Chokmah was a chain reaction and did not need the active creative effort of the Divine. At a more human level, when we complete the work of Chokmah we have achieved a point of self-development where we are ready to move into an existence that is not wholly bounded by physical reality.

If we look at the total value of the title Chokmah, we find the letters Ayin (70) and Gimel (3). The letter Ayin literally means "eye," and the letter Gimel means "camel." For Christian Kabbalists, this provides interesting possibilities in terms of the parable of the camel passing through the eye of a needle. It has been interpreted as Jesus referring to the idea of a person passing through the Sephira of Chokmah and achieving a vision of the Divine. We can also look at the reference to the "eye" as referring to Chokmah's role as being the first Sephira that is separated from the Divine itself; in this sense, it is the means by which the Divine can watch over its creation.

Up to this point in the Tree of Life, each Sephira has been associated with a particular planet. Kabbalah is an ancient mystical system, and so it does not feature the most recently discovered planets of Uranus, Neptune, and Pluto. Instead, the Sephira of Chokmah is associated with the zodiac or the so-called fixed stars. In Hermetic Kabbalah, one of the aims of the Great Work is to free ourselves from the influence of our astrological destiny because this is not the direct result of the Divine will operating through our Higher Self. Chokmah is associated with the whole notion of destiny and the need to challenge the destiny that the stars and our environment offer us, while learning to accept the inner plan of our Higher Self. So it's appropriate that Chokmah is associated with the zodiac or *Masloth,* as it is known in Kabbalah.

The key Divine name of Chokmah is Yah, which is pronounced exactly as it is spelled. Its literal translation is "Lord." More specifically it refers to the Divine in the act of creating the physical universe, and so is often referred to as "Lord of Creation." This is perhaps why one of the alternative titles for Chokmah is the "crown of creation." The Hebrew spelling of Yah is Yod Heh. These are the first two letters in the spelling of the Divine name YHVH. This four-lettered name of God is hugely significant in Kabbalah, and among other things, each letter represents one of the four elements. The two elements represented in the God name Yah are Fire and Water. When we consider that Chokmah is concerned with the duality inherent in the physical universe, the association with the two extremes of Fire and Water makes sense. In addition, if we consider the esoteric meaning of the two letters Yod and Heh, we can see this God name as referring directly to the creation of the universe. In Chokmah, the Divine takes its creative power (Yod) and makes it visible (Heh).

One becomes Two and Two becomes Three; and by means of the Third, the Fourth achieves Unity. Thus the two create nothing but One.
—From a fragment written by Christianus, an ancient Greek alchemist

Areas of Empowerment

You won't be surprised to learn that when working with Chokmah, most of the areas in our lives where we should expect change tend to relate to more general and potentially spiritual dimensions rather than directly impacting our career or relationships, for instance. Having said that, the changes that do occur will inevitably affect the way you live your life.

The key word that could be used to sum up the responsibility of Chokmah is *destiny*. When we are working with Chokmah, we are empowered in two distinct ways. On the one hand, we should learn to realize our true purpose or higher will; this is the result of being fully open to the influence of Chokmah as a positive shaper of our destiny. On the other hand, we need to try to rid ourselves of those forces that shape our lives that are not the result of a direct relationship between our Higher Self and the Divine.

By the time you reach the end of this chapter, you will have achieved a level of internal balance between an acceptance of those things that we cannot change and a determination to change those things that don't advance you on a personal or spiritual level. The realization of this balance can be referred to as the wisdom that is the translation of the Hebrew name Chokmah. It may be hard to accept the idea of a hidden inner purpose to your life while being encouraged to develop ways of escaping from the controlling forces of destiny. However, wisdom lies in being able to see where the line between these two competing forces needs to be drawn. This line is unique for every one of us, and the techniques in this chapter are designed to help you find where that line is for you.

Practical Activities

You will feel the impact of the next two exercises in areas of your life that are above your usual day-to-day concerns. These activities help you to embody the wisdom that we associate with those people who have achieved a real degree of spiritual insight or enlightenment. When we think of "enlightened" people, we tend to think of a calm accepting nature, an ability to understand the deep meaning of things, and a genuinely benevolent and compassionate approach to the whole world. We should also remember that wisdom is a very active quality. Wisdom does not require us to be somber or always serious in our dealings with people. In fact, the wisest people I have met, whether Kabbalists or Buddhists or followers of some other mystical tradition, have all been open, cheerful, and above all, curious and inquisitive.

Shifting Sun Signs

For this activity, you need some paper and a pen and an introductory book on astrology. Many books provide a summary of the basic characteristics of each sun sign. I recommend *The Complete Idiot's Guide to Astrology, Third Edition* (see Appendix C). If you have access to the Internet, a simple search using the key words "zodiac signs" will bring up a wide range of interesting sites.

Most of us know our sun sign and have at least a general idea of the traits associated with it. However, if we are honest, there are certain traits that we would like to change. For instance, Taureans often wish they were a little more dynamic, Librans a little more decisive, and so forth. In addition, although we may be happy with the traits that we have developed because of our sun sign, it is important that we develop the freedom to behave in ways that do not fall in line with our expected personality. The aim of this activity is to assist you in beginning to choose your behavior rather than it being the unconscious result of your astrological destiny.

1. Locate your sun sign in your introductory astrology book and make sure that you are fully familiar with all the key personality traits of your sign. You may well find that you do not immediately recognize some characteristics as being "you." However, especially when it comes to negative aspects, if you think objectively you may find that you do come to see yourself in your sun sign description.

2. Select the personality trait you believe to be the most positive aspect of your particular sign. Write down your understanding of this personality aspect in a short paragraph. This will help make the characteristic more personal to you. For the next week, make a point of

highlighting this aspect of your personality in your dealings with others.

3. We are now going to begin to operate outside our own sun sign. Select a sun sign at random from your astrology book and read about how that sign engages with practical matters. Try to incorporate this way of being practical into your daily life. In doing so you will not only be developing new skills at a day-to-day level, you will also be causing subtle shifts in your deep understanding of yourself.

4. If we are going to free ourselves from the "Wheel of Fortune" as the ancients used to refer to the signs of the zodiac, we need to progress one step at a time. Pick another sun sign at random, and this time look at the hobbies and pastimes that it suggests someone of that sign would enjoy. Select the one that least appeals to you and spend a week trying it out. Don't just grin and bear it, but really try to enjoy yourself!

5. The next stage involves trying to consciously take control of your sensory preferences. If you are an Aries, for instance, you are likely to prefer the color red, but you want to try to persuade your Aries mind that it can like the color blue equally well. Although this may seem like a trivial aim, our sensory preferences indirectly control much of our behavior. If we can exercise some control over these preferences, we become more genuinely in control of ourselves.

6. Choose another sun sign from your book, ideally this should be from the opposite half of the year from the one in which you were born. Determine the favorite color, smell, and taste of your chosen sun sign and then make sure that you wear clothes in that color, cologne of that scent, and eat the sorts of food associated with that sun sign. Again, the key to this activity is that you make an effort to genuinely enjoy these sensory experiences.

7. Choose another sun sign and read about how this sign interacts with other people, then try to emulate this behavior for a few days. For example, Leos are outgoing and like to be the center of attention. If possible, instead of just acting, try to locate a part of you deep down that can relate to the motivation for responding to people in that way and allow that to guide you.

8. By now you're probably reasonably familiar with a number of different sun signs. Go back to your own sun sign and find one characteristic that you would like to change about yourself. Rather than just suppressing that characteristic, try to find that sun sign that you feel offers a personality type that most contradicts the negative aspect you are trying to remove.

9. After you have found an appropriate sun sign, try to emulate the specific sort of behavior that counteracts the negative behavior associated with your own sun sign. In addition, wear the color associated with this other sun sign until you feel that you have achieved some measure of success in controlling the negative behavior.

10. The final challenge is to pick a sun sign and try to incorporate all the aspects that typify that sign into the way you live your life for at least a few days. Don't expect to succeed at this on your first attempt. This really is a challenge that will draw on all your skills that you have learned in earlier chapters. However, when you can achieve this level of control, you really will have freed yourself from your astrological destiny.

The Coin Trick

One of the biggest difficulties that we face in life is making the right decision. Often the most difficult part is not so much living with the decision that we've made, but actually making the decision in the first place. The ability to make decisions sits within the responsibility of Chokmah in two ways. First, the ability to choose appropriately helps us to embody the wisdom associated with Chokmah. Second, when we make decisions with the assistance of our Higher Self, we are allowing the positive forces of Divine destiny to play a role in the way we live our lives.

As you might guess from its title, you need a coin for this activity as well as some paper and a pen. It can be any sort of coin you want as long as you can differentiate between the two sides, so that you can call heads or tails and see which way it has landed.

As you work through this exercise, you will begin to let the influence of the Divine, as it communicates with your Higher Self, into your life. One of the overall aims of working with Chokmah is to develop an awareness of our true purpose in life. This is not something we can achieve in one great leap, but tends to happen very gradually. Our true purpose is not something we can realize just by thinking, but has to be accessed by opening ourselves up to the influence of higher forces. This exercise encourages us to allow those forces into our lives.

This is one of the simplest activities that you will come across in this book. In spite of its simplicity, it can also be one of the most powerful tools that you can use to empower your life. Although the activity is simple in terms of what you actually have to do, it does require you to be honest with yourself. This can be a lot more difficult than you might initially think.

1. Before using the coin, you need to take some preparatory steps. The next time you are thinking about a possible course of action, focus deeply on what you really want to do. You will find this easier if, instead of thinking about whether to take the possible action, you focus on the sort of long-term outcome you are hoping for. For some decisions, you may find that by paying special attention to your thoughts you will be able to reach a decision without any further ado.

2. If you still really can't decide, write down both possible courses of action. For instance, you may be trying to decide whether to spend a work bonus on a vacation. Write a paragraph describing what will happen depending on whether you do or don't take the action in question. Write the paragraphs in an imaginative storytelling way rather than in a factual manner. Read through the two accounts and see which one appeals to you the most.

3. These initial attempts at making a decision are designed to quiet your conscious mind and allow your intuition to have a voice. However, you may still have trouble making some decisions. Take your coin and assign one course of action to heads and the other course of action to tails.

4. Flip the coin and as you do so call out, without thinking, heads or tails. It doesn't actually matter on which side the coin lands. The key is that when you call out which way it is going to land, you are bypassing your normal conscious decision-making processes. As a result, the side that you call out is likely to be the decision that on a deep intuitive level you know to be right.

5. When you have used this technique for some time, you will probably reach a point where you can dispense with using an actual coin. Instead of tossing the coin, just visualize the coin spinning in the air

and call out heads or tails. (Obviously, if you are not alone you might want to call this in your head rather than out loud.) Again, don't think about it, just let your intuition guide you. The more you rely on your Higher Self, the easier it will be for you to listen to it. Eventually you will not even need to visualize the coin.

Meditations

The two meditations in this section help to embed the positive energies associated with Chokmah within your consciousness. Because you are now on the threshold of the final Sephira, these meditations work on the spiritual aspect of your understanding of the world. Try to perform one of the meditations every two or three days as a preparation for moving into the final Sephira of Kether. The Chokmah meditations work together to create an unconscious appreciation of both the workings of Divine destiny and the need for the individual to allow his or her Higher Self to take control of his or her life. This is itself yet another duality—the tension between the individual freedom of choice and the will of the Divine.

Chokmah is the point on the Tree of Life where it becomes possible for physical creation to begin. Above Chokmah we have the undifferentiated oneness of the Divine; in Chokmah, however, we find the pure creative spark. This is a very powerful force, and because it is only the potential for creation rather than creation itself, it represents an uncontrolled force, or a force that has yet to receive any form. It's helpful to enter your temple in Tiphareth by performing the Building an Astral Kingdom in Tiphareth meditation described in Chapter 6 before beginning these meditations; this will help to provide an appropriate form to the high levels of energy released when working with Chokmah.

Destiny Meditation

This meditation stimulates your Higher Self into challenging the external forces that have had a part in shaping your destiny. These forces, such as the planets or the impact of your parental upbringing, operate in your unconscious, and this meditation causes shifts in your unconscious to counteract their effects. You don't need any candles or incense for this meditation because it focuses solely on you and not on any other symbols, such as a planet of elemental energy.

1. Lie on the floor with your arms outstretched and your legs together. Visualize a circle around you touching your head and your feet. If it helps you with visualization, mark out a circle of chalk or salt before lying down and beginning your meditation.

2. After establishing your breathing rhythm, visualize a ring of 12 illuminated spheres hovering above you. The outline of this ring matches the circle surrounding your body on the ground. Within this ring is a smaller ring in which there are seven illuminated spheres. Both of the rings are spinning at a gentle and steady pace.

3. As you watch the rings spinning above you, a ray of light emerges from each of the illuminated spheres. The rays are white but shaded with subtle colors, and each ray is slightly different. The spheres represent the planets and the signs of the zodiac. The rays, which symbolize their power, all combine in a single point just above the center of the circle in which you are lying.

4. Beneath the glowing light of these 19 combined rays of energy is a small infant. It is curled up and sleeping. As it sleeps, tendrils of light emanate from the glowing ray of the planets and the zodiac. These tendrils wrap themselves around the body of the infant.

5. You hear a rumbling sound like slow thunder, and two dark gray stone pillars emerge from the ground on either side of the infant's body. Although you cannot make out what is written, both pillars are covered with writing. The pillar on the left appears to be covered with handwriting, whereas the text on the pillar on the right looks as though it has been carefully engraved with capital letters.

6. Your attention is now drawn back to the infant as it starts to move within the tendrils of light. It is growing, and before your eyes it develops into a fully mature adult. You recognize this adult as an exact image of yourself. As this person struggles to be free of the tendrils of light, the coils of light themselves attach to the stone pillars so that this image of you is now entirely trapped.

7. As you become aware at a deep level that you are now trapped, not only by planetary forces but also by the combined restraints of your parents and your society, you see an equal-armed cross hovering just in view. It begins to slowly float down until it is level with the two rings of light that contain the spheres.

8. This silvery gray cross now begins to spin on its axis, faster and faster, much like a Catherine wheel firework. As it spins, a silver light radiates out from its center. This light fills you with a sense of enormous energy and excitement. At the peak of this excitement, the light radiating from the cross completely fills your field of vision and all the bonds holding your mirror image are shattered.

9. At this point, the newly freed image of you turns around so that you are facing each other. You feel your consciousness enter the body of this image. As it does so, you become acutely aware of a sense of absolute freedom and complete responsibility. Energized by this realization, you give thanks to the Divine. When you are ready, you can return to your normal waking state.

Duality Meditation

When you perform this meditation a number of times, you will be increasing your unconscious appreciation of the innate duality that fills the universe. This duality is not only present in the universe, but the friction and contrast that duality creates provide the motivating energy for the universe to be continually creative.

Before you begin, light a black candle in the west of your meditation space and a white candle in the east of your meditation space. It may also be helpful to burn some musk-scented incense in the east.

1. Sit cross-legged on the floor with one hand on the floor and one in the air or on your right knee. As you establish your breathing rhythm, visualize before you a black-and-white checkered floor. In the center of this room are two tall pillars. One is made of black onyx and the other of white marble. You stand up and walk toward the two pillars. As you do so, you become aware that you are wearing a silvery gray cloak and are holding a lantern in your right hand.

2. Between the two pillars, you see a low stone table. On this table lay all the letters of the Hebrew alphabet carved out of silver. You pick up the letter Yod and place it inside your lantern. Immediately the lantern gives off a bright reddish light and you find yourself in a large templelike building.

3. Holding the lantern out in front of you, advance slowly toward the far end of the temple. Notice that the walls are decorated with a series of circles and crosses separated by images of a silver flash of lightning. At the far end, you come to a double door, one half of which is white, and the other half black.

4. Open this doorway by pushing both doors away from you and step into a narrow corridor, which has black walls and a white floor and ceiling. At the end of the corridor is a plain gray wall on which hangs a seven-spoke wheel. You turn the wheel clockwise once and then counterclockwise once.

5. The wall slides away, revealing another room much like the room you first entered. However, this room is like a mirror image; the colors of the floor and the pillars have been swapped. In addition, the wall decorations now have the cross placed inside the circle with the silver lightning flash coming from the bottom of the circle.

6. In the center of this room stands a silver pillar roughly the height of your shoulders. Stand in front of this pillar and watch as a triangle of blue flame emerges from the top of the pillar. At the same time, a triangle of red flame descends from the ceiling. The two triangles unite to form a hexagram hovering above the pillar.

7. As you stand in front of the pillar, you are approached by a tall bearded man wearing a gray robe and carrying a staff of gnarled wood in each hand. He stands in front of you and points up with the staff in his left hand and down with the staff in his right hand.

8. A beam of energy jets out of the ends of each of the staves and moves in a circular direction so that there is a circle of moving energy linking the staves together. As you look closely at this swiftly moving flow of pure energy, you can see that it contains every color imaginable. You can see scenes of life and organic growth flitting in and out of focus in this symbol of eternal creation. You may watch this display of dualistic creativity for as long as you wish before returning to your normal waking state.

Empowerment Technique for Chokmah: Communication with the Higher Self

One of the names that Kabbalists have traditionally given to Chokmah is "abba," which means "father." This label is especially suitable because of Chokmah's status as the source of the pure creative force that is shaped and given form by Binah. The special empowerment technique for Chokmah relates strongly to this notion of abba as a creative force. We can see Chokmah as the father because it is the source of the symbolic seed that then grows and develops in the womb of Binah. However, that does not mean that only men can access these energies; it is very important to remember that gender themes are used in Kabbalah as a way of expressing ideas and not as an attempt to assign certain roles to one gender or another.

As mentioned previously, one of the fundamental concepts of Hermetic Kabbalah is the idea of "As above, so below." Now that we have reached the Sephira of wisdom, we can see this as meaning that although there is a Divine being that exists completely beyond our understanding and outside us, there is also within each of us what we might call a Divine spark. This Divine spark is "below," and it constantly strives to be reunited with the Divine, which is "above." When we talk about our Higher Self, we are really talking a personalized version of this Divine spark that we all contain. The coexistence of a Divine spark in a mortal body is perhaps the most fundamental form of dualism that we could imagine.

For this technique, you need a piece of paper, a pen, a large piece of white fabric that you can fashion into a simple robe or tabard, two silver or gray candles, and some musk-scented incense.

Up to now, when we have been trying to establish a link with our Higher Self we have been opening ourselves up to the influence of the Higher Self rather than actively seeking to make contact with it. Because Chokmah is the seat of raw creative force—the "father" of creation so to speak—it is now time for us to try to proactively engage with our Higher Self. When we try to do this, we are right on the edge of the boundary between Kabbalistic mysticism and Kabbalistic magic.

1. Before you begin, take a clean sheet of paper and write the following statement of intent, "In the name of Yah, the Father of Creation, I assert my will to communicate with my Higher Self." Beneath this draw an equal-armed cross within a circle, as shown in Appendix B.

Using the white fabric, fashion a robe or tabard. This can be as simple as a single strip of material with a hole that fits over your head.

2. Starting on a Sunday, read your statement of intent out aloud first thing in the morning and last thing at night. In addition, when you are dropping off to sleep focus your mind on the notion of communicating with your Higher Self. Your white robe or tabard should also be completed in this week. It's better if you make this yourself, even if it means having a simpler design than you would ideally like.

3. On the following Sunday, take a bath and put on your robe or tabard. Then prepare your ritual space: In the center place a high-backed chair. On two low tables or other stands, one on either side of the chair, place the silver or gray candles. Burn some musk-scented incense in front of and behind the chair.

4. Sit in the chair and place your hands on top of your legs, keeping your back straight. Place your written statement of intent on your lap. Before you begin, read your statement of intent out loud. After doing so, enter your temple in Tiphareth.

5. Focus on your physical body. Be aware of the feelings of your muscles, of your breathing, and of your heart beating. When your whole consciousness is concentrated on your body, suddenly shut off this attention and focus instead on the visualization of a flame-colored letter Yod at the crown of your head and declare, "I have balanced the physical element of Earth and now seek the Divine spark."

6. Focus on your thoughts, allowing your mind to wander. Again, after this is established, immediately shut it out and focus on the flaming letter Yod as you declare, "I have balanced the physical element of Air and now seek the Divine spark."

7. Focus on your emotions, allowing feelings of sadness, happiness, loss, and contentment to roll over you in waves. As before, shut out these sensations with a sudden vigor and declare, "I have balanced the physical element of Water and now seek the Divine spark."

8. Turn your focus to thoughts of your desires, passions, ideas that you have had, and your artistic creativity. Again shut out these thoughts in a single instant and declare, "I have balanced the physical element of Fire and now it is my will to make contact with my Higher Self."

9. Change your breathing rhythm so that you inhale for a count of three, hold for a count of three, and exhale for a count of three, immediately followed by another inhale. This breathing should be deep, vigorous, and controlled. After you have established this rhythm, you will begin to feel a sense of swirling energy around the top of your head and the base of your spine.

10. Visualize a red upward-pointing triangle at the base of your spine and a downward-pointing triangle at the crown of your head. Declare, "The Divine element of Fire moves within me, the Divine element of Water guides me." Feel the energy from the top of your head and the base of your spine begin to circulate. Focus on the intense energy that is being built up and visualize a white light above the top of your head getting increasingly intense. Focus all your awareness in this white light and as the energy circulates within you, you will be able to hear inside your consciousness the voice of your Higher Self.

Kabbalistic Rituals

The two rituals that follow help you reach a point of genuine freedom in your life. In the first ritual, you free yourself from the negative influences of your astrological destiny. In the second ritual, you ensure that you are able to receive the positive influences that will allow you to discover your true inner purpose in life.

Zodiac Ritual

For this ritual, you need some musk-scented incense, a red candle, a blue bowl filled with water, and an earthenware plate upon which you've placed some salt.

In the Shifting Sun Signs activity earlier in this chapter, you worked on freeing yourself from the forces of astrological destiny by making active and conscious changes in your behavior. This ritual builds on that exercise by using the power of your Higher Self to set yourself free from the Wheel of Fortune on every level of your existence, from the physical to the spiritual. In addition, it enables you to attract the positive forces of each zodiac sign while repelling their more negative aspects.

Before preparing your ritual space, determine which element is associated with your sun sign:

Sun Signs	Element
Gemini, Libra, Aquarius	Air
Aries, Leo, Sagittarius	Fire
Cancer, Scorpio, Pisces	Water
Taurus, Virgo, Capricorn	Earth

1. Set up your ritual space by placing the musk incense in the east to represent Air, the red candle in the south to represent Fire, the blue bowl of water in the west to represent Water, and the plate with salt in the north to represent Earth. Having set up your ritual space, enter your temple in Tiphareth.

2. Move to the east and holding out your arms in the form of a cross declare, "In the name of Yah, the Divine ruler of the crown of creation, I declare my will and intent to be free from the Wheel of Fortune in all aspects of my life."

3. Walk clockwise around your ritual space until you reach the element that is linked with your sun sign. Visualize a large cube of the type described in the Rite of Protection (see Chapter 2) directly in front of you. Point both hands at this cube and declare, "In the name of Yah, the source of wisdom and the creative force, I declare that any negative influences emanating from [insert the name of your sun sign] shall return to their source."

4. Walk to the east. If you are already standing in the east, walk clockwise around your ritual space and return to the east. Stand with your arms in a cross and declare, "In the name of Yah, let the positive attributes of the Air signs flourish within me."

5. Walk to the south and with your arms in the same position declare, "In the name of Yah, let the positive energies of the Fire signs be active within me."

6. Walk to the west and with your arms in the same position declare, "In the name of Yah, let the harmony of the Water signs grow within me."

7. Walk to the north and with your arms in the same position declare, "In the name of Yah, may the sense and solidity of the Earth signs manifest within me." Continue this circuit of your ritual space until you are again standing in the east.

8. From the east turn so that you are facing west. Before you extends a glowing red path. Declare, "Now shall I enter the path of Heh, the domain of the emperor." You walk to the west of your ritual space and as you do so you are flanked on either side by two large rams. On arriving in the west, you turn to face east again and declare, "I stand within the path of the Constituting Intelligence and I am a victorious emperor, having rid myself of all negative influence."

9. A rose-colored path extends before you. Declare, "Now shall I pass through the path of Daleth the doorway to the crown of creation." Walking to the center of your ritual space, you are flanked on each side by two streams in which swim two graceful swans. On arriving in the center you declare, "I stand within the path of the Illuminating Intelligence and I embody all the positives of the wheel of the zodiac."

10. Stretch your arms in the form of a cross and see a cross in a circle hovering above your head. Declare, "In the name of Yah, the crown of creation, I declare myself free from the Wheel of Fortune and influenced only by the Divine with whom I shall find union through my Higher Self." Ensure that you feel balanced within your temple in Tiphareth before returning to your normal wakeful state.

Every man and every woman is a star.
—Aleister Crowley, British Kabbalist and occultist (1875–1947)

Ritual to Remove Blockages

For this ritual, you need some parchment paper, a ribbon or string, a pen, two gray candles, some musk-scented incense, a lantern (ideally red), and some clover.

The purpose of this ritual is to ensure that you can work toward achieving your true will without any form of distraction or blockage getting in the way. In the Zodiac ritual we remove negative astrological influences, but we also need to ensure that there are no other sources of negativity interfering with our attempts to form a union with our Higher Self. Perform this ritual whenever you are feeling as though you are stuck in a rut.

1. Write on the parchment paper, "In the name of Yah, I shall remove all obstacles that stand between me and my achievement of my true inner will." Roll up the parchment and tie it closed with the ribbon or string.

2. Set up your ritual space by lighting the two gray candles and placing them in the east, along with the musk incense. Light the lantern and place it in the south. Place your parchment scroll in the west, and place the bell and clover in the north.

3. Stand in the east and enter your temple in Tiphareth. Then stand with your arms extended in the shape of a cross and declare, "In the name of Yah, I call upon Raziel (Ratz-Ee-Al) to guide me to the completion of my true inner purpose and will."

4. Walk around to the south and declare, "In the name of Yah, I call upon the great archangel Raziel to assist me as I drive out all distractions from the achievement of my true will." As you say this, visualize a red flame burning in the south.

5. Now move to the west where you see a tall white pillar on which rests your parchment scroll. While facing the pillar and scroll declare, "In the name of Yah, I call upon Raziel, the herald of the Divine, to help me to see through all false feelings that may disturb my pursuit of my true purpose."

6. Walk around to the north. Visualize a mound of treasure and declare, "In the name of Yah, I call upon Raziel to help me to see the wisdom in being free of lust for material wealth." As you say this, you see the pile of treasure crumbling to dust.

7. Continue around to the east and then walk to the center of your ritual space. Stretch out your arms in the form of a cross and declare, "It is my intent, in the name of Yah, to achieve my true will and to choose only those paths that will lead me to a union with my Higher Self."

8. Turn so that you are facing north. A rich reddish-brown path extends before you leading to the north. As you walk along this path, you are aware of many enticing images on your left, and on your right you hear angry voices challenging you. As you walk you feel yourself stumbling and being forced backward.

9. When you arrive in the north, strike the bell twice and declare, "In the name of Yah, I call upon Raziel to send forth the Ophaunim, the angelic choir of the crown of creation. Let the Ophaunim manifest

in my life and assist me in my aim." As you complete this declaration, you are surrounded by a host of brightly shining spinning wheels of light.

10. Surrounded by these wheels of light, you walk back to the center of your ritual space along the path of Vau, but this time there are no distractions or challenges. When you arrive in the center, say a short prayer to Yah, thanking the Divine force for its guidance. You can then return to your normal waking state after you have balanced yourself in your temple of Tiphareth.

Signs and Symbols of Chokmah

This section lists symbols, colors, and other associations with Chokmah. These are interesting in their own right and can be meditated on to arrive at your own deep understanding of their meaning. Additionally, while you are working with the energies of Chokmah or when you want to attract positive energies relating to a matter governed by Chokmah, you may want to wear or carry with you something that relates to Chokmah. If you feel that you need an extra boost to your levels of energy, for example, you may want to keep a piece of turquoise with you.

Appendix A shows the pathway correspondences at a glance, and Appendix B lists more symbols, including easy-to-copy planetary and elemental symbols.

- **Symbols:** Cross within a circle, wheel of the zodiac, obelisks, pillars, and lanterns
- **Colors:** Gray, silvery gray, white flecked with yellow, red, and blue
- **Numbers and letters:** 2, 6, 12, 15, 19, 73, 248, 477, Daleth (D), Heh (H), Vau (V), Yod (Y)
- **Crystals and stones:** Turquoise
- **Plants and incense:** Musk, clover, geranium, mallow
- **Archangel:** Raziel
- **Direction:** South
- **Element:** Fire, whose archangel is Michael and whose spirits are the salamanders
- **Planet:** None; Chokmah rules over the zodiac (Mazloth)

Chapter 11

Kether: The Kingdom of the Divine

It will have taken you some months to reach this point, and in working through all the lower Sephiroth you will have learned a lot about yourself. Although Hermetic Kabbalah is all about self-development, you will also have developed a much deeper appreciation of the world around you and indeed of the nature of the Divine. In one sense the purpose of climbing the Tree of Life is to achieve all those positive changes in your outlook and in the way that you experience your life. However, from a purely spiritual point of view, all those lower Sephiroth are just staging posts on your journey toward the crown of the Tree.

In our Four World model of the Tree of Life, Kether occupies a very special position. In the Physical world, or *Assiah* as it is called in Hebrew, this Sephira represents the realm of the Divine as it is manifested in the physical universe. At the same time, the Kether of the purely physical universe can also be seen as the Malkuth of the Tree of Life in the Astral or Angelic world known as the world of *Yetzirah* in Hebrew. What this means is that when you have fully embodied the energies of Kether, you will be able to begin to see the practical world around you in terms of its spiritual origins. It is this ability to see beyond the purely physical that allows us to begin working in what we might call a genuinely magical way.

In the Kabbalistic model of the universe, the Yetziratic or Angelic world contains what we could describe as blueprints for everything that ultimately manifests in physical reality. In other words, in the Angelic world there is the blueprint of an apple that leads to apples actually existing in the Physical world. If the Kether of the world of Assiah is also the Malkuth of the world of Yetzirah, we can access these blueprints and construct a reality in the Angelic world that can be brought into material existence in the Physical world. This is the principle behind much of the magic in Hermetic Kabbalah.

We pronounce Kether "Ke-Tur," with the emphasis on the second syllable and the initial *e* like the *e* in bet. Kether is spelled Kaph Tau Resh, and the title Kether translates as "crown." We can reach Kether by three paths. From Tiphareth we follow the path of Gimel, from Binah the path of Beth, and from Chokmah the path of Aleph. The path of Gimel is associated with the High Priestess card in Tarot and represents the secret wisdom found in the realm of the Divine. The path of Gimel is also known as "the Uniting Intelligence," and this emphasizes the fact that our aim is to unite with the Divine.

The path of Beth is also referred to as "the Intelligence of Transparency," indicating that as we move from Binah, which is "understanding," and toward the Crown of Kether our understanding deepens to a level where the Divine design of creation begins to be transparent for us. The letter Beth literally means "home." This links both to the maternal and domestic associations with Binah and to the sense in which our journey toward Kether is really a journey back home. The path of Beth is linked with the Tarot card the Magician, connecting the idea of Kether with a magical level of spiritual insight that we touched on earlier.

The path of Aleph is also called "the Scintillating Intelligence." Its title emphasizes the difficulty of climbing this far up the Tree of Life. In addition, the path of Aleph is associated with the Tarot card the Fool. The Fool does not represent stupidity but rather symbolizes the pure innocence that cannot be learned consciously. To fully experience Kether, we need to embody this perfect innocence. The path of Aleph is also scintillating or stimulating because it is the first path and carries with it the very first emanation from the Divine, a force so powerful and complex that it can never be fully understood.

When we look at the shape of the letters in the Hebrew spelling of Kether, as shown in the Tree of Life diagram in Chapter 1, and bear in mind their symbolic meaning, we can see that the name of Kether symbolizes the very creation of the universe. In ancient mythology, the origins of the universe are often depicted in sexual terms. The central letter Tau was traditionally regarded as a phallic symbol, whereas the final letter Resh represents the pure creative energy of the Divine. This is the symbolism attributed to the letter Yod, and when we look at the letter Resh we can see that in many ways it represents an expanded Yod. The letter Kaph is linked with notions of activity and movement. When we combine the symbolism of these three letters, we have a centrally placed symbol of generative power that, when activated, leads to an emanation of pure creative energy.

When I consider the spelling of Kether, I find a message that reminds us that the physical creation is as much a part of the Divine as Kether itself. This relates strongly to the Kabbalistic belief that "Kether is in Malkuth and Malkuth is in Kether, but after another fashion." The hand of the Divine (Kaph) moves and activates the four elements (Tau) as a sign of Divine love and benevolence (Resh).

The value of the Hebrew word Kether is 620. This can be reduced to the number 8 (6 + 2 + 0 = 8). This value is appropriate for the Sephira Kether in a number of ways. The number 8 is symbolic of eternity, and as the location of the Divine spirit, Kether is clearly associated with notions of immortality and eternity. The number 8 is also the value of the Hebrew letter Cheth. The letter Cheth means "fence" and is associated with ideas of protection and boundaries. The Divine is an obvious source of protection, and additionally we can see the Sephira of Kether as a boundary between one level of existence and the next.

If we look at the total value of the title Kether, we find the letters Mem (600) and Kaph (20). The letter Mem literally means "water," and the letter Kaph means "palm of the hand." This is reminiscent of the first moment of creation when the Divine moves its hand over the face of the waters. Mem is also associated with themes of maternal protection, and Kaph is associated with vigorous activity. We can therefore see the home of the Divine as neither male or female, but a combination of the archetypal energies of both genders.

All forms of Kabbalah hold that the Divine is ultimately unknowable. If the Divine could be fully understood, it would no longer be beyond us;

in fact, it would be of a lower level of complexity than the human intelligence that could reach a full understanding of its nature. This means that for the Divine to be genuinely Divine, it must by definition be unknowable. It is because of this quality that Kether is known as the "Hidden Intelligence." Another reason for this title goes back to the idea that Malkuth is in Kether and Kether is in Malkuth. Although the energy of Kether is deeply hidden, it is still possible to access it while remaining in the Physical world.

Like Chokmah, the Sephira Kether is not linked to any particular planet because these are all the responsibility of the lower Sephiroth. Because Kether is the realm of the Divine, it cannot be attributed to any particular planet or even to the solar system or galaxy in which we live. Kether is the home of what was traditionally called the "primum mobile" or "prime mover," what we would today call the first and ultimate cause in the infinite chain of cause and effect. When we think of Kether in this way and think of ourselves as seeking to emulate the energy and effect of Kether in our own lives, we can begin to see why attaining this level of creative power has been seen as a magical as well as mystical achievement.

The key Divine name of Kether is Eheieh (A-Hay-Eh), which is spelled AHYH in Hebrew and pronounced the same way, A-Hay-Eh. This name translates as "I am what I am" or "I am that which is." Both of these alternative translations point directly to the notion of the Divine as being essentially unknowable except to itself. The second possible translation also draws attention to the fact that the entire universe is part of the body of the Divine—the idea that because the Divine is everywhere, everything that exists is a part of the Divine. The value of the name Eheieh is 21, and this is the same value as words meaning "innocence" and "meditation." These connections are another reminder of the fact that if we are to access the energies of Kether, we need to approach it with an attitude of innocence and trust.

Areas of Empowerment

As you are now operating in the realm of the Divine, the areas in which your life will be empowered are likely to be more profound and wide-ranging than in the lower, elemental Sephiroth. The responsibilities of Kether include the unity of the universe, eternity, and the spiritual order of existence. The main changes that you will see in your life will be in how you feel about yourself and indeed about the whole purpose of life in general.

Spirituality as we experience it is always hugely individual, because we are all unique spiritual beings. Your exact response to the energies of Kether can't be fully predicted.

To see a world in a grain of sand
And a heaven in a wild flower,
Hold infinity in the palm of your hand
And eternity in an hour …
—William Blake, "Auguries of Innocence"

Practical Activities

It might seem a little odd to think of practical activities in terms of the Sephira that is regarded as the "crown" of the Tree of Life. However, we need to take into account two things here. The first is that we are using the Four World model of the Tree of Life, and so, even when we enter Kether, we are still in the physical universe, albeit in its very upper reaches. The other important consideration is best summed up in a Buddhist phrase, "Before enlightenment chop wood carry water, after enlightenment chop wood carry water." Even when we are in the presence of the spiritual, we should not forget the practical and actual nature of our existence on Earth. In addition, it reminds us of the need to retain our humility.

Who Am I?

The ultimate aim of the Great Work is to achieve a sense of union with the Divine. However, a complete link with the Divine can be forged only when we are working with the Kether of the Atziluthic or Divine world. Remember that we're using the Four World model of the Tree of Life and are working with the Tree that exists in the Physical world in this book. In the Physical world or the world of Assiah as it is known, we make a partial link with the Divine by coming to understand its impact in our lives. We also help ourselves to make that link by fulfilling our true potential.

For this next activity, you need some paper, a pen, and a mirror.

If we are to fulfill our true potential, we must first know ourselves very thoroughly indeed. One of the traditional axioms of Hermetic Kabbalah is "Know thyself." The following activities will help you get closer to that complete sense of self-knowledge. Now that you are in the realm of the Divine, it will also help you to reflect on how you have changed as you have worked your way through this book.

1. Stand in front of the mirror and look directly into your own eyes. Ask yourself, "Who am I?" The first answer you should give ought to be appropriate to the Sephira Malkuth in some way. In other words, it should be related to a practical or material aspect of your personality.

2. Repeat the question nine times. Each time you ask the question, the answer should be one that is appropriate to one of the remaining nine Sephiroth. Work through the Sephiroth in order, until you arrive at an answer that relates to your spiritual identity that is appropriate for the Sephira of Kether.

3. List 10 statements that describe the 10 most important things in your life. They might be things, or people, or elements of your work. Then write down how you relate to each of these things.

4. Think back to how you felt when you first began your journey through this book. Reflect on how you have changed and developed and the ways your priorities have shifted. Compare the lists you made in the Life Inventory exercise in Chapter 2 with the lists you've just made.

5. Now let's get a little deeper into who you are now and how you feel about yourself. Stand in front of the mirror again and continually ask yourself "Who am I?" Give one-sentence answers and keep going until you really feel that you cannot offer any further answers. When you reach that point, keep going for at least another 10 questions, no matter how silly the answers you end up giving may seem.

6. Sit down with a pen and piece of paper. Write at least a half page describing yourself as though you were writing about someone else and needed to describe as much about the person as you possibly could. This writing should include ways in which you have changed since beginning your journey on the Tree of Life.

7. Read through this description carefully. Taking into account the answers you have given when asking "Who am I?" consider what aspects of the description could be removed and it still be able to describe the essential you. Also consider what other aspects of your life and your possessions you could lose and still be able to say that you were still you.

8. There will inevitably be some things you feel you cannot remove from the description and still retain the "you-ness" of you. Reflect on what those things are and why they seem so essential and intrinsic to your sense of identity.

9. The next part of the exercise is difficult, but useful as a way of figuring out what you see as the essential you. Think deeply on the issue of whether your identity is made up of all the different things that various people think go together to making you, or whether your identity is something you can have without the need for anyone else to interact with and respond to that identity.

10. Whatever view you end up with—even if it is the view that both answers are correct—try to get it completely clear in your head. Write down a defense of your point of view that makes it very clear why you have taken that particular position.

Acts of Random Kindness

In each Sephira that we work with, we are seeking to emulate its qualities in the way we behave both toward ourselves and in how we behave toward others. Kether is the home of the Divine in so far as it can be understood within the confines of the Physical world. One of the best ways for us to emulate the Divine is to demonstrate to others an unconditional and universal benevolence.

The most important thing you need for this activity is a genuine desire to spread a sense of happiness in the world. Don't attach this to any desire for thanks or appreciation. Of course, by helping anonymously you can also make sure that no one feels obliged to return any favors. It is still hugely empowering to you as a person, though. When you experience the feeling that comes with helping others without any thought for yourself, you will find that it gives a deeper sense of purpose to your life.

Even boring essentials become meaningful when we realize that by keeping the necessities going, we are able to make the world a brighter place to live in.

The aim of this activity is to take the influx of positive energy from Kether and share it with others. In so doing, you assist in the creation of a more harmonious and understanding world. If you do it without any thought for yourself, you will also experience a profound sense of spiritual insight. It is in small acts of concern and kindness like these that we come to a better appreciation of the true nature of Divine love.

1. Many of the people we meet in life are strangers whom we may never see again. Even though we don't know a person, however, we can still bring a sense of happiness and well-being into his or her life. Try smiling at people who catch your glance as you are walking to work or standing in line at a grocery store.

2. People always appreciate simple kindness, so the next time you are riding on a train or bus, give up your seat to someone, not just if the person is elderly or pregnant or laden with shopping bags, but just because you have a seat and that person doesn't.

3. Write down the names of everyone in your workplace. Then go to the store and buy a little gift of some sort. When you get home, randomly pick a name from your list and the next day give the gift to that person. If possible, find a way for the person to receive the gift without knowing it was from you.

4. The next time you are at the store and see someone struggling with a lot of bags, go over and offer to help carry some bags for them to the car. It doesn't take very long, and the more of us who make a point of just being nice to other people without any ulterior motive, the happier the world will become.

5. Do something nice for people you will never even see. The next time you see a row of parked cars, leave a dollar bill under the windshield wiper of four or five cars. It isn't much, but that's not what matters. The important thing for you is that you don't let yourself worry about who actually ends up with the dollar bill, even if one person comes along and takes them all. The important thing is the spirit in which you gave.

6. It might seem old-fashioned, but it's still a nice thing to make your neighbors feel cared about. Next weekend bake some cakes and take them around the neighborhood. The best way to do this is to tell them that another member of your family actually made them and you are just delivering the cakes.

7. An even better way to be kind to your neighbors is to save them a tedious job. If you have the means, the next time it snows you could clear all the snow from the sidewalk and the road. If you live in an area that never gets snow, you could clean neighbors' cars (with their permission) and donate any contributions to a charity chosen by the neighborhood.

8. You can also do your bit for the community as a whole. Spend a few hours each weekend for a month or so just picking up litter around your local area. Don't just do the areas that are close to your home, also choose places that you don't normally spend much time in.

9. The nature of Divine concern is that it is not restricted. In the summer, invest in some dog bowls and make sure that you put some bowls of water in your local parks for thirsty pets. The Divine cares for the whole of creation and not just people. Of course, most people will have provided for their pets, but there are many unwanted animals. Another good idea is to donate old, clean towels and blankets to your local animal shelter.

10. In the winter, put food out for the birds—not just in your own backyard, but in places where other people are unlikely to feed them. Remember, though, that the birds will come to depend on this food; so once you begin to feed them, you are making a long-term commitment. This makes the exercise all the more valuable for your own long-term development.

Meditations

The two meditations in this section help you to manifest the power of the Sephira Kether in your life. Because we are now operating at the very top or "crown" of the Tree of Life, these meditations are very spiritual in nature. When you are performing these meditations, you are trying to access the most spiritual aspect of yourself. This is very different from the earlier meditations when you were trying to awaken very specific elemental powers within yourself. The realm of Kether is wholly concerned with the unity of creation, and these meditations encourage and enhance your sense of the interconnectedness of all things.

Continue the practice you began in Chokmah of first entering your temple in Tiphareth by performing the Building an Astral Kingdom in Tiphareth meditation in Chapter 6 before beginning this meditation. Additionally, you will find that the spiritual aspect of the meditations is felt more strongly if you also fast for half a day or even a whole day if you are able to. You may also wear the white robe or tabard that you made in Chapter 10.

Universe Meditation

The aim of this meditation is to help your inner self unite with the symbolism of the Tree of Life. This will help you see the way all things and all experiences can be related to the Tree, which in turn promotes a realization of the unity of the created universe. Nothing is needed for this meditation because you are concentrating on your own inner universe.

1. This meditation is best performed in a seated position with legs crossed. Sit comfortably on a large soft cushion and support your back with a large cushion.

2. After establishing your breathing rhythm, visualize a cone of white light surrounding you. Within this cone you see swirling clouds of stars that seem to dance in complex patterns above your head.

3. You feel your consciousness ascending into the cone. You drift upward and arrive in a large white room. The floor of the room is a black-and-white tiled floor, and there are no other features to the room except a very plain black door in the center of the far wall.

4. You walk to the far end of the room and open the door. Facing you is a swirling vortex of blue light, and within the center of the vortex you can make out shapes like miniature galaxies. You step through the doorway into the vortex.

5. Now you are floating in absolute blackness, having passed into the center of the vortex. There is no sound, no movement, and no color.

Despite this, you feel completely calm. You look up above your head and see a golden crown shining in the darkness. Beneath the crown the blackness seems to be slightly shaded to give the impression of a face in profile.

6. A lightning flash illuminates the center of the crown. Its light is so bright that the blackness is replaced by blindingly white light. After the initial blinding flash, the darkness gradually returns. However, in the middle of your field of vision you can see that the path of the lightning has traced an outline of the Tree of Life.

7. Watching this outline, you see that at the points where the Sephiroth would be positioned, the white light seems to throbbing and pulsating. As you watch, 10 individual spheres begin to form and as they are completed, the two-dimensional image of the Tree becomes a three-dimensional solid object made of pure light.

8. From the bottom Sephira of Malkuth, you see a scarlet light begin to climb its way back up the Tree of Life. As the light passes through each Sephira, it takes on the color with which it is associated: Malkuth (earth tones), Yesod (violet), Hod (orange), Netzach (emerald green), Tiphareth (gold), Geburah (red), Chesed (blue), Binah (black), Chokmah (gray), Kether (white).

9. As the head of this serpentlike trail of red light passes into Kether and causes its white brilliance to shine out, the image of the Tree rapidly expands until it is no longer possible to make out the paths or the Sephiroth. Your whole vision is filled with the white glow of Kether. Remain in this state experiencing the emanation of the Divine until you feel ready to return to your normal waking state.

Affirmation Meditation

Try to perform this next meditation at least once a week. You should find that it leaves you feeling refreshed both physically and spiritually and that it enhances your sense of your own unity with the universe as a whole.

1. Before you begin, light two white candles, one in the east and one in the west of your meditation space. In addition, you can burn some ambergris or frankincense in the east while you are meditating.

There is no fixed position for this meditation; the key thing is that you feel comfortable. I always find that lying curled on my side is very effective.

2. After establishing your breathing rhythm, visualize yourself bathed in a golden light. This light represents the power of Tiphareth in your life. Stretching out before you is a pale blue path of light. This is the path of Gimel, which leads into Kether.

3. Walking up the path, you notice that as you get higher the path gets steeper and steeper. You see a tall elegant woman walking toward you. She is wearing a blue gown and a starry crown on her head. She offers you her hand and you walk together in a sphere of bright white light. As you walk with her, you feel filled with a strong sense of wisdom.

4. Now visualize yourself curled up inside a black egg. A shaft of gray penetrates the egg and causes it to break open. You stand up, but initially you feel very weak and have to consciously think about exactly how to climb out of the now-open eggshell.

5. The shaft of gray light forms itself into a set of steps. You begin to walk up these ethereal stairs that lead from the Great Mother Binah into Kether. As you walk you feel your muscles and coordination improving. A group of swallows surrounds you as you near the top of the steps. When you enter the white light, you have a strong sense of being held and protected by the Divine.

6. You now find yourself balancing on a gray pillar that seems to be standing in a great chasm. Before you stands a series of emerald and blue pillars, and in the distance at the far side of the chasm a brilliant white light.

7. As you carefully step from pillar to pillar, you are aware of a strong smell of peppermint in the air. Above you an eagle flies slightly ahead, guiding you from one pillar to the next. As you step off each pillar, it turns black or white in an alternating sequence.

8. When you reach the far side of the chasm, you are lifted up in the air by the brilliant white light. As you hover suspended in this immense brilliant glow, you feel a sense of absolute trust and certainty both in yourself and in the Divine.

9. The cloud of light gently descends and you are standing on a rocky outcrop. As you look down you can see stars and planets as though you are standing above the whole of creation. Around your body, seven diamond stars steadily circle. Your body is surrounded by a pinkish-white aura. You can stand like this absorbing the positive energy from the Divine until you feel ready to return to your normal waking state.

Empowerment Technique for Kether: Invocations

The empowerment techniques of the previous chapters were designed in part to help you develop your mystical and magical abilities as you progressed from one Sephira to the next. The following empowerment technique brings together all those skills that you have learned for a single purpose. Just as Kether crowns the Tree of Life, this empowerment technique can be seen as the crowning glory of your personal empowerment.

An invocation is the process of bringing the energy of a Divine or angelic force into the center of your own consciousness. From the most ancient civilizations, the art of invocation has been seen as the highest form of practical mysticism or magic. In terms of the commands "to know, to will, to dare, to be silent," the process of invocation can be seen as an ideal combination of all four requirements. When we invoke the energy of an entity that is more than human into ourselves, we are undoubtedly being daring. Its achievement requires strength of will and that we know the nature of the force that we are trying to invoke. Additionally, invocations only work properly when they are the result of a communication solely between the invoker and the entity being invoked. In other words, silence is an absolute must.

The main thing that you need to succeed with an invocation is complete sincerity and a genuine heartfelt desire to communicate with the Divine.

The aim of the Great Work is the genuine completion of the self by the forging of a link with the Higher Self and the Divine will. The aim of invocation is to make an actual connection between ourselves and a Divine force in such a way that we can feel its presence within our consciousness.

There are a number of ways in which we can invoke the energy of a Divine being into ourselves. Prayer, emulation, and dramatic ritual are methods that have been used over the centuries. This technique uses a combination of methods, which increases the level of impact on all aspects of your consciousness when you make the link with the spiritual.

1. Decide which spirit or force you wish to invoke. Initially start with one of the archangels of the Sephiroth. When you are successful with this, you can move on to invoking the Divine names of the Sephiroth or the planetary and elemental spirits and angels.

2. When you have selected your chosen spiritual entity, offer up a prayer declaring your intention. Choose the exact words yourself, but it should be along these lines: "In the name of AHYH (A-Hay-Eh), I pledge myself to the invocation of [insert name of spiritual entity]. It is my will that the energies of [insert name of spiritual entity] shall enter my life and bring me closer to the completion of the Great Work in accordance with the will of the Divine AHYH."

3. For the next week or two, spend time emulating the characteristics of the force that you intend to invoke. This may mean making some very definite changes in lifestyle. If you intend to invoke the archangel of the Sephira Hod, for example, make a point of taking a rational and intellectual attitude toward the world in general for the next two weeks. At a symbolic level, you should also emulate the energy of your chosen spirit, and so you might wear an item of clothing in a color appropriate to its associated Sephira or planet. For Hod, for instance, you might wear an orange tie or belt.

4. While you are emulating the characteristics of your chosen spiritual being, also engage in earnest and committed prayer. Ideally, pray to your chosen spiritual force every morning, lunchtime, and evening. These prayers should be of your own making and be said with great intensity and passion.

5. Do as much reading as possible about the nature of your selected spirit. Also read about the characteristics with which the spirit is linked. If you are invoking the archangel of Netzach, for example, you might read about the history of dance or drama.

6. After two to three weeks of praying, emulating, and reading about the subject, you will be ready to begin the actual ritual. Ideally, fast for a day before starting the ritual process. On the day of the ritual, take a long bath, and then put on your white robe or tabard and a stone or crystal that is linked to the spiritual force you are trying to

attract. You can buy special stone cages and chains from many crystal shops so that you can wear it as a necklace. Or if you prefer, you can just keep the stone near you all day.

7. Perform the Rite of Protection (see Chapter 2) and then enter your temple in Tiphareth. During the meditation, make sure you are using correct breathing techniques and that you are in a state of physical stillness. Begin to build up a projected image of the appearance of your chosen spiritual entity. If you prefer, you can just use shapes and colors rather than a personalized or human image.

8. Visualize a white candle burning at each of the four quarters. Starting in the east you stand before each candle and say, "In the name of AHYH, let the spirit of [insert name of spiritual entity] enter my psyche and fill my consciousness. Let [insert name of spiritual entity] and I become as one—a perfect unity under the guidance of AHYH."

9. As you utter each declaration, a ray of white light emanates from the candle in question. When you have completed all four declarations, you will be standing in the center of a cross made of pure white light. Make sure that you clear your mind completely and then repeat the declaration one final time. Then intone repeatedly the name of the being whom you wish to invoke while using your trained will to urge its essence to manifest within your consciousness. Although it may take time, you will ultimately feel something tangible, almost like a door opening, and you will be aware that your consciousness is being filled with a Divine presence.

10. You can remain in this state for as long as you wish. When you are ready, you can return to your normal waking state. It's always a good idea to perform the Rite of Protection after as well as before any invocations.

Whatever is in the earth has its parallel in the world above. There is not a single thing, however small, in the world that does not depend on something that is higher ... He made this world to match the world above, and whatever exists above has its counterpart below ... and all is one.

—From the *Zohar*

Kabbalistic Rituals

The two rituals that follow awaken and enliven the spiritual dimension of your existence. One is a magical active ritual that will mainly help you to continue striving forward with the Great Work. The second is more passive and mystical in nature and encourages an acceptance of the Divine will and an understanding of the way in which the universal unity operates in our lives.

Ritual to Awaken the Divine Spark

For this ritual, you need a white candle, some ambergris or frankincense incense, a red lantern or candle, a blue bowl filled with water, an earthenware plate, and some salt.

The purpose of this ritual is to activate the connection that we all have to the Divine. This connection exists through the awareness of our Higher Self. In this ritual you bring the awareness of this link into your conscious mind. It is an ideal precursor to any other ritual or meditation.

1. Set up your ritual space: Place the white candle and incense in the east, the lit red lantern or candle in the south, the blue bowl of water in the west, and the salt on the earthenware plate in the north.

2. Enter your temple in Tiphareth and then perform the Rite of Protection. Afterward, stand in the east and declare, "It is my Will to ignite the spark of the Divine within my eternal soul. It is my will in the name of AHYH to breathe life into that spark and light a burning flame within my Higher Self. The illuminating glow of that flame shall be a beacon in all that I think, feel, and do—in the name of AHYH."

3. Walk clockwise around your ritual space three times. As you do, say a prayer of your own making in your head. The focus of the prayer should be the Divine presence in Kether and your joy at realizing the ultimate unity of the universe.

4. After the third circuit, stand facing east with your hands by your sides and ensure that you are using deep meditative breathing and have achieved a level of complete physical stillness. Visualize a ball of white light above your head. As you do so declare, "AHYH awaken the force of the Divine within me."

5. Visualize a glowing white sphere at your left temple and intone, "Yah awaken the force of the Divine within me." Visualize a similar sphere at your right temple and intone, "YHVH Elohim (Yod-Hay-Vow-Hay El-Oh-Heem) awaken the force of the Divine within me."

6. At your left shoulder, visualize another glowing sphere and declare, "Al awaken the force of the Divine within me." Following this, visualize a ball of white light at your right shoulder and declare, "Elohim Gibor (El-Oh-Heem Gi-Boor) awaken the force of the Divine within me."

7. A ball of golden light now shines in your heart area and you declare, "YHVH Eloah Ve Da'ath (Yod-Hay-Vow-Hay El-Oh-Ah Vee De-Arth) awaken the force of the Divine within me." Next visualize a ball of white light at your left hip as you intone, "YHVH Tzabaoth (Yod-Hay-Vow-Hay Za-Ba-Oht) awaken the force of the Divine within me." Now as a sphere of light appears at your right hip you declare, "Elohim Tzabaoth awaken the force of the Divine within me."

8. Another shining sphere of white light now forms at the level of your groin and you declare, "Shaddai Al Chai (Sha-Dy Al Ky) awaken the Divine force within me and prepare within me the foundation on which I shall build my understanding."

9. A final ball of light now appears covering your feet and ankles. Intone, "Adonai Ha Aretz (Ah-Doh-Ny Haa Ah-Retz) awaken the Divine force within me. In the name of Adonai Ha Aretz may the Divine force manifest in every aspect of my life that I may draw closer to the completion of the Great Work and unite my soul with the will of the Divine."

10. Remain standing and focus on your deep breathing. As you inhale, each of the spheres of light glows with a greater intensity. As you exhale, rays of white light emanate from each sphere so that you are surrounded by an aura of brilliant white light. As you inhale, feel energy flowing into you; as you exhale, feel the energy circulating throughout your body.

Ritual of Unity and Acceptance

For this ritual, you need some ambergris or frankincense incense, four white candles, a bell or cymbal, and your white robe or tabard. The aim of this ritual is to bring a greater awareness and felt experience of the spiritual into your life. The exact results of this ritual will vary from person to person because the realm of Kether operates directly on our Higher Self and this is the seat of our individuality.

1. Set up your ritual space: Place the incense in the east, one white candle in each of the four directions (east, south, north, and west), and the bell or cymbal in the east. Put on your white robe or tabard.

2. Enter your temple of Tiphareth and then perform the Rite of Protection. After re-establishing a strong deep-breathing rhythm, repeat the following dedication three times, striking your bell or cymbal after each speech: "In the name of AHYH, I call upon the great archangel Metatron (Met-Ah-Tron) to assist me in my working that I may achieve the true wisdom of the Great Work and understand the nature of Divine unity."

3. Walk from the east to the center of your ritual space. You see a silver path extending into the west. Declare, "Now shall I enter the path of Gimel." As you walk forward, a female figure appears and demands that you tell her the nature of the secret wisdom. You reply, "True wisdom is beyond words and can only be received, never given."

4. At this reply you are free to continue into the west. Now repeat the declaration you gave in Step 2, before walking clockwise from the west around to the south of your ritual space.

5. In the south, you see a purple path of light leading toward the north. Declare, "Now shall I enter the path of Beth." As you walk forward, a tall man appears in a black robe and demands that you give him the secret signs of initiation before you can continue. You reply, "The true sign of initiation and understanding lies in the soul and can be seen only by the Divine."

6. The tall man stands aside and you are free to continue into the north. When standing in the north, repeat the declaration from Step 2. Then turn so that you are facing east.

7. Before you, running from north to east, is a pathway of sky-blue light. You declare, "Now I shall enter the path of Aleph." As you walk forward, you are aware of strong winds buffeting you and the sound of wild dogs barking close behind. On the wind you hear a voice asking, "Are you not scared, should you not turn back?" You

reply, "I am guided only by my Higher Self and the Divine, my soul knows no fear and so I shall pass into the crown."

8. You are now able to continue into the east. When you arrive in the east, strike the bell or cymbal three times and repeat the declaration from Step 2. As you strike the bell, you are aware of an intense white light shining above your head. This grows in intensity as you recite the declaration.

9. Feeling the white light begin to spread over you, open your arms in the form of a cross and declare, "In the name of AHYH, may the great angel Metatron send forth the angelic choir of the Chayoth Ha Qadosh (Chy–Ot Hah Ka-Dosh) that they may lift me into the arms of the Divine."

10. Having made this declaration, feel your consciousness almost physically lifting so that your sense of your center of awareness is above your physical body. Remain in this state for as long as you wish. You can then return to your normal waking state after you have balanced yourself in your temple of Tiphareth.

Signs and Symbols of Kether

This section lists symbols, colors, and other associations with Kether. These are interesting in their own right and can be meditated on to arrive at your own deep understanding of their meaning. Additionally, while you are working with the energies of Kether or when you want to attract positive energies relating to a matter governed by Kether, you may want to wear or carry with you something that relates to Kether. If you are going through a difficult time in your life you might use almond-scented oil in your bath each night to soothe you and increase a sense of connection to the Divine.

Appendix A shows the pathway correspondences at a glance, and Appendix B lists more symbols, including easy-to-copy planetary and elemental symbols.

- **Symbols:** A point within a circle, a single line, a figure eight
- **Colors:** Brilliant white, the clear glow of pure diamond, white flecked with gold

- **Numbers and letters:** 1, 8, 9, 12, 32, 72, 620, Aleph (A), Beth (B), Gimel (G)
- **Crystals and stones:** Diamond
- **Plants and incense:** Ambergris, frankincense, almond, peppermint
- **Archangel:** Metatron
- **Direction:** East
- **Element:** Air, whose archangel is Raphael and whose spirits are the sylphs
- **Planet:** None; Kether is the origin of the physical universe, the first cause

Chapter 12

Beyond Balance

What lies beyond Kether? It may seem strange to think of continuing with your self-exploration after you have fulfilled the work of Kether. After all, if Kether is the realm of the Divine, how can we move any further on? At this point, we need to remember that throughout this book we have used the Four World model of the Tree of Life. This means that although we have reached an appreciation of the Divine at the level of physical existence, we can still move on to greater levels of spiritual awareness by developing an understanding of the next world of existence, which is the Astral or Angelic plane, known as the Yetziratic world in Kabbalah.

As well as trying to increase our level of spiritual understanding, it's important that we don't see our journey up the Tree of Life as a one-time experience. If you work out regularly, you will increase your level of fitness, but if you stop exercising, eventually your level of fitness will drop right back to where you started. Kabbalah is much the same, and so from time to time it will be very helpful to return to the various activities you have experienced throughout this book.

There is no need, necessarily, to work all the way through the book again. It's likely that the level of self-awareness that you have acquired by climbing the Tree of Life will mean that you will have an intuitive sense of which area you need to work on. Of course, if there are particular exercises that you found especially enjoyable or helpful, feel free to include them as an integral part of your life.

In many ways we have only scratched the surface of Kabbalah in this book. This is because Kabbalah covers a vast range of practices and beliefs, and because as Kabbalah has developed over the centuries, numbers of different schools of Kabbalistic thought have emerged. Kabbalah has provided generations of mystics with lifetime after lifetime of spiritual wisdom and hidden knowledge. If you'd like to continue your journey into Kabbalah and the Western Mystery Tradition, the resources in Appendix C give you a good starting point.

The wish for prayer is a prayer in itself.
—Georges Bernanos, French novelist (1888–1948)

Creating Your Own Rituals

One of the best ways to maintain the positive impact of the energies of each Sephira in your life is to continue to use the meditations from the various chapters on a reasonably regular basis. By using the existing activities in this book to strengthen the energies of individual Sephiroth in your life, you can also create your own rituals for specific purposes.

Rituals can be as complicated as you want to make them. Some Kabbalistic groups build hugely ornate and beautiful rituals using every possible association with a particular Sephira or planetary energy. When working on your own, however, it's best to keep the ritual simple. This ensures that you don't create a confusion of energies that could muddy or dilute the effect of the ritual, and it also helps you to keep your focus on the specific aim of the ritual in question.

To create your own ritual for a specific purpose, follow these steps:

1. Decide what the purpose of your ritual is. It could be to increase your creativity, get a job promotion, or ensure that you stay motivated

in your new exercise program. Review the descriptions of the Sephiroth to determine which one is appropriate for your ritual. (If you are unsure, send me an e-mail at jonathansharp3621@hotmail.com and I will be happy to advise you.)

2. Look at the symbols in Appendix B and choose one that feels appropriate to you. As long as the symbol is linked with the Sephira that's appropriate for your ritual, you can leave the choice of the exact symbol to your intuition. After you have chosen your symbol, trace it onto a piece of blank paper.

3. Arrange your ritual space: The incense appropriate to the Sephira in question should be in the east. A red candle or lantern is placed in the south, a blue bowl of water in the west, and some salt or bread placed on a plate (ideally of wood or ceramic) in the north. If you wish, you can add additional touches such as colors or precious stones or plants that are appropriate to the Sephira or planetary energy that you will be working with.

4. Begin your ritual with a prayer to the Divine energy associated with the Sephira related to your ritual's purpose. So a ritual utilizing the energy of Malkuth, for instance, would begin with a prayer to Adonai Ha Aretz.

5. After your prayer, walk clockwise around your ritual space. Do this the number of times that corresponds with one of the numbers associated with your selected Sephira.

6. When you arrive back in the east, recite a declaration that you have prewritten. This declaration should ask the Divine energy of your Sephira to send the archangel of that Sephira to assist you in achieving the goal of your ritual. Then visualize that archangel appearing and a ray of light passing from it to your heart center.

7. Focus all your concentration on the traced symbol without thinking directly of the outcome that you are hoping for. When your intuition tells you that you have achieved a sufficient level of concentration, burn the traced symbol in the flame of the candle in the south while focusing on a sense of success in your ritual's aims.

8. Finally, return to the east and offer a prayer of thanks to the Divine.

With these eight steps, you can construct a whole variety of rituals. As you read more about Kabbalah and your experience grows, you will no doubt find yourself creating your own particular style or flavor and adding little complexities here and there. That's great—Kabbalah is meant to be a creative process, so allow yourself to experiment!

Exploring the Paths on the Tree of Life

As you now know, the 10 Sephiroth that make up the Tree of Life are connected by 22 pathways. Each pathway represents a particular aspect of our inner development and, when fully explored, helps us to gain an even deeper level of self-knowledge.

Thirty-two wondrous paths were engraved by Yah, the Lord of Hosts, the God of Israel, the living God, God almighty … who … created his world by three principles: by limit, by letter and by number. There are ten primordial numbers and twenty-two fundamental letters.

—From the *Sefer Yetzirah*

The exploration of the paths on the Tree of Life forms an important part of the work of many groups within the Western Mystery Tradition. These path workings, as they are often called, can be very complex and incorporate magic ritual and symbols to help the practitioner gain access to deeper and deeper levels of mystical significance.

Each of the 22 paths is linked to a letter in the Hebrew alphabet, value, meaning, color, Tarot card, and astrological or elemental association (see Appendix A). The paths actually have a different color in each of the four worlds, but we will only be using the Physical world colors of the paths for these workings.

To further explore the paths, follow these steps:

1. Select which path you want to explore. There is a certain merit in starting at the bottom of the Tree and working your way up in order, but this is not essential.

2. Refer to the Tree of Life diagram in Chapter 1 to see which Sephira the path emanates from. As we are working up the Tree toward the Divine, the Sephira that the path belongs to will be the lower one. So the path of Teth, for instance, links the Sephiroth Geburah and

Chesed, the relevant Sephira for our path working will be Geburah because it is the first Sephira of the two that we pass through when climbing up the Tree of Life.

3. Select one of the symbols associated with this Sephira and trace it onto a large piece of paper. If the path is also associated with a planetary energy or an elemental force, also trace one of the symbols associated with the particular element or planet above the Sephira symbol that you have selected.

4. Write the name of the path below your symbol. If you like, copy the Hebrew letter rather than writing out the name of the Hebrew letter, using Appendix A as a guide.

5. Now perform the Rite of Protection from Chapter 2 and then enter the astral kingdom of the Sephira that is linked to this path. If you are dealing with Sephiroth above Tiphareth, enter your temple in Tiphareth by performing the Building an Astral Kingdom in Tiphareth meditation described in Chapter 6.

6. When you are in your astral temple, hold up the symbol that you have drawn in front of you and concentrate on it. Focus on the symbol for at least 10 to 15 minutes.

7. Close your eyes. You should still be able to see the image of the symbol in your mind's eye. This symbol should now grow and grow until it's big enough that you can walk through it like a portal.

8. Visualize yourself stepping through this portal and into a vast expanse of light that is the color given for the path you are exploring.

9. As you stand in the light, ask the Divine essence linked with the Sephira associated with this pathway for permission to explore the path in question. Formulate this question in a style similar to the declarations that you have been making in Kabbalistic rituals.

10. You are now free to explore the pathway. You will find that you meet all kinds of interesting creatures and often that you will just have a sense of information and intuitive knowledge passing into your consciousness. Offer a short prayer of thanks to the Divine before you return to your astral temple and then back to your normal waking state.

You now have the map and some initial directions to start out on the most exciting journey that anyone can ever make: the journey to the heart of ourselves and to the heart of the universe. The more you explore the pathways of the Tree of Life, the more you will learn about yourself and about the nature of the universe. At one level this will increase your sense of inner purpose and your connection to your own Divine spark. In your day-to-day life, every path that you explore will enrich the way in which you live. So when people spend time exploring the path of Tzaddi, for example, they tend to find that they are much more cheerful and more tenacious. Very often a thorough exploration of Tzaddi leads to a promotion at work or the final achievement of some long-held ambition.

The Tree of Life and Kabbalah as a whole is like an ever-changing landscape: Every time you look at an aspect of it you find something new. Be sure that you keep exploring. If you persevere with your quest, you may even find yourself penetrating the very deepest mystical secrets. I wish you well as a fellow seeker after truth. If you seek with genuine sincerity, you will surely find the wisdom that you aspire to achieve.

Appendix A

Pathway Correspondences

The following table gives you all the main information associated with each of the 22 paths on the Tree of Life. Each path is known by its Hebrew letter. So looking at the Tree of Life diagram in Chapter 1, for instance, path number 1 is known as the path of Aleph because Aleph is the first letter in the Hebrew alphabet. Path 11 is the path of Kaph because Kaph is the eleventh letter in the Hebrew alphabet.

Next to the name of the letter is the way the letter is written in Hebrew; the shapes of the letters are said to be sacred and symbolic in their own right. The values that follow relate to the fact that in ancient times Hebrew letters were also used as numbers, and so each letter has a value. Nowadays Hebrew letters do not tend to be used for counting, but they still retain the potential to be used as numbers. Some letters have a different shape when they are used at the end of a word, and these different-shaped letters also have their own values. This applies to the letters Kaph, Mem, Nun, Ayin, Peh, and Tzaddi.

After the value, the literal meaning of each letter is listed. Often these meanings relate to the shape of the letter, but they always have a symbolic meaning. Every path has a color, and you will have seen some of these colors in the meditations that you have performed in this book. The colors are also very useful when doing the pathway explorations in Chapter 12. The last two columns give a flavor of the particular links that each path has with other mystical systems such as Tarot and astrology.

Name	Hebrew	Value(s)	Meaning	Color(s)	Tarot Card	Elements/ Planets/ Signs
Aleph	א	1	Ozxen	Ezzzmerald, gold	The Fool	Air
Beth	ב	2	Home	Indigo, violet	Magician	Mercury
Gimel	ג	3	Camel	Silver, blue	High Priestess	Moon
Daleth	ד	4	Doorway	Pale green	Empress	Venus
Heh	ה	5	Window	Flame red	Emperor	Mars
Vau	ו	6	Nail	Rich brown	Hierophant	Taurus
Zayin	ז	7	Sword	Reddish-gray	Lovers	Gemini
Cheth	ח	8	Fence	Greenish-brown	Chariot	Cancer
Teth	ט	9	Serpent	Reddish-amber	Force	Leo
Yod	י	10	Hand	Plum	Hermit	Virgo
Kaph	כ ך	20, 500	Palm of hand	Bright blue, yellow	Wheel of Fortune	Jupiter
Lamed	ל	30	Ox goad	Pale green	Justice	Libra
Mem	מ ם	40, 600	Water	Pearl white	Hanged Man	Water
Nun	נ ן	50, 700	Fish	Bluish-black	Death	Scorpio

Name	Hebrew	Value(s)	Meaning	Color(s)	Tarot Card	Elements/ Planets/ Signs
Samech	ס	60	Prop	Dark blue	Temperance	Sagittarius
Ayin	ע	70	Eye	Dark gray	Devil	Capricorn
Peh	פ ף	80, 800	Mouth	Bright red	The Tower	Mars
Tzaddi	צ ץ	90, 900	Fish hook	White, purple	The Star	Aquarius
Qoph	ק	100	Head	Stone	The Moon	Pisces
Resh	ר	200	Back of head	Amber	The Sun	Sun
Shin	ש	300	Tooth	Crimson, emerald	Judgment	Fire
Tau	ת	400	Cross	White, red, yellow, blue	Universe	Saturn/ Earth

Appendix B

Useful Kabbalistic Symbols
and Their Meanings

The symbols shown in this appendix have existed since ancient times and have a number of uses. In many civilizations, the practice of esoteric arts such as Kabbalah was forbidden and could lead to excommunication or even death. By using symbols to describe ideas, it was possible for the study of Kabbalah to continue without persecution. Symbols are also a very handy way to represent a complex idea in a single image. Throughout this book, you use these symbols as aids in your meditations or as ways to enhance the energy of your rituals.

The Sephiroth

Kether

A single point. The single point represents the potential for creation that lies hidden within Kether.   •

Point within a circle. The whole universe is contained within Kether; the circle around the point can be seen as the limit of the physical universe that will ultimately emanate from Kether.

The line. Kether is the primal force of creation, and the single line emphasizes both its unity and the dynamic nature of the power that lies within Kether.

Horizontal figure eight. This symbol represents the idea of eternity. The line of the figure eight has no beginning and no end. Because it contains two circular shapes, it also reminds us of the eternal link between the spiritual and the material.

Chokmah

Cross in a circle. The cross in a circle indicates the four elements that are contained within the force emanating from Chokmah.

Two lines. Chokmah is the Sephira of duality, and is the point in the creation of the universe where the Divine is able to reflect itself. The two lines symbolize this moment. In addition, the two lines form a channel down which the creative energy can flow into the rest of the universe.

Binah

Triangle in a circle. Binah is the Great Mother and the ability to create a genuinely new life. The number 3 symbolizes creation, and so the triangle in a circle represents the creation taking place at the heart of the universe.

Cup made of a semicircle, circle, and triangle. In many myths, we hear about a chalice, grail, or cup that is supposed to contain great mystery and wisdom. Binah is referred to as the Sephira of understanding and so the grail of mystery is linked to Binah.

Archway. The symbol represents the two vertical lines of Chokmah being linked by a circular line. This circular line symbolizes the feminine and maternal energy connecting the two lines of masculine power from Chokmah. The resulting archway also symbolizes the role of Binah as the Great Mother.

Vertical line facing a horizontal line linked to a vertical line.
This symbol emphasizes the role of Binah as a source of form
and shape in the universe. The light from Chokmah enters in
through a very narrow pathway in the top-left corner where it
is then formed into a definite shape in the womb of Binah.

Chesed

Square in a circle. Chesed is seen as the home of those energies
that we associate with paternalistic deities. The square symbolizes
the certainty and solidity that we expect from such gods. The circle is a way of showing that these very solid and definite energies
exist within the context of an overseeing eternal Divine power.

Square-based pyramid. The square at the base of the pyramid
symbolizes the just nature of the Divine energy associated with
Chesed. The pyramid shape itself links our modern ideas of a
paternal and merciful God all the way back to the beliefs of
the ancient Egyptians.

Equal-armed cross. The equal-armed cross is symbolic of the
four elements, and because of its balanced shape, the just nature
of Chesed.

Vertical line ending in a curved shape. This shape is a symbolic
representation of a shepherd's crook and points to the role of the
Chesed as a protective and merciful force in our lives.

Geburah

Five-pointed star in a circle. The five-pointed star or pentagram
represents the four elements ruled by spirit. For us to use the
power of Geburah wisely, it is important that we only ever wield
this strong force in support of a spiritually appropriate cause.

Pentagon. Geburah is associated with the planet Mars, and the
pentagon has long been the symbol of this warlike planet. We can
see this represented even in modern times in the Pentagon building in Washington, D.C.

Five circles arranged in pentagon shape. The energy of Geburah can be harsh and severe. However, the inevitable nature of decay, destruction, and even death needs to be understood as an essential part of the Divine structure of the universe. The circles from which this symbol is made remind us of the presence of God in even the most warlike of symbols.

Tiphareth

Unicursal hexagram (six-pointed star made from one continuous line). The number 6 is symbolic of the balance between the Divine world and the Physical world. Six-pointed figures have always been seen as a way of representing the Divine as manifested in the physical universe. The fact that this symbol can be drawn with one continuous line emphasizes the eternal nature of the Divine.

Two interlocking triangles. This symbol is also known as the Star of David and is a traditional symbol of God in the Jewish faith. In Hermetic Kabbalah, it also represents the union of the two elements of Fire and Water that leads to the creation of the physical universe.

Calvary cross (horizontal bar two thirds up vertical line). This symbol represents the self-sacrifice needed for us to achieve a level of mystical understanding that will lead us to a realization of the presence of the Divine. In Christian Kabbalah, this symbol also has very obvious links to the idea of Christ suffering on the Cross.

Truncated pyramid. This symbol is rather like the pyramid symbol of Chesed but with a flat square top rather than the usual point of a pyramid. This is symbolic of the fact that having reached Tiphareth, we are able to stand on the top of the pyramid that is made of the four elements and are therefore closer to the Divine.

The cube. In Hermetic Kabbalah, the symbol of an altar made from one cube placed on top of another is often used to represent the union of the spiritual and the material universes. The symbol of a single cube in Tiphareth represents the presence of the Divine within the material universe. The material is symbolized by the square sides of the cube, and the spiritual is represented by the presence of the number 6.

Circle containing a point. This symbol is the same as one of the symbols of Kether. This is because Tiphareth in some ways represents the energy of Kether when it is brought down to a material level.

Netzach

Heptagram. This seven-pointed symbol can be drawn with a single continuous line, and this emphasizes the presence of the Divine even in the lower reaches of the Tree of Life. The number 7 is the number of the Sephira Netzach, and because it is also the number of dynamic intense activity, it also refers directly to the associations between Netzach and the creative arts and passions.

Elliptical circle with vertical line. The Sephira Netzach is associated with the planet Venus. The girdle is one of the traditional associations with both the Sephira Netzach and Venus. This shape is a symbolic representation of a girdle and symbolizes the direction and control of the emotions and passions.

Horizontal crescent with vertical line and ellipse on the right. This rather strange-looking shape is a symbolic drawing of an ancient oil lamp. The obvious connection in this symbol is to the element of Fire, which rules the Sephira of Netzach. In addition, it connects to the idea of our personal creative spark that burns in the darkness of the material world.

Hod

Octogram. As you can see, the octogram is made by placing one square over another at an angle. The number 8 is linked with Hod, which is the eighth Sephira if we count down from Kether. In addition, it is connected with the intellect and thought. This is symbolized by the way the second square has shifted position, which represents the way we "turn things over" in our minds.

Triangular-based pyramid. The number 3 represents creativity, and pyramids represent manifestation. This symbol represents the way in which we can think creatively and make new ideas appear, which in turn can lead to the creation and manifestation of new objects and ways of living.

Cross made of 13 squares. The number 13 is a number of change, and the cross represents the four elements. This symbol points to our ability to change the world around us by the processes of thought. The 13 squares represent the signs of the zodiac and the sun, which occupies the central square. This represents the need for our thinking processes to be connected to the Divine structure of the universe.

Yesod

Enneagram. The number 9 is the number of Yesod, and so this nine-pointed symbol is traditionally associated with it. Notice that like the heptagram, this enneagram can be drawn with a single continuous line.

Cubical cross. The equal-armed cross here, as always, represents a sense of balance. The cross is made out of five cubes arranged together. The reason they are three-dimensional is that now that you have entered Yesod, you can see the world in a more solid and genuinely real way because you are beginning to see the spiritual dimension of the universe.

Malkuth

Circle divided into four quarters. The circle here represents the presence of the Divine, and the fact that it is divided into quarters symbolizes the four elements that are the body of the Divine in the material universe.

Cross within a square. Malkuth is the world of physical existence, and this is symbolized by the square. The small cross in the center of the square symbolizes the fact that even within the material world we can still find balance and evidence of the Divine if we look properly and carefully.

The Planetary Symbols

The planetary symbols are the traditional planetary symbols that have been used by astrologers for hundreds of years with the exception of the nine-pointed star, which symbolizes the moon, and the seven-pointed star, which represents Venus, as well as the additional symbol for Mercury. These two star shapes have been used in the Western Mystery Tradition in addition to the traditional planetary symbols that you may have seen before in astrology books. Because the traditional symbols of the moon and Venus are quite well known, you might find it easier to use the star symbols for meditations of rituals.

The additional symbol for Mercury may be familiar to you because it is used by many medical associations and companies. Properly known as the caduceus, this symbol represents the positive uniting of opposing elements (represented by the two serpents wrapped around the central staff). The circle at the top of the staff symbolizes the Sephira Kether. The wings symbolize the fact that when we possess the secret wisdom, we will be able to fly up to Kether.

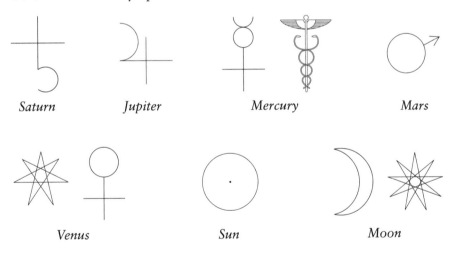

Saturn Jupiter Mercury Mars

Venus Sun Moon

The Elemental Symbols

The origin of these four simple symbols is not fully known. It seems sensible that the Fire triangle is upright to represent a flame. Because water falls from the sky, it makes sense for the Water element to be symbolized by a downward-pointing triangle. Earth is said to be cold and dry, and so its triangle of Earth also points downward. Similarly, Air is hot and moist, whereas Fire is hot and dry, and so the triangle of Air is also upward-pointing.

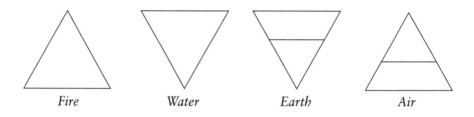

Fire   *Water*   *Earth*   *Air*

Appendix C

Resources

If you'd like to expand your exploration of Kabbalah and the Western Mystery Tradition, the following books and online resources are good places to continue your journey.

Books

Agrippa, Cornelius. *Three Books of Occult Philosophy.* St Paul, MN: Llewellyn Publications, 1997.

Bardon, Franz. *Initiation into Hermetics.* Berlin, Germany: Dieter Ruggeberg, 1971.

Budge, E. A. Wallis. *Egyptian Magic.* New York: Dover Publications, 1971.

Cicero, Chic, and Sarah Tabatha Cicero. *Self Initiation into the Golden Dawn Tradition.* St. Paul, MN: Llewellyn Publications, 2003.

Crowley, Aleister. *Liber 777.* York Beach, Maine: Samuel Weiser, 1997.

Denning, Melita, and Osborne Phillips. *Astral Projection.* St. Paul, MN: Llewellyn Publications, 1996.

Douglas, Alfred. *The Tarot*. Reading, UK: Penguin, 1987.

Evola, Julius. *The Hermetic Tradition*. Rochester, Vermont: Inner Traditions, 1995.

Fortune, Dion. *The Mystical Qabalah*. New York: Ibis Books, 1981.

Frater A.H.E.H.'O. *Angelic Images*. Leeds, UK: The Sorcerer's Apprentice Press, 1996.

Gerwick-Brodeur, Madeline, and Lisa Lenard. *The Complete Idiot's Guide to Astrology, Third Edition*. Indianapolis, IN: Alpha Books, 2003.

Godwin, David. *Godwin's Cabalistic Encyclopedia*. St. Paul, MN: Llewellyn Publications, 1989.

Grey, Eden. *The Complete Guide to the Tarot*. New York: Bantam Books, 1982.

Halevi, Z'Ev Ben Shimon. *The Way of Kabbalah*. New York: Red Wheel/Weiser, 1991.

James, William. *The Varieties of Religious Experience*. Carmichael, CA: Touchstone Books, 1997.

Jung, Carl Gustav. *The Archetypes and the Collective Unconscious*. London, UK: Routledge, 1990.

Kaplan, Aryeh. *Sefer Yetzirah*. York Beach, ME: Samuel Weiser, 1990.

King, Francis. *Modern Ritual Magic*. New York: Prism Unity, 1990.

Knight, Gareth. *A Practical Guide to Qabbalistic Symbolism*. New York: Samuel Weiser, 1983.

Knight, Sirona. *Empowering Your Life with Dreams*. Indianapolis, IN: Alpha Books, 2003.

Mathers, S. L. MacGregor, trans. *The Kabbalah Unveiled*. London, UK: Penguin, 1991.

McClain, Gary, and Eve Adamson. *Empowering Your Life with Joy*. Indianapolis, IN: Alpha Books, 2003.

Regardie, Israel. *The Tree of Life*. York Beach, ME: Samuel Weiser, 1972.

Scholem, Gershom G. *Major Trends in Jewish Mysticism*. New York: Schocken Books, 1995.

Sharp, Jonathan. *Divining Your Dreams*. New York: Fireside Books, 2002.

The Three Initiates. *The Kybalion.* Whitefish, MT: Kessinger Publishing, 1997.

Tognetti, Arlene, and Lisa Lenard. *The Complete Idiot's Guide to the Tarot, Second Edition.* Indianapolis, IN: Alpha Books, 2003.

Online Suppliers

alternativemarketplace.com. Provides a whole range of New Age supplies and books.

www.azothart.com/cgi-bin/main.pl. Specializes in making magical tools and paraphernalia.

www.druidskeep.co.uk. Good source of books and incense.

www.omegactr.com/flore.html. Suppliers of a wide range of incense and crystals.

www.sacredsource.com. Provides a wide range of New Age supplies.

www.sorcerersapprentice.co.uk. Specialists in serious occult and Kabbalistic texts along with specially prepared incense and crystals.

www.wanderomen.com/incense.htm. Incense specialists.

www.whisperedprayers.com. Provides a wide range of New Age supplies.

Online Kabbalah Resources

digital-brilliance.com/kab. Features links to orthodox Kabbalah resources and documents on practical Kabbalah.

www.esotericarchives.com. Contains many documents from the Western Mystery Tradition.

www.hermetic.com. Features links to documents relating to Hermetic Kabbalah.

www.hermeticfellowship.org. An organization dedicated to practical application of Hermetic wisdom.

www.hermeticgoldendawn.org. Contains excellent resources on Hermetic Kabbalah and the Western Mystery Tradition in general.

www.ucalgary.ca/~elsegal/RelS_365/Kabbalah_Guide.html. A scholarly guide to Kabbalah.

Index

T